Combine: Asynchronous Programming with Swift

By Shai Mishali, Florent Pillet

& Marin Todorov

Combine: Asynchronous Programming with Swift

By Shai Mishali, Florent Pillet & Marin Todorov

Copyright ©2021 Razeware LLC.

Notice of Rights

All rights reserved. No part of this book or corresponding materials (such as text, images, or source code) may be reproduced or distributed by any means without prior written permission of the copyright owner.

Notice of Liability

This book and all corresponding materials (such as source code) are provided on an "as is" basis, without warranty of any kind, express of implied, including but not limited to the warranties of merchantability, fitness for a particular purpose, and noninfringement. In no event shall the authors or copyright holders be liable for any claim, damages or other liability, whether in action of contract, tort or otherwise, arising from, out of or in connection with the software or the use of other dealing in the software.

Trademarks

All trademarks and registered trademarks appearing in this book are the property of their own respective owners.

ISBN: 978-1-950325-49-8

Table of Contents

Book License 11
Before You Begin 13
What You Need 15
Book Source Code & Forums 17
    About the Authors 20
Acknowledgments 21
Section I: Introduction to Combine 23
Chapter 1: Hello, Combine! 25
    Asynchronous programming 26
    Swift's Modern Concurrency 29
    Foundation of Combine 30
    Combine basics 31
    What's the benefit of Combine code over "standard" code? 36
    App architecture 37
    Book projects 38
    Key points 41
    Where to go from here? 41
Chapter 2: Publishers & Subscribers 43
    Getting started 44
    Hello Publisher 44
    Hello Subscriber 47
    Hello Cancellable 52
    Understanding what's going on 53
    Creating a custom subscriber 56
    Hello Future 59
    Hello Subject 61

Dynamically adjusting demand 68
Type erasure 70
Bridging Combine publishers to async/await 71
Challenge 73
Key points 76
Where to go from here? 77

Section II: Operators 79

Chapter 3: Transforming Operators 81
Getting started 82
Collecting values 82
Mapping values 85
Flattening publishers 89
Replacing upstream output 91
Incrementally transforming output 95
Challenge 97
Key points 99
Where to go from here? 99

Chapter 4: Filtering Operators 101
Getting started 102
Filtering basics 102
Compacting and ignoring 105
Finding values 107
Dropping values 111
Limiting values 116
Challenge 121
Key points 122
Where to go from here? 122

Chapter 5: Combining Operators 123
Getting started 124
Prepending 124

  Appending 131
  Advanced combining 136
  Key points 148
  Where to go from here? 148

Chapter 6: Time Manipulation Operators 149
  Getting started 150
  Shifting time 152
  Collecting values 156
  Collecting values (part 2) 159
  Holding off on events 160
  Timing out 168
  Measuring time 171
  Challenge 173
  Key points 176
  Where to go from here? 176

Chapter 7: Sequence Operators 177
  Getting started 178
  Finding values 178
  Querying the publisher 188
  Key points 198
  Where to go from here? 198

Chapter 8: In Practice: Project "Collage Neue" 199
  Getting started with "Collage Neue" 201
  Presenting views 206
  Wrapping a callback function as a future 210
  Sharing subscriptions 214
  Operators in practice 216
  Challenges 216
  Key points 218
  Where to go from here? 218

Section III: Combine in Action 219

Chapter 9: Networking 221
URLSession extensions 222
Codable support 223
Publishing network data to multiple subscribers 224
Key points 226
Where to go from here? 226

Chapter 10: Debugging 227
Printing events 228
Acting on events — performing side effects 230
Using the debugger as a last resort 231
Key points 232
Where to go from here? 232

Chapter 11: Timers 233
Using RunLoop 234
Using the Timer class 235
Using DispatchQueue 236
Key points 238
Where to go from here? 238

Chapter 12: Key-Value Observing 239
Introducing publisher(for:options:) 240
Preparing and subscribing to your own KVO-compliant properties ... 240
ObservableObject 244
Key points 245
Where to go from here? 245

Chapter 13: Resource Management 247
The share() operator 248
The multicast(_:) operator 250
Future 252

    Key points 255
    Where to go from here? 255

Chapter 14: In Practice: Project "News" 257
    Getting started with the Hacker News API 258
    Getting a single story 259
    Multiple stories via merging publishers 264
    Getting the latest stories 267
    Challenges 273
    Key points 274
    Where to go from here? 274

Section IV: Advanced Combine 275

Chapter 15: In Practice: Combine & SwiftUI 277
    Hello, SwiftUI! 279
    Getting started with "News" 281
    A first taste of managing view state 282
    Fetching the latest stories 284
    Using ObservableObject for model types 286
    Displaying errors 288
    Subscribing to an external publisher 289
    Initializing the app's settings 292
    Editing the keywords list 295
    Challenges 301
    Key points 302
    Where to go from here? 302

Chapter 16: Error Handling 303
    Getting started 304
    Never 304
    Dealing with failure 314
    Key points 332
    Where to go from here? 332

Chapter 17: Schedulers 333
- An introduction to schedulers..................................... 334
- Operators for scheduling... 335
- Scheduler implementations 340
- Challenges.. 354
- Key points 356
- Where to go from here? 356

Chapter 18: Custom Publishers & Handling Backpressure 357
- Creating your own publishers 358
- Publishers as extension methods................................... 358
- The subscription mechanism 360
- Publishers emitting values 362
- Publishers transforming values 371
- Handling backpressure... 387
- Key points 394
- Where to go from here? 394

Chapter 19: Testing....................................... 395
- Getting started 396
- Testing Combine operators... 397
- Testing production code... 406
- Challenges.. 413
- Key points 416
- Where to go from here? 416

Section V: Building a Complete App 417

Chapter 20: In Practice: Building a Complete App 419
- Getting started 420
- Setting goals... 422
- Implementing JokesViewModel....................................... 423
- Wiring JokesViewModel up to the UI 429
- Implementing Core Data with Combine 434

    Challenge 443
    Key points 444
    Where to go from here? 445
Conclusion 447

Book License

By purchasing *Combine: Asynchronous Programming with Swift*, you have the following license:

- You are allowed to use and/or modify the source code in *Combine: Asynchronous Programming with Swift* in as many apps as you want, with no attribution required.

- You are allowed to use and/or modify all art, images and designs that are included in *Combine: Asynchronous Programming with Swift* in as many apps as you want, but must include this attribution line somewhere inside your app: "Artwork/images/designs: from *Combine: Asynchronous Programming with Swift*, available at www.raywenderlich.com".

- The source code included in *Combine: Asynchronous Programming with Swift* is for your personal use only. You are NOT allowed to distribute or sell the source code in *Combine: Asynchronous Programming with Swift* without prior authorization.

- This book is for your personal use only. You are NOT allowed to sell this book without prior authorization, or distribute it to friends, coworkers or students; they would need to purchase their own copies.

All materials provided with this book are provided on an "as is" basis, without warranty of any kind, express or implied, including but not limited to the warranties of merchantability, fitness for a particular purpose and noninfringement. In no event shall the authors or copyright holders be liable for any claim, damages or other liability, whether in an action or contract, tort or otherwise, arising from, out of or in connection with the software or the use or other dealings in the software.

All trademarks and registered trademarks appearing in this guide are the properties of their respective owners.

Before You Begin

This section tells you a few things you need to know before you get started, such as what you'll need for hardware and software, where to find the project files for this book, and more.

What You Need

To follow along with this book, you'll need the following:

- A Mac running **macOS Big Sur** (11.0) or later. Catalina and earlier versions might work, but they're untested for this edition.

- **Xcode 13 or later**. Xcode is the main development tool for iOS. You'll need Xcode 13 or later for the tasks in this book. Since Combine was introduced with the iOS 13 SDK, Xcode 12 should work as well - but the code in this book was tested against Xcode 13. You can download the latest version of Xcode from Apple's developer site here: apple.co/2asi58y

- **An intermediate level knowledge of Swift**. This book teaches you how to write declarative and reactive iOS applications using Apple's Combine framework. Combine uses a multitude of advanced Swift features such as generics, so you should have at least an intermediate-level knowledge of Swift.

If you want to try things out on a physical iOS device, you'll need a developer account with Apple, which you can obtain for free. However, all the sample projects in this book will work just fine in the iOS Simulator bundled with Xcode, so a paid developer account is completely optional.

Book Source Code & Forums

Where to download the materials for this book

The materials for this book can be cloned or downloaded from the GitHub book materials repository:

- https://github.com/raywenderlich/comb-materials/tree/editions/3.0

Forums

We've also set up an official forum for the book at https://forums.raywenderlich.com/c/books/combine-asynchronous-programming-with-swift. This is a great place to ask questions about the book or to submit any errors you may find.

"For my wife Elia and Baby Ethan—my love, inspiration, and rock 🩶. To my family and friends for their support: Dad, Mom, Ziv, Adam, and everyone else, you're the best!"

— *Shai Mishali*

"To Fabienne and Alexandra 🩶."

— *Florent Pillet*

"To my father. To my mom. To Mirjam and our beautiful daughter."

— *Marin Todorov*

About the Authors

Shai Mishali is an author and the final pass editor on this book. He's an experienced, award-winning iOS specialist; as well as an international speaker, and a highly active open-source contributor and maintainer on several high-profile projects - namely, the RxSwift Community and RxSwift projects, but also releases many open-source endeavors around Combine such as CombineCocoa, RxCombine and more. As an avid enthusiast of hackathons, Shai took 1st place at BattleHack Tel-Aviv 2014, BattleHack World Finals San Jose 2014, and Ford's Developer Challenge Tel-Aviv 2015. You can find him on GitHub (https://github.com/freak4pc) and Twitter as @freak4pc (https://twitter.com/freak4pc).

Florent Pillet is an author of this book. He has been developing for mobile platforms since the last century and moved to iOS on day 1. He adopted reactive programming before Swift was announced, using it in production since 2015. A freelance developer, Florent also uses reactive programming on the server side as well as on Android and likes working on tools for developers like the popular NSLogger when he's not contracting, training or reviewing code for clients worldwide. Say hello to Florent on Twitter (https://twitter.com/fpillet) and GitHub (https://github.com/fpillet) at @fpillet.

Marin Todorov is an author of this book. Marin is one of the founding members of the raywenderlich.com team and has worked on eight of the team's books. He's an independent contractor and has worked for clients like Roche, Realm, and others. Besides crafting code, Marin also enjoys blogging, teaching and speaking at conferences. He happily open-sources code. You can find out more about Marin at www.underplot.com.

Acknowledgments

We would like to thank **Scott Gardner** for his work as an author on the previous editions of this book.

Section I: Introduction to Combine

In this part of the book, you're going to ramp up over the basics of Combine and learn about some of the building blocks it comprises. You'll learn what Combine aims to solve and what are some of the abstractions it provides to help you solve them: `Publisher`, `Subscriber`, `Subscription`, `Subject` and much more.

Chapter 1: Hello, Combine!

By Marin Todorov

This book aims to introduce you to the Combine framework and to writing declarative, reactive apps with Swift for Apple platforms.

In Apple's own words: "*The Combine framework provides a declarative approach for how your app processes events. Rather than potentially implementing multiple delegate callbacks or completion handler closures, you can create a single processing chain for a given event source. Each part of the chain is a Combine operator that performs a distinct action on the elements received from the previous step.*"

Although very accurate and to the point, this delightful definition might sound a little too abstract at first. That's why, before delving into coding exercises and working on projects in the following chapters, you'll take a little time to learn a bit about the problems Combine solves and the tools it uses to do so.

Once you've built up the relevant vocabulary and some understanding of the framework in general, you'll move on to covering the basics while coding.

Gradually, as you progress in the book, you'll learn about more advanced topics and eventually work through several projects.

When you've covered everything else you will, in the last chapter, work on a complete app built with Combine.

Asynchronous programming

In a simple, single-threaded language, a program executes sequentially line-by-line. For example, in pseudocode:

```
begin
  var name = "Tom"
  print(name)
  name += " Harding"
  print(name)
end
```

Synchronous code is easy to understand and makes it especially easy to argue about the state of your data. With a single thread of execution, you can always be sure what the current state of your data is. In the example above, you know that the first `print` will always print "Tom" and the second will always print "Tom Harding".

Now, imagine you wrote the program in a multi-threaded language that is running an asynchronous event-driven UI framework, like an iOS app running on Swift and UIKit.

Consider what could potentially happen:

```
--- Thread 1 ---
begin
  var name = "Tom"
  print(name)

--- Thread 2 ---
name = "Billy Bob"

--- Thread 1 ---
  name += " Harding"
  print(name)
end
```

Here, the code sets `name`'s value to `"Tom"` and then adds `"Harding"` to it, just like before. But because another thread could execute at the same time, it's possible that some other part of your program could run between the two mutations of `name` and set it to another value like `"Billy Bob"`.

When the code is running concurrently on different cores, it's difficult to say which part of the code is going to modify the shared state first.

The code running on "Thread 2" in the example above might be:

- executing at exactly the same time on a different CPU core as your original code.
- executing just before `name += " Harding"`, so instead of the original value `"Tom"`, it gets `"Billy Bob"` instead.

What exactly happens when you run this code depends on the system load, and you might see different results each time you run the program.

Managing mutable state in your app becomes a loaded task once you run asynchronous concurrent code.

Foundation and UIKit/AppKit

Apple has been continually improving asynchronous programming for their platforms over the years. They've created several mechanisms you can use, on different system levels, to create and execute asynchronous code.

You can use APIs as low-level as managing your own threads with `NSThread` all the way up to using Swift's modern concurrency with the `async/await` construct.

You've probably used at last some of the following in your apps:

- `NotificationCenter`: Executes a piece of code any time an event of interest happens, such as when the user changes the orientation of the device or when the software keyboard shows or hides on the screen.

- **The delegate pattern**: Lets you define an object that acts on behalf of, or in coordination with, another object. For example, in your app delegate, you define what should happen when a new remote notification arrives, but you have no idea when this piece of code will run or how many times it will execute.

- **Grand Central Dispatch** and **Operations**: Helps you abstract the execution of pieces of work. You can use them to schedule code to run sequentially in a serial queue or to run a multitude of tasks concurrently in different queues with different priorities.

- **Closures**: Create detached pieces of code that you can pass around in your code, so other objects can decide whether to execute it, how many times, and in what context.

Since most typical code performs some work asynchronously, and all UI events are inherently asynchronous, it's impossible to make assumptions about which order the **entirety** of your app code will execute.

And yet, writing good asynchronous programs is possible. It's just more complex than... well, we'd like it to be.

Certainly, one of the causes for these issues is the fact that a solid, real-life app most likely uses all the different kinds of asynchronous APIs, each with its own interface, like so:

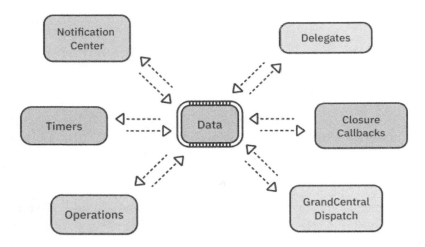

Combine introduces a common, high-level language to the Swift ecosystem to design and write asynchronous code.

Apple has integrated Combine into its other frameworks too, so `Timer`, `NotificationCenter` and core frameworks like **Core Data** already speak its language. Luckily, Combine is also very easy to integrate into your own code.

Finally, last but definitely not least, Apple designed their amazing UI framework, **SwiftUI**, to integrate easily with Combine as well.

To give you an idea of how committed Apple is to reactive programming with Combine, here's a simple diagram showing where Combine sits in the system hierarchy:

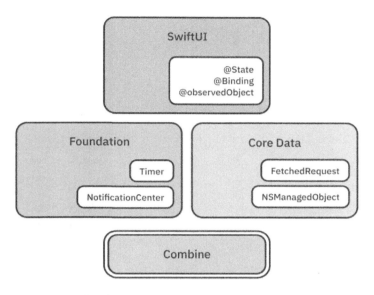

Various system frameworks, from Foundation all the way up to SwiftUI, depend on Combine and offer Combine integration as an alternative to their more "traditional" APIs.

Swift's Modern Concurrency

Swift 5.5 introduces a range of APIs for developing asynchronous and concurrent code which, thanks to a new threading-pool model, allows your code to safely and quickly suspend and resume asynchronous work at will.

The modern concurrency APIs make many of the classic async problems fairly easy to solve - for example waiting on a network response, running multiple tasks in parallel, and more.

These APIs solve some of the same problems as Combine does, but Combine's strength lays in its rich set of operators. The operators that Combine offers for processing events over time make a lot of complex, common scenarios easy to address.

Reactive operators directly address a variety of common problems in networking, data processing, and handling UI events so for more complex applications there's a lot of benefit in developing with Combine.

And, speaking of Combine's strengths, let's have a quick look at reactive programming's excellent track so far.

Foundation of Combine

Declarative, reactive programming isn't a new concept. It's been around for quite a while, but it's made a fairly noticeable comeback in the last decade.

The first "modern-day" reactive solution came in a big way in 2009 when a team at Microsoft launched a library called **Reactive Extensions** for .NET (Rx.NET).

Microsoft made that Rx.NET implementation open source in 2012, and since then, many different languages have started to use its concepts. Currently, there are many ports of the Rx standard like RxJS, RxKotlin, RxScala, RxPHP and more.

For Apple's platforms, there have been several third-party reactive frameworks like RxSwift, which implements the Rx standard; ReactiveSwift, directly inspired by Rx; Interstellar, which is a custom implementation and others.

Combine implements a standard that is different but similar to Rx, called Reactive Streams. Reactive Streams has a few key differences from Rx, but they both agree on most of the core concepts.

If you haven't previously used one or another of the frameworks mentioned above — don't worry. So far, reactive programming has been a rather niche concept for Apple's platforms, and especially with Swift.

In iOS 13/macOS Catalina, however, Apple brought reactive programming support to its ecosystem via the built-in system framework, **Combine**.

With that said, start by learning some of Combine's basics to see how it can help you write safe and solid asynchronous code.

Combine basics

In broad strokes, the three key moving pieces in Combine are publishers, operators and subscribers. There are, of course, more players in the team, but without those three you can't achieve much.

You'll learn in detail about publishers and subscribers in Chapter 2, "Publishers & Subscribers," and the complete second section of the book guides you through acquainting you with as many operators as humanly possible.

In this introductory chapter, however, you're going to get a simple crash course to give you a general idea of the purpose those types have in the code and what their responsibilities are.

Publishers

Publishers are types that can emit values over time to one or more interested parties, such as subscribers. Regardless of the internal logic of the publisher, which can be pretty much anything including math calculations, networking or handling user events, every publisher can emit multiple events of these three types:

1. An output value of the publisher's generic `Output` type.

2. A successful completion.

3. A completion with an error of the publisher's `Failure` type.

A publisher can emit zero or more output values, and if it ever completes, either successfully or due to a failure, it will not emit any other events.

Here's how a publisher emitting `Int` values could look like visualized on a timeline:

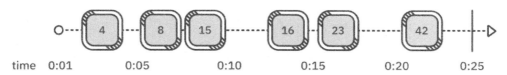

The blue boxes represent values that were emitted at a given time on the timeline, and the numbers represent the emitted values. A vertical line, like the one you see on the right-hand side of the diagram, represents a successful stream completion.

The simple contract of three possible events is so universal that it could represent any kind of dynamic data in your program. That's why you can address any task in your app using Combine publishers — regardless of whether it's about crunching numbers, making network calls, reacting to user gestures or displaying data on-screen.

Instead of always looking in your toolbox for the right tool to grab for the task at hand, be it adding a delegate or injecting a completion callback — you can just use a publisher instead.

One of the best features of publishers is that they come with error handling built in; error handling isn't something you add optionally at the end, if you feel like it.

The `Publisher` protocol is generic over two types, as you might have noticed in the diagram earlier:

- `Publisher.Output` is the type of the output values of the publisher. If it's an `Int` publisher, it can never emit a `String` or a `Date` value.
- `Publisher.Failure` is the type of error the publisher can throw if it fails. If the publisher can never fail, you specify that by using a `Never` failure type.

When you subscribe to a given publisher, you know what values to expect from it and which errors it could fail with.

Operators

Operators are methods declared on the `Publisher` protocol that return either the same or a new publisher. That's very useful because you can call a bunch of operators one after the other, effectively chaining them together.

Because these methods, called "operators", are highly decoupled and composable, they can be combined (aha!) to implement very complex logic over the execution of a single subscription.

It's fascinating how operators fit tightly together like puzzle pieces. They cannot be mistakenly put in the wrong order or fit together if one's output doesn't match the next one's input type:

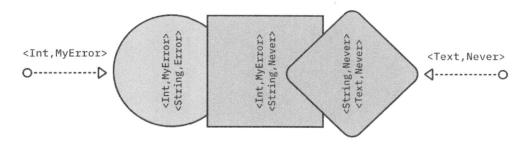

In a clear deterministic way, you can define the order of each of those asynchronous abstracted pieces of work alongside with the correct input/output types and built-in error handling. It's almost too good to be true!

As an added bonus, operators always have input and output, commonly referred to as **upstream** and **downstream** — this allows them to avoid shared state (one of the core issues we discussed earlier).

Operators focus on working with the data they receive from the previous operator and provide their output to the next one in the chain. This means that no other asynchronously-running piece of code can "jump in" and change the data you're working on.

Subscribers

Finally, you arrive at the end of the subscription chain: Every subscription ends with a subscriber. Subscribers generally do "something" with the emitted output or completion events.

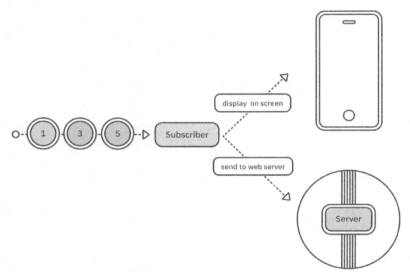

Currently, Combine provides two built-in subscribers, which make working with data streams straightforward:

- The **sink** subscriber allows you to provide closures with your code that will receive output values and completions. From there, you can do anything your heart desires with the received events.

- The **assign** subscriber allows you to, without the need of custom code, *bind* the resulting output to some property on your data model or on a UI control to display the data directly on-screen via a key path.

Should you have other needs for your data, creating custom subscribers is even easier than creating publishers. Combine uses a set of very simple protocols that allow you to be able to build your own custom tools whenever the workshop doesn't offer the right one for your task.

Subscriptions

> **Note**: This book uses the term **subscription** to describe both Combine's `Subscription` protocol and its conforming objects, as well as the complete chain of a publisher, operators and a subscriber.

When you add a subscriber at the end of a subscription, it "activates" the publisher all the way at the beginning of the chain. This is a curious but important detail to remember — publishers do not emit any values if there are no subscribers to potentially receive the output.

Subscriptions are a wonderful concept in that they allow you to *declare* a chain of asynchronous events with their own custom code and error handling **only once**, and then you never have to think about it again.

If you go full-Combine, you could describe your whole app's logic via subscriptions and once done, just let the system run everything without the need to push or pull data or call back this or that other object:

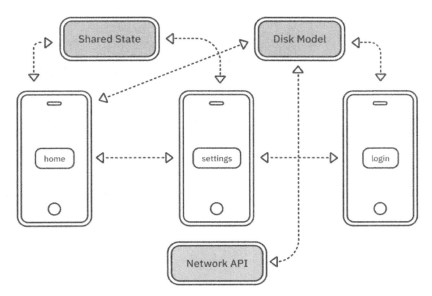

Once the subscription code compiles successfully and there are no logic issues in your custom code — you're done! The subscriptions, as designed, will asynchronously "fire" each time some event like a user gesture, a timer going off or something else awakes one of your publishers.

Even better, you don't need to specifically memory manage a subscription, thanks to a protocol provided by Combine called `Cancellable`.

Both system-provided subscribers conform to `Cancellable`, which means that your subscription code (e.g. the whole publisher, operators and subscriber call chain) returns a `Cancellable` object. Whenever you release that object from memory, it cancels the whole subscription and releases its resources from memory.

This means you can easily "bind" the lifespan of a subscription by storing it in a property on your view controller, for example. This way, any time the user dismisses the view controller from the view stack, that will deinitialize its properties and will also cancel your subscription.

Or to automate this process, you can just have an `[AnyCancellable]` collection property on your type and throw as many subscriptions inside it as you want. They'll all be automatically canceled and released when the property is released from memory.

As you see, there's plenty to learn, but it's all logical when explained in detail. And that's exactly what the plan is for the next chapters — to bring you slowly but steadily from zero to Combine hero by the end of this book.

What's the benefit of Combine code over "standard" code?

You can, by all means, never use Combine and still create the best apps out there. There's no argument about that. You can also create the best apps without Core Data, `URLSession`, or even UIKit. But using those frameworks is more convenient, safe and efficient than building those abstractions yourself.

Combine (and other system frameworks) aim to add another abstraction to your async code. Another level of abstraction on the system level means tighter integration that's well tested and a safe-bet technology.

It's up to you to decide whether Combine is a great fit for your project or not, but here are just a few "pro" reasons you might not have considered yet:

- Combine is integrated on the system level. That means Combine itself uses language features that are not publicly available, offering you APIs that you couldn't build yourself.
- Combine abstracts many common operations as methods on the `Publisher` protocol and they're already well tested.
- When all of your asynchronous pieces of work use the same interface — `Publisher` — composition and reusability become extremely powerful.
- Combine's operators are highly composable. If you need to create a new one, that new operator will instantly plug-and-play with the rest of Combine.
- Combine'a asynchronous operators are already tested. All that's left for you to do is test your own business logic.

As you see, most of the benefits revolve around safety and convenience. Combined with the fact that the framework comes from Apple, investing in writing Combine code looks promising.

App architecture

As this question is most likely already sounding alarms in your head, take a look at how using Combine will change your pre-existing code and app architecture.

Combine is not a framework that affects how you structure your apps. Combine deals with asynchronous data events and unified communication contract — it does not alter, for example, how you would separate responsibilities in your project.

You can use Combine in your MVC (Model-View-Controller) apps, you can use it in your MVVM (Model-View-ViewModel) code, in VIPER and so forth and so on.

This is one of the key aspects of adopting Combine that is important to understand early — you can add Combine code iteratively and selectively, using it only in the parts you wish to improve in your codebase. It's not an "all or nothing" choice you need to make.

You could start by converting your data models, or adapting your networking layer, or simply using Combine only in new code that you add to your app while keeping your existing functionality as-is.

It's a slightly different story if you're adopting Combine and SwiftUI at the same time. In that case, it really does make sense to drop the C from an MVC architecture. But that's thanks to using Combine and SwiftUI in tandem — those two are simply on fire when in the same room.

View controllers just don't have any chance against a Combine/SwiftUI team. When you use reactive programming all the way from your data model to your views, you don't need to have a special controller just to control your views:

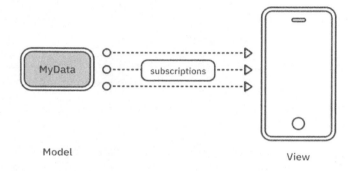

If that sounds interesting, you're in for a treat, as this book includes a solid introduction to using the two frameworks together in Chapter 15, "In Practice: Combine & SwiftUI."

Book projects

In this book, you'll start with the concepts first and move on to learning and trying out a multitude of operators.

Unlike other system frameworks, you can work pretty successfully with Combine in the isolated context of a playground.

Learning in an Xcode playground makes it easy to move forward and quickly experiment as you progress through a given chapter and to see instantly the results in Xcode's Console:

Combine does not require any third-party dependencies, so usually, a few simple helper files included with the starter playground code for each chapter will suffice to get you running. If Xcode ever gets stuck while you experiment in the playground, a quick restart will likely solve the issue.

Once you move to more complex concepts than playing with a single operator, you'll alternate between working in playgrounds and real Xcode projects like the Hacker News app, which is a newsreader that displays news in real time:

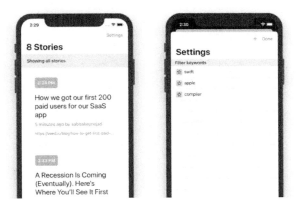

It's important that, for each chapter, you begin with the provided starter playground or project, as they might include some custom helper code which isn't relevant to learning Combine. These tidbits are pre-written so you don't distract yourself from the focus of that chapter.

In the last chapter, you'll make use of all the skills you learned throughout the book as you finish developing a complete iOS app that relies heavily on Combine and Core Data. This will give you a final push on your road to building real-life applications with Combine!

Key points

- Combine is a declarative, reactive framework for processing asynchronous events over time.

- It aims to solve existing problems, like unifying tools for asynchronous programming, dealing with mutable state and making error handling a starting team player.

- Combine revolves around three main types: **publishers** to emit events over time, **operators** to asynchronously process and manipulate upstream events and **subscribers** to consume the results and do something useful with them.

Where to go from here?

Hopefully, this introductory chapter has been useful and has given you an initial understanding of the issues Combine addresses as well as a look at some of the tools it offers to make your asynchronous code safer and more reliable.

Another important takeaway from this chapter is what to expect from Combine and what is out of its scope. Now, you know what you're in for when we speak of reactive code or asynchronous events over time. And, of course, you don't expect using Combine to magically solve your app's problems with navigation or drawing on-screen.

Finally, having a taste of what's in store for you in the upcoming chapters has hopefully gotten you excited about Combine and reactive programming with Swift. Upwards and onwards, here we go!

Chapter 2: Publishers & Subscribers

By Marin Todorov

Now that you've learned some of the basic concepts of Combine, it's time to jump in and play with two of Combine's core components — publishers and subscribers.

In this chapter, you'll experiment with various ways to create publishers and subscribe them so that you feel right at home when you need to do so throughout the book.

> **Note**: There are starter and final versions of the playgrounds and projects that you'll use in each of the chapters in this book. The starter is ready for you to enter the code for each example and challenge. You can compare your work with the final version at the end or along the way if you get stuck.

Getting started

For this chapter, you'll use an Xcode playground with Combine imported. Open **Starter.playground** in the **projects** folder and you'll see the following:

```
1  import Foundation
2  import Combine
3
4  var subscriptions = Set<AnyCancellable>()
5
6  Add your code here
7
8  /// Copyright (c) 2020 Razeware LLC
```

Open **Sources** in the **Project navigator** (**View ▸ Navigators ▸ Show Project Navigator** and twist down the **Combine** playground page), and select **SupportCode.swift**. It contains the following helper function example(of:):

```
public func example(of description: String,
                    action: () -> Void) {
  print("\n—— Example of:", description, "——")
  action()
}
```

You'll use this function to encapsulate each example you'll work on in a plauyground throughout the book.

However, before you begin playing with those examples, you first need to look at publishers, subscribers and subscriptions in a bit more detail. They form the foundation of Combine and enable you to *send* and *receive* data, typically asynchronously.

Hello Publisher

At the heart of Combine is the `Publisher` protocol. This protocol defines the requirements for a type to be able to transmit a sequence of values over time to one or more subscribers. In other words, a publisher publishes or emits events that can include values of interest.

The idea of subscribing a publisher is similar to subscribing for a specific notification from `NotificationCenter`. With `NotificationCenter` you express interest in certain events and then you're notified asynchronously whenever a new event comes through.

In fact, they are so similar, that `NotificationCenter` has a method named `publisher(for:object:)` that provides a `Publisher` type that can publish notifications.

To check this out in practice, go back to the starter playground and replace the `Add your code here` placeholder with the following code:

```
example(of: "Publisher") {
  // 1
  let myNotification = Notification.Name("MyNotification")

  // 2
  let publisher = NotificationCenter.default
    .publisher(for: myNotification, object: nil)
}
```

In this code, you:

1. Create a notification name.

2. Access `NotificationCenter`'s default instance, call its `publisher(for:object:)` method and assign its return value to a local constant.

Option-click on `publisher(for:object:)`, and you'll see that it returns a `Publisher` that emits an event when the default notification center broadcasts a notification.

So what's the point of publishing notifications when a notification center is already capable of broadcasting its notifications *without* a publisher? **Glad you asked**!

You can think of these types of methods as a bridge from the older async APIs to the newer alternatives — a way to *Combine-ify* them, if you will.

A publisher emits two kinds of events:

1. Values, also referred to as elements.

2. A completion event.

A publisher can emit zero or more values but only one completion event, which can either be a normal completion event or an error. Once a publisher emits a completion event, it's finished and can **no longer emit** any more events.

> **Note**: In that sense, a publisher is somewhat similar to a Swift iterator. One very valuable difference is that a `Publisher`'s completion could be either successful or a failure, and also that you need to actively *pull* values from an iterator, while a `Publisher` *pushes* values to its consumers.

Next, you'll wrap up the current example by using `NotificationCenter` to observe for and post a notification. You'll also unregister that observer when you're no longer interested in receiving that notification.

Append the following code to what you already have in the example's closure:

```
// 3
let center = NotificationCenter.default

// 4
let observer = center.addObserver(
  forName: myNotification,
  object: nil,
  queue: nil) { notification in
    print("Notification received!")
}

// 5
center.post(name: myNotification, object: nil)

// 6
center.removeObserver(observer)
```

With this code, you:

3. Get a handle to the default notification center.

4. Create an observer to listen for the notification with the name you previously created.

5. Post a notification with that name.

6. Remove the observer from the notification center.

Run the playground. You'll see this output printed to the console:

```
——— Example of: Publisher ———
Notification received!
```

The example's title is a little misleading because the output is not actually coming from a publisher. For that to happen, you need a subscriber.

Hello Subscriber

`Subscriber` is a protocol that defines the requirements for a type to be able to receive input from a publisher. You'll dive deeper into conforming to the `Publisher` and `Subscriber` protocols shortly; for now, you'll focus on the basic flow.

Add a new example to the playground that begins like the previous one:

```
example(of: "Subscriber") {
  let myNotification = Notification.Name("MyNotification")
  let center = NotificationCenter.default

  let publisher = center.publisher(for: myNotification, object: nil)
}
```

If you were to post a notification now, the publisher wouldn't emit it because there is no subscription to consume the notification yet.

Subscribing with sink(_:_:)

Continue in the previous example and add the following code:

```
// 1
let subscription = publisher
  .sink { _ in
    print("Notification received from a publisher!")
  }
// 2
center.post(name: myNotification, object: nil)
// 3
subscription.cancel()
```

With this code, you:

1. Create a subscription by calling `sink` on the publisher.

2. Post the notification.

3. Cancel the subscription.

Don't let the obscurity of the `sink` method name give you a *sinking* feeling. **Option-click** on `sink` and you'll see that it provides an easy way to attach a subscriber with closures to handle output from a publisher. In this example, you just print a message to indicate that a notification was received. You'll learn more about canceling a subscription shortly.

Run the playground and you'll see the following:

```
——— Example of: Publisher ———
Notification received from a publisher!
```

The `sink` operator will continue to receive as many values as the publisher emits - this is known as *unlimited demand*. And although you ignored them in the previous example, the `sink` operator actually provides two closures: one to handle receiving a completion event (a success or a failure), and one to handle receiving values.

To try those out, add this new example to your playground:

```
example(of: "Just") {
  // 1
  let just = Just("Hello world!")

  // 2
  _ = just
    .sink(
      receiveCompletion: {
        print("Received completion", $0)
      },
      receiveValue: {
        print("Received value", $0)
    })
}
```

Here, you:

1. Create a publisher using `Just`, which lets you create a publisher from a single value.

2. Create a subscription to the publisher and print a message for each received event.

Run the playground. You'll see the following:

```
——— Example of: Just ———
Received value Hello world!
Received completion finished
```

Option-click on `Just` and the Quick Help explains that it's a publisher that emits its output to each subscriber once and then finishes.

Try adding another subscriber by adding the following code to the end of your example:

```
_ = just
  .sink(
    receiveCompletion: {
      print("Received completion (another)", $0)
    },
    receiveValue: {
      print("Received value (another)", $0)
  })
```

Run the playground. True to its word, a `Just` happily emits its output to each new subscriber exactly once and then finishes.

```
Received value (another) Hello world!
Received completion (another) finished
```

Subscribing with assign(to:on:)

In addition to `sink`, the built-in `assign(to:on:)` operator enables you to assign the received value to a KVO-compliant property of an object.

Add this example to see how this works:

```
example(of: "assign(to:on:)") {
  // 1
  class SomeObject {
    var value: String = "" {
      didSet {
        print(value)
      }
    }
  }

  // 2
  let object = SomeObject()

  // 3
  let publisher = ["Hello", "world!"].publisher

  // 4
  _ = publisher
    .assign(to: \.value, on: object)
}
```

From the top:

1. Define a class with a property that has a `didSet` property observer that prints the new value.

2. Create an instance of that class.

3. Create a publisher from an array of strings.

4. Subscribe to the publisher, assigning each value received to the `value` property of the object.

Run the playground and you will see printed:

```
——— Example of: assign(to:on:) ———
Hello
world!
```

> **Note**: In later chapters you'll see that `assign(to:on:)` is **especially** useful when working on UIKit or AppKit apps because you can assign values directly to labels, text views, checkboxes and other UI components.

Republishing with assign(to:)

There is a variation of the `assign` operator that you can use to *republish* values emitted by a publisher through another property marked with the `@Published` property wrapper. To try this add this new example to your playground:

```swift
example(of: "assign(to:)") {
  // 1
  class SomeObject {
    @Published var value = 0
  }
  
  let object = SomeObject()
  
  // 2
  object.$value
    .sink {
      print($0)
    }
  
  // 3
  (0..<10).publisher
    .assign(to: &object.$value)
}
```

With this code, you:

1. Define and create an instance of a class with a property annotated with the `@Published` property wrapper, which creates a publisher for `value` in addition to being accessible as a regular property.

2. Use the `$` prefix on the `@Published` property to gain access to its underlying publisher, subscribe to it, and print out each value received.

3. Create a publisher of numbers and assign each value it emits to the `value` publisher of `object`. Note the use of `&` to denote an `inout` reference to the property.

The `assign(to:)` operator doesn't return an `AnyCancellable` token, because it manages the lifecycle internally and cancels the subscription when the `@Published` property deinitializes.

You might wonder how is this useful compared to simply using `assign(to:on:)`? Consider the following example (you don't need to add this to the playground):

```
class MyObject {
  @Published var word: String = ""
  var subscriptions = Set<AnyCancellable>()

  init() {
    ["A", "B", "C"].publisher
      .assign(to: \.word, on: self)
      .store(in: &subscriptions)
  }
}
```

In this example, using `assign(to: \.word, on: self)` and storing the resulting AnyCancellable results in a strong reference cycle. Replacing `assign(to:on:)` with `assign(to: &$word)` prevents this problem.

You'll focus on using the `sink` operator for now, but you'll learn more about the use of `@Published` properties in Chapter 8, "In Practice: Project "Collage"," and in later chapters.

Hello Cancellable

When a subscriber finishes its work and no longer wants to receive values from a publisher, it's a good idea to cancel the subscription to free up resources and stop any corresponding activities from occurring, such as network calls.

Subscriptions return an instance of `AnyCancellable` as a "cancellation token," which makes it possible to cancel the subscription when you're done with it. `AnyCancellable` conforms to the `Cancellable` protocol, which requires the `cancel()` method exactly for that purpose.

At the bottom of the **Subscriber** example earlier, you added the code `subscription.cancel()`. You're able to call `cancel()` on the subscription because the `Subscription` protocol inherits from `Cancellable`.

If you don't explicitly call `cancel()` on a subscription, it will continue until the publisher completes, or until normal memory management causes a stored subscription to deinitialize. At that point it cancels the subscription for you.

> **Note**: It's also fine to ignore the return value from a subscription in a playground (for example, `_ = just.sink...`). However, one caveat: if you don't store a subscription in full projects, that subscription will cancel as soon as the program flow exits the scope in which it was created!

These are good examples to start with, but there's a lot more going on behind the scenes. It's time to lift the curtain and learn more about the roles of publishers, subscribers and subscriptions in Combine.

Understanding what's going on

They say a picture is worth a thousand words, so let's kick things off with one to explain the interplay between publishers and subscribers:

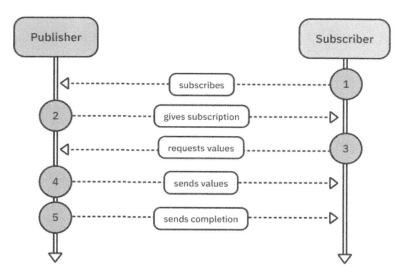

Walking through this UML diagram:

1. The subscriber subscribes to the publisher.
2. The publisher creates a subscription and gives it to the subscriber.
3. The subscriber requests values.
4. The publisher sends values.
5. The publisher sends a completion.

> **Note**: The above diagram provides a streamlined overview of what's going on. Later, you'll gain a deeper understanding of this process in Chapter 18, "Custom Publishers & Handling Backpressure."

Take a look at the `Publisher` protocol and one of its most important extensions:

```swift
public protocol Publisher {
  // 1
  associatedtype Output

  // 2
  associatedtype Failure : Error

  // 4
  func receive<S>(subscriber: S)
    where S: Subscriber,
    Self.Failure == S.Failure,
    Self.Output == S.Input
}
extension Publisher {
  // 3
  public func subscribe<S>(_ subscriber: S)
    where S : Subscriber,
    Self.Failure == S.Failure,
    Self.Output == S.Input
}
```

Here's a closer look:

1. The type of values that the publisher can produce.

2. The type of error a publisher may produce, or `Never` if the publisher is guaranteed to not produce an error.

3. A subscriber calls `subscribe(_:)` on a publisher to attach to it.

4. The implementation of `subscribe(_:)` will call `receive(subscriber:)` to attach the subscriber to the publisher, i.e., create a subscription.

The associated types are the publisher's interface that a subscriber must match in order to create a subscription. Now, look at the `Subscriber` protocol:

```swift
public protocol Subscriber: CustomCombineIdentifierConvertible {
  // 1
  associatedtype Input

  // 2
  associatedtype Failure: Error

  // 3
  func receive(subscription: Subscription)

  // 4
```

```
    func receive(_ input: Self.Input) -> Subscribers.Demand
    // 5
    func receive(completion: Subscribers.Completion<Self.Failure>)
}
```

Here's a closer look:

1. The type of values a subscriber can receive.
2. The type of error a subscriber can receive; or `Never` if the subscriber won't receive an error.
3. The publisher calls `receive(subscription:)` on the subscriber to give it the subscription.
4. The publisher calls `receive(_:)` on the subscriber to send it a new value that it just published.
5. The publisher calls `receive(completion:)` on the subscriber to tell it that it has finished producing values, either normally or due to an error.

The connection between the publisher and the subscriber is the subscription. Here's the `Subscription` protocol:

```
public protocol Subscription: Cancellable,
CustomCombineIdentifierConvertible {
    func request(_ demand: Subscribers.Demand)
}
```

The subscriber calls `request(_:)` to indicate it is willing to receive more values, up to a max number or unlimited.

> **Note**: We call the concept of a subscriber stating how many values it's willing to receive **backpressure management**. Without it, or some other strategy, a subscriber could get flooded with more values from the publisher than it can handle.

In `Subscriber`, notice that `receive(_:)` returns a `Demand`. Even though `subscription.request(_:)` sets the initial max number of values a subscriber is willing to receive, you can adjust that max each time a new value is received.

> **Note**: Adjusting max in `Subscriber.receive(_:)` is additive, i.e., the new max value is *added* to the current max. The max value must be positive, and passing a negative value will result in a `fatalError`. This means that you can increase the original max each time a new value is received, but you cannot decrease it.

Creating a custom subscriber

Time to put what you just learned to practice. Add this new example to your playground:

```swift
example(of: "Custom Subscriber") {
  // 1
  let publisher = (1...6).publisher

  // 2
  final class IntSubscriber: Subscriber {
    // 3
    typealias Input = Int
    typealias Failure = Never

    // 4
    func receive(subscription: Subscription) {
      subscription.request(.max(3))
    }

    // 5
    func receive(_ input: Int) -> Subscribers.Demand {
      print("Received value", input)
      return .none
    }

    // 6
    func receive(completion: Subscribers.Completion<Never>) {
      print("Received completion", completion)
    }
  }
}
```

What you do here is:

1. Create a publisher of integers via the range's `publisher` property.

2. Define a custom subscriber, `IntSubscriber`.

3. Implement the type aliases to specify that this subscriber can receive integer inputs and will never receive errors.

4. Implement the required methods, beginning with `receive(subscription:)`, called by the publisher; and in that method, call `.request(_:)` on the subscription specifying that the subscriber is willing to receive up to three values upon subscription.
5. Print each value as it's received and return `.none`, indicating that the subscriber will not adjust its demand; `.none` is equivalent to `.max(0)`.
6. Print the completion event.

For the publisher to publish anything, it needs a subscriber. Add the following at the end of the example:

```
let subscriber = IntSubscriber()

publisher.subscribe(subscriber)
```

In this code, you create a subscriber that matches the `Output` and `Failure` types of the publisher. You then tell the publisher to subscribe, or attach, the subscriber.

Run the playground. You'll see the following printed to the console:

```
——— Example of: Custom Subscriber ———
Received value 1
Received value 2
Received value 3
```

You did not receive a completion event. This is because the publisher has a finite number of values, and you specified a demand of `.max(3)`.

In your custom subscriber's `receive(_:)`, try changing `.none` to `.unlimited`, so your `receive(_:)` method looks like this:

```
func receive(_ input: Int) -> Subscribers.Demand {
  print("Received value", input)
  return .unlimited
}
```

Run the playground again. This time you'll see that the output contains all values, along with the completion event:

```
——— Example of: Custom Subscriber ———
Received value 1
Received value 2
Received value 3
Received value 4
Received value 5
Received value 6
Received completion finished
```

Try changing `.unlimited` to `.max(1)` and run the playground again.

You'll see the same output as when you returned `.unlimited`, because each time you receive an event, you specify that you want to increase the max by 1.

Change `.max(1)` back to `.none`, and change the definition of `publisher` to an array of strings instead. Replace:

```
let publisher = (1...6).publisher
```

With:

```
let publisher = ["A", "B", "C", "D", "E", "F"].publisher
```

Run the playground. You get an error that the `subscribe` method requires types `String` and `IntSubscriber.Input` (i.e., `Int`) to be equivalent. You get this error because the `Output` and `Failure` associated types of a publisher must match the `Input` and `Failure` types of a subscriber in order to create a subscription between the two.

Change the `publisher` definition back to its original range of integers to resolve the error.

Hello Future

Much like you can use `Just` to create a publisher that emits a single value to a subscriber and then complete, a `Future` can be used to *asynchronously* produce a single result and then complete. Add this new example to your playground:

```
example(of: "Future") {
  func futureIncrement(
    integer: Int,
    afterDelay delay: TimeInterval) -> Future<Int, Never> {

  }
}
```

Here, you create a factory function that returns a future of type `Int` and `Never`; meaning, it will emit an integer and never fail.

You also add a `subscriptions` set in which you'll store the subscriptions to the future in the example. For long-running asynchronous operations, not storing the subscription will result in the cancelation of the subscription as soon as the current code scope ends. In the case of a Playground, that would be immediately.

Next, fill the function's body to create the future:

```
Future<Int, Never> { promise in
  DispatchQueue.global().asyncAfter(deadline: .now() + delay) {
    promise(.success(integer + 1))
  }
}
```

This code defines the future, which creates a promise that you then execute using the values specified by the caller of the function to increment the `integer` after the `delay`.

A `Future` is a publisher that will eventually produce a single value and finish, or it will fail. It does this by invoking a closure when a value or error is available, and that closure is, in fact, the promise. **Command-click** on `Future` and choose **Jump to Definition**. You'll see the following:

```
final public class Future<Output, Failure> : Publisher
  where Failure: Error {
  public typealias Promise = (Result<Output, Failure>) -> Void
  ...
}
```

`Promise` is a type alias to a closure that receives a `Result` containing either a single value published by the `Future`, or an error.

Head back to the main playground page, and add the following code after the definition of `futureIncrement`:

```
// 1
let future = futureIncrement(integer: 1, afterDelay: 3)

// 2
future
  .sink(receiveCompletion: { print($0) },
        receiveValue: { print($0) })
  .store(in: &subscriptions)
```

Here, you:

1. Create a future using the factory function you created earlier, specifying to increment the integer you passed after a three-second delay.

2. Subscribe to and print the received value and completion event, and store the resulting subscription in the `subscriptions` set. You'll learn more about storing subscriptions in a collection later in this chapter, so don't worry if you don't entirely understand that portion of the example.

Run the playground. You'll see the example title printed, followed by the output of the future after a three-second delay:

```
——— Example of: Future ———
2
finished
```

Add a second subscription to the future by entering the following code in the playground:

```
future
  .sink(receiveCompletion: { print("Second", $0) },
        receiveValue: { print("Second", $0) })
  .store(in: &subscriptions)
```

Before running the playground, insert the following print statement immediately before the `DispatchQueue` block in the `futureIncrement` function:

```
print("Original")
```

Run the playground. After the specified delay, the second subscription receives the same value. The future does not re-execute its promise; instead, it shares or replays its output.

```
——— Example of: Future ———
Original
2
finished
Second 2
Second finished
```

The code prints `Original` right away before the subscriptions occur. This happens because a future is *greedy*, meaning executes as soon as it's created. It does not require a subscriber like regular publishers that are *lazy*.

In the last few examples, you've been working with publishers that have a finite number of values to publish, which are sequentially and synchronously published.

The notification center example you started with is an example of a publisher that can keep on publishing values indefinitely and asynchronously, provided:

1. The underlying notification sender emits notifications.
2. There are subscribers to the specified notification.

What if there was a way that you could do the same thing in your own code? Well, it turns out, there is! Before moving on, comment out the entire "Future" example, so the future isn't invoked every time you run the playground — otherwise its delayed output is printed after the last example.

Hello Subject

You've already learned how to work with publishers and subscribers, and even how to create your own custom subscribers. Later in the book, you'll learn how to create custom publishers. For now, though, there's just a couple more things standing between you and a well-deserved <insert your favorite beverage> break. First is a **subject**.

A subject acts as a go-between to enable non-Combine imperative code to send values to Combine subscribers. That <favorite beverage> isn't going to drink itself, so it's time to get to work!

Add this new example to your playground:

```
example(of: "PassthroughSubject") {
  // 1
  enum MyError: Error {
    case test
  }

  // 2
  final class StringSubscriber: Subscriber {
    typealias Input = String
    typealias Failure = MyError

    func receive(subscription: Subscription) {
      subscription.request(.max(2))
    }

    func receive(_ input: String) -> Subscribers.Demand {
      print("Received value", input)
      // 3
      return input == "World" ? .max(1) : .none
    }

    func receive(completion: Subscribers.Completion<MyError>) {
      print("Received completion", completion)
    }
  }

  // 4
  let subscriber = StringSubscriber()
}
```

With this code, you:

1. Define a custom error type.

2. Define a custom subscriber that receives strings and `MyError` errors.

3. Adjust the demand based on the received value.

4. Create an instance of the custom subscriber.

Returning `.max(1)` in `receive(_:)` when the input is `"World"` results in the new max being set to 3 (the original max plus 1).

Other than defining a custom error type and pivoting on the received value to adjust demand, there's nothing new here. Here comes the more interesting part.

Add this code to the example:

```
// 5
let subject = PassthroughSubject<String, MyError>()

// 6
subject.subscribe(subscriber)

// 7
let subscription = subject
  .sink(
    receiveCompletion: { completion in
      print("Received completion (sink)", completion)
    },
    receiveValue: { value in
      print("Received value (sink)", value)
    }
  )
```

This code:

5. Creates an instance of a `PassthroughSubject` of type `String` and the custom error type you defined.

6. Subscribes the subscriber to the subject.

7. Creates another subscription using `sink`.

Passthrough subjects enable you to publish new values on demand. They will happily pass along those values and a completion event. As with any publisher, you must declare the type of values and errors it can emit in advance; subscribers must match those types to its input and failure types in order to subscribe to that passthrough subject.

Now that you've created a passthrough subject that can send values and subscriptions to receive them, it's time to send some values. Add the following code to your example:

```
subject.send("Hello")
subject.send("World")
```

This sends two values (one at a time) using the subject's `send` method.

Run the playground. You'll see:

```
 ——— Example of: PassthroughSubject ———
Received value Hello
Received value (sink) Hello
Received value World
Received value (sink) World
```

Each subscriber receives the values as they're published.

Add the following code:

```
// 8
subscription.cancel()

// 9
subject.send("Still there?")
```

Here, you:

8. Cancel the second subscription.

9. Send another value.

Run the playground. As you might have expected, only the first subscriber receives the value. This happens because you previously canceled the second subscriber's subscription:

```
 ——— Example of: PassthroughSubject ———
Received value Hello
Received value (sink) Hello
Received value World
Received value (sink) World
Received value Still there?
```

Add this code to the example:

```
subject.send(completion: .finished)
subject.send("How about another one?")
```

Run the playground. The second subscriber does not receive the "How about another one?" value, because it received the completion event right before the subjects sends the value. The first subscriber does not receive the completion event or the value, because its subscription was previously canceled.

```
——— Example of: PassthroughSubject ———
Received value Hello
Received value (sink) Hello
Received value World
Received value (sink) World
Received value Still there?
Received completion finished
```

Add the following code immediately before the line that sends the completion event.

```
subject.send(completion: .failure(MyError.test))
```

Run the playground, again. You'll see the following printed to the console:

```
——— Example of: PassthroughSubject ———
Received value Hello
Received value (sink) Hello
Received value World
Received value (sink) World
Received value Still there?
Received completion failure(...MyError.test)
```

> **Note**: The error type is abbreviated for readability.

The first subscriber receives the error, but not the completion event sent *after* the error. This demonstrates that once a publisher sends a *single* completion event — whether it's a normal completion or an error — it's done, as in fini, kaput! Passing through values with a PassthroughSubject is one way to bridge imperative code to the declarative world of Combine. Sometimes, however, you may also want to look at the current value of a publisher in your imperative code — for that, you have an aptly named subject: CurrentValueSubject.

Instead of storing each subscription as a value, you can store multiple subscriptions in a collection of AnyCancellable. The collection will then automatically cancel each subscription added to it shortly before the collection deinitializes.

Add this new example to your playground:

```
example(of: "CurrentValueSubject") {
  // 1
  var subscriptions = Set<AnyCancellable>()

  // 2
  let subject = CurrentValueSubject<Int, Never>(0)

  // 3
  subject
    .sink(receiveValue: { print($0) })
    .store(in: &subscriptions) // 4
}
```

Here's what's happening:

1. Create a `subscriptions` set.
2. Create a `CurrentValueSubject` of type `Int` and `Never`. This will publish integers and never publish an error, with an initial value of `0`.
3. Create a subscription to the subject and print values received from it.
4. Store the subscription in the `subscriptions` set (passed as an `inout` parameter instead of a copy).

You must initialize current value subjects with an initial value; new subscribers immediately get that value or the latest value published by that subject. Run the playground to see this in action:

```
——— Example of: CurrentValueSubject ———
0
```

Now, add this code to send two new values:

```
subject.send(1)
subject.send(2)
```

Run the playground again. Those values are also received and printed to the console:

```
1
2
```

Unlike a passthrough subject, you can ask a current value subject for its value at any time. Add the following code to print out the subject's current value:

```
print(subject.value)
```

As you might have inferred by the subject's type name, you can get its current value by accessing its `value` property. Run the playground, and you'll see 2 printed a second time.

Calling `send(_:)` on a current value subject is one way to send a new value. Another way is to assign a new value to its `value` property. Whoah, did we just go all imperative here or what? Add this code:

```
subject.value = 3
print(subject.value)
```

Run the playground. You'll see 2 and 3 each printed twice — once by the receiving subscriber and once from printing the subject's `value` after adding that value to the subject.

Next, at the end of this example, create a new subscription to the current value subject:

```
subject
    .sink(receiveValue: { print("Second subscription:", $0) })
    .store(in: &subscriptions)
```

Here, you create a subscription and print the received values. You also store that subscription in the `subscriptions` set.

You read a moment ago that the `subscriptions` set will automatically cancel the subscriptions added to it, but how can you verify this? You can use the `print()` operator, which will log all publishing events to the console.

Insert the `print()` operator in both subscriptions, between `subject` and `sink`. The beginning of each subscription should look like this:

```
subject
    .print()
    .sink...
```

Run the playground again and you'll see the following output for the entire example:

```
——— Example of: CurrentValueSubject ———
receive subscription: (CurrentValueSubject)
request unlimited
receive value: (0)
0
receive value: (1)
1
receive value: (2)
2
```

```
2
receive value: (3)
3
3
receive subscription: (CurrentValueSubject)
request unlimited
receive value: (3)
Second subscription: 3
receive cancel
receive cancel
```

The code prints each event along with the values printed in the subscription handlers, and when you printed the subject's `values`. The `receive cancel` events appear because the `subscriptions` set is defined within the scope of this example, so it cancels the subscriptions it contains when deinitialized.

So, you may be wondering, can you also assign a completion event to the `value` property? Try it out by adding this code:

```
subject.value = .finished
```

Nope! That produces an error. A `CurrentValueSubject`'s `value` property is for just that: values. You still need to send completion events by using `send(_:)`. Change the erroneous line of code to the following:

```
subject.send(completion: .finished)
```

Run the playground again. This time you'll see the following output at the bottom:

```
receive finished
receive finished
```

Both subscriptions receive the completion event instead of the cancel event. Since they've finished, you no longer need to cancel those.

Dynamically adjusting demand

You learned earlier that adjusting demand in `Subscriber.receive(_:)` is additive. You're now ready to take a closer look at how that works in a more elaborate example. Add this new example to the playground:

```
example(of: "Dynamically adjusting Demand") {
  final class IntSubscriber: Subscriber {
    typealias Input = Int
```

```
  typealias Failure = Never

  func receive(subscription: Subscription) {
    subscription.request(.max(2))
  }

  func receive(_ input: Int) -> Subscribers.Demand {
    print("Received value", input)

    switch input {
    case 1:
      return .max(2) // 1
    case 3:
      return .max(1) // 2
    default:
      return .none // 3
    }
  }

  func receive(completion: Subscribers.Completion<Never>) {
    print("Received completion", completion)
  }
}

let subscriber = IntSubscriber()

let subject = PassthroughSubject<Int, Never>()

subject.subscribe(subscriber)

subject.send(1)
subject.send(2)
subject.send(3)
subject.send(4)
subject.send(5)
subject.send(6)
}
```

Most of this code is similar to example you've previously worked on in this chapter, so instead you'll focus on the `receive(_:)` method. You continually adjust the demand from within your custom subscriber:

1. The new max is 4 (original max of 2 + new max of 2).

2. The new max is 5 (previous 4 + new 1).

3. max remains 5 (previous 4 + new 0).

Run the playground and you'll see the following:

```
 ——— Example of: Dynamically adjusting Demand ———
Received value 1
Received value 2
Received value 3
Received value 4
Received value 5
```

As expected, the code emits five values but the sixth is not printed.

There is one more important thing you'll want to know about before moving on: hiding details about a publisher from subscribers.

Type erasure

There will be times when you want to let subscribers subscribe to receive events from a publisher without being able to access additional details about that publisher.

This would be best demonstrated with an example, so add this new one to your playground:

```
example(of: "Type erasure") {
  // 1
  let subject = PassthroughSubject<Int, Never>()

  // 2
  let publisher = subject.eraseToAnyPublisher()

  // 3
  publisher
    .sink(receiveValue: { print($0) })
    .store(in: &subscriptions)

  // 4
  subject.send(0)
}
```

With this code you:

1. Create a passthrough subject.

2. Create a type-erased publisher from that subject.

3. Subscribe to the type-erased publisher.

4. Send a new value through the passthrough subject.

Option-click on `publisher` and you'll see that it is of type `AnyPublisher<Int, Never>`.

`AnyPublisher` is a type-erased struct that conforms the `Publisher` protocol. Type erasure allows you to hide details about the publisher that you may not want to expose to subscribers — or downstream publishers, which you'll learn about in the next section.

Are you experiencing a little *déjà vu* right now? If so, that's because you saw another case of type erasure earlier. `AnyCancellable` is a type-erased class that conforms to `Cancellable`, which lets callers cancel the subscription without being able to access the underlying subscription to do things like request more items.

One example of when you would want to use type erasure for a *publisher* is when you want to use a pair of public and private properties, to allow the owner of those properties to send values on the private publisher, and let outside callers only access the public publisher for subscribing but not be able to send values.

`AnyPublisher` does not have a `send(_:)` operator, so you cannot add new values to that publisher directly.

The `eraseToAnyPublisher()` operator wraps the provided publisher in an instance of `AnyPublisher`, hiding the fact that the publisher is actually a `PassthroughSubject`. This is also necessary because you cannot specialize the `Publisher` protocol, e.g., you cannot define the type as `Publisher<UIImage, Never>`.

To prove that `publisher` is type-erased and you cannot use it to send new values, add this code to the example.

```
publisher.send(1)
```

You get the error `Value of type 'AnyPublisher<Int, Never>' has no member 'send'`. Comment out that line of code before moving on.

Bridging Combine publishers to async/await

Two great additions to the Combine framework in Swift 5.5, available in iOS 15 and macOS 12, help you effortlessly use Combine with the new `async/await` syntax in Swift.

In other words — *all* publishers, futures and subjects you learn about in this book can used from your modern Swift code at no cost.

Add one last example to your playground:

```
example(of: "async/await") {
  let subject = CurrentValueSubject<Int, Never>(0)
}
```

In this example you will use a `CurrentValueSubject` but as said the APIs are available on `Future` and any type that conforms to `Publisher`.

You will use `subject` to emit elements and a `for` loop to iterate over the asynchronous sequence of those elements.

You will subscribe for the values in a new asynchronous task. To do this, add:

```
Task {
  for await element in subject.values {
    print("Element: \(element)")
  }
  print("Completed.")
}
```

`Task` creates a new asynchronous task — the closure code will run asynchronously to the rest of your code in this code example.

The key API in this code block is the `values` property on your subject. `values` returns an asynchronous sequence with the elements emitted by the subject or publisher. You can iterate that asynchronous sequence in a simple `for` loop like you do above.

Once the publisher completes, either successfully or with a failure, the loop ends and the execution continues on the next line.

Next, add also this code to the current example to emit some values:

```
subject.send(1)
subject.send(2)
subject.send(3)

subject.send(completion: .finished)
```

This will emit 1, 2 and 3 and then complete the subject.

That wraps nicely this example — sending the `finished` event will also end the loop in your asynchronous task. Run again the playground code and you will see this output:

```
——— Example of: async/await ———
Element: 0
Element: 1
Element: 2
Element: 3
Completed.
```

In the case of `Future` which emits a single element (if any) a `values` property wouldn't make so much sense. That's why `Future` has a `value` property which you can use with `await` to get the future's result asynchronously.

Fantastic job! You've learned a lot in this chapter, and you'll put these new skills to work throughout the rest of this book and beyond. But not so fast! It's time to practice what you just learned. So, grab yourself a `<insert your favorite beverage>` to enjoy while you work through the challenges for this chapter.

Challenge

Completing challenges helps drive home what you learned in the chapter. There are starter and final versions of the challenge in the exercise files download.

Challenge: Create a Blackjack card dealer

Open **Starter.playground** in the **challenge** folder, and twist down the playground page and **Sources** in the **Project navigator**. Select **SupportCode.swift**.

Review the helper code for this challenge, including

- A `cards` array that contains 52 tuples representing a standard deck of cards.

- Two type aliases: `Card` is a tuple of `String` and `Int`, and `Hand` is an array of `Cards`.

- Two helper properties on `Hand`: `cardString` and `points`.

- A `HandError` error enumeration.

In the main playground page, add code immediately below the comment `// Add code to update dealtHand here` that evaluates the result returned from the hand's `points` property. If the result is greater than 21, send the `HandError.busted` through the `dealtHand` subject. Otherwise, send the hand value.

Also in the main playground page, add code immediately after the comment `// Add subscription to dealtHand here` to subscribe to `dealtHand` and handle receiving both values and an error.

For received values, print a string containing the results of the hand's `cardString` and `points` properties.

For an error, print it out. A tip though: You can receive either a `.finished` or a `.failure` in the `receivedCompletion` block, so you'll want to distinguish whether that completion is a failure or not.

`HandError` conforms to `CustomStringConvertible` so printing it will result in a user-friendly error message. You can use it like this:

```
if case let .failure(error) = $0 {
  print(error)
}
```

The call to `deal(_:)` currently passes 3, so you deal three cards each time you run the playground.

In a *real* game of Blackjack, you're initially dealt two cards, and then you have to decide to take one or more additional cards, called *hits*, until you either hit 21 or bust. For this simple example, you're just getting three cards straight away.

See how many times you go bust versus how many times you hit Blackjack or stay in the game. Are the odds stacked up against you in Vegas or what?

The card emoji characters are small when printed in the console. You can temporarily increase the font size of the **Executable Console Output** for this challenge. To do so, select **Xcode ▸ Preferences… ▸ Themes/Console**.

Then, select **Executable Console Output**, and click the **T** button in the bottom right to change it to a larger font, such as 48.

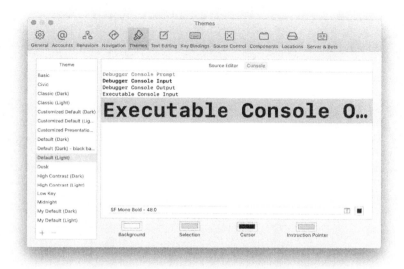

Solution

How'd you do? There were two things you needed to add to complete this challenge. The first was to update the `dealtHand` publisher in the `deal` function, checking the hand's points and sending an error if it's over 21:

```
// Add code to update dealtHand here
if hand.points > 21 {
  dealtHand.send(completion: .failure(.busted))
} else {
  dealtHand.send(hand)
}
```

Next, you needed to subscribe to `dealtHand` and print out the value received or the completion event if it was an error:

```
_ = dealtHand
  .sink(receiveCompletion: {
    if case let .failure(error) = $0 {
      print(error)
    }
  }, receiveValue: { hand in
    print(hand.cardString, "for", hand.points, "points")
  })
```

Each time you run the playground, you'll get a new hand and output similar to the following:

```
—— Example of: Create a Blackjack card dealer ——
🂡🂢🂣 for 21 points
```

Blackjack!

Key points

- Publishers transmit a sequence of values over time to one or more subscribers, either synchronously or asynchronously.

- A subscriber can subscribe to a publisher to receive values; however, the subscriber's input and failure types must match the publisher's output and failure types.

- There are two built-in operators you can use to subscribe to publishers: `sink(_:_:)` and `assign(to:on:)`.

- A subscriber may increase the demand for values each time it receives a value, but it cannot decrease demand.

- To free up resources and prevent unwanted side effects, cancel each subscription when you're done.

- You can also store a subscription in an instance or collection of `AnyCancellable` to receive automatic cancelation upon deinitialization.

- You use a future to receive a single value asynchronously at a later time.

- Subjects are publishers that enable outside callers to send multiple values asynchronously to subscribers, with or without a starting value.

- Type erasure prevents callers from being able to access additional details of the underlying type.

- Use the `print()` operator to log all publishing events to the console and see what's going on.

Where to go from here?

Congratulations! You've taken a huge step forward by completing this chapter. You learned how to work with publishers to send values and completion events, and how to use subscribers to receive those values and events. Up next, you'll learn how to manipulate the values coming from a publisher to help filter, transform or combine them.

Section II: Operators

If you think of Combine as a language, such as the English language, operators are its words. The more operators you know, the better you can articulate your intention and the logic of your app. Operators are a huge part of the Combine ecosystem which lets you manipulate values emitted from upstream publishers in meaningful and logical ways.

In this section, you'll learn the majority of operators Combine has to offer, divided into useful groups: transforming, filtering, combining, time manipulation and sequence. Once you've got your operator chops down, you'll wrap up this section with a hands-on project to practice your newly-acquired knowledge.

Chapter 3: Transforming Operators

By Marin Todorov

Having completed section 1, you've already learned a lot. You should feel pretty good about that accomplishment! You've laid a solid foundation on the fundamentals of Combine, and now you're ready to build upon it.

In this chapter, you're going to learn about one of the essential categories of operators in Combine: Transforming operators. You'll use transforming operators all the time, to manipulate values coming from publishers into a format that is usable for your subscribers. As you'll see, there are parallels between transforming operators in Combine and regular operators in the Swift standard library, such as `map` and `flatMap`.

By the end of this chapter, you'll be transforming all the things!

Getting started

Open the starter playground for this chapter, which already has Combine imported and is ready for you to start coding.

Operators are publishers

In Combine, we call methods that perform an operation on values coming from a publisher "**operators**".

Each Combine operator returns a publisher. Generally speaking, the publisher receives upstream events, manipulates them, and then sends the manipulated events downstream to consumers.

To simplify this concept, in this chapter you'll focus on using operators and working with their output. Unless an operator's purpose is to handle upstream errors, it will just re-publish said errors downstream.

> **Note:** You'll focus on transforming operators in this chapter, so error handling will not appear in each operator example. You'll learn all about error handling in Chapter 16, "Error Handling."

Collecting values

Publishers can emit individual values or collections of values. You'll frequently work with collections, for example when you want to populate list or grid views. You'll learn how to do this later in the book.

collect()

The `collect` operator provides a convenient way to transform a stream of individual values from a publisher into a single array. To help understand how this and all other operators you'll learn about in this book, you'll use **marble diagrams**.

Marble diagrams help visualize how operators work. The top line is the upstream publisher. The box represents the operator. And the bottom line is the subscriber, or more specifically, what the subscriber will *receive* after the operator manipulates the values coming from the upstream publisher.

The bottom line could also be another operator that receives the output from the upstream publisher, performs its operation, and sends those values downstream.

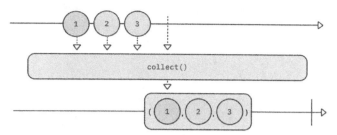

This marble diagram depicts how `collect` buffers a stream of individual values until the upstream publisher completes. It then emits that array downstream.

Add this new example to your playground:

```
example(of: "collect") {
  ["A", "B", "C", "D", "E"].publisher
    .sink(receiveCompletion: { print($0) },
          receiveValue: { print($0) })
    .store(in: &subscriptions)
}
```

This code is not using the `collect` operator just yet. Run the playground, and you'll see each value appears on a separate line followed by a completion event:

```
——— Example of: collect ———
A
B
C
D
E
finished
```

Now use `collect` just before calling `sink`. Your code should now look like this:

```
["A", "B", "C", "D", "E"].publisher
  .collect()
  .sink(receiveCompletion: { print($0) },
        receiveValue: { print($0) })
  .store(in: &subscriptions)
```

Run the playground again and you'll now see that `sink` receives a single array value, followed by the completion event:

```
——— Example of: collect ———
["A", "B", "C", "D", "E"]
finished
```

> **Note**: Be careful when working with `collect()` and other buffering operators that do not require specifying a count or limit. They will use an unbounded amount of memory to store received values as they won't emit before the upstream finishes.

There are a few variations of the `collect` operator. For example, you can specify that you only want to receive up to a certain number of values, effectively chopping the upstream into "batches".

Replace the following line:

```
.collect()
```

With:

```
.collect(2)
```

Run the playground, and you'll see the following output:

```
——— Example of: collect ———
["A", "B"]
["C", "D"]
["E"]
finished
```

The last value, E, is also an array. That's because the upstream publisher completed before `collect` filled its prescribed buffer, so it sent whatever it had left as an array.

Mapping values

In addition to collecting values, you'll often want to transform those values in some way. Combine offers several mapping operators for that purpose.

map(_:)

The first you'll learn about is map, which works just like Swift's standard map, except that it operates on values emitted from a publisher. In the marble diagram, map takes a closure that multiplies each value by 2.

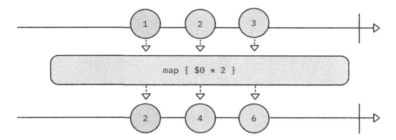

Notice how, unlike collect, this operator re-publishes values as soon as they are published by the upstream.

Add this new example to your playground:

```
example(of: "map") {
  // 1
  let formatter = NumberFormatter()
  formatter.numberStyle = .spellOut

  // 2
  [123, 4, 56].publisher
    // 3
    .map {
      formatter.string(for: NSNumber(integerLiteral: $0)) ?? ""
    }
    .sink(receiveValue: { print($0) })
    .store(in: &subscriptions)
}
```

Here's the play-by-play:

1. Create a number formatter to spell out each number.

2. Create a publisher of integers.

3. Use map, passing a closure that gets upstream values and returns the result of using the formatter to return the number's spelled out string.

Run the playground, and you will see this output:

```
——— Example of: map ———
one hundred twenty-three
four
fifty-six
```

Mapping key paths

The map family of operators also includes three versions that can map into one, two, or three properties of a value using key paths. Their signatures are as follows:

- map<T>(_:)
- map<T0, T1>(_:_:)
- map<T0, T1, T2>(_:_:_:)

The T represents the type of values found at the given key paths.

In the next example, you'll use the Coordinate type and quadrantOf(x:y:) method defined in **Sources/SupportCode.swift**. Coordinate has two properties: x and y. quadrantOf(x:y:) takes x and y values as parameters and returns a string indicating the quadrant for the x and y values.

> **Note:** Quadrants are part of coordinate geometry. For more information you can visit mathworld.wolfram.com/Quadrant.html.

Feel free to review these definitions if you're interested, otherwise just use
map(_:_:) with the following example to your playground:

```swift
example(of: "mapping key paths") {
    // 1
    let publisher = PassthroughSubject<Coordinate, Never>()

    // 2
    publisher
        // 3
        .map(\.x, \.y)
        .sink(receiveValue: { x, y in
            // 4
            print(
                "The coordinate at (\(x), \(y)) is in quadrant",
                quadrantOf(x: x, y: y)
            )
        })
        .store(in: &subscriptions)

    // 5
    publisher.send(Coordinate(x: 10, y: -8))
    publisher.send(Coordinate(x: 0, y: 5))
}
```

In this example you're using the version of map that maps into two properties via key paths.

Step-by-step, you:

1. Create a publisher of Coordinates that will never emit an error.

2. Begin a subscription to the publisher.

3. Map into the x and y properties of Coordinate using their key paths.

4. Print a statement that indicates the quadrant of the provide x and y values.

5. Send some coordinates through the publisher.

Run the playground and the output from this subscription will be the following:

```
——— Example of: map key paths ———
The coordinate at (10, -8) is in quadrant 4
The coordinate at (0, 5) is in quadrant boundary
```

tryMap(_:)

Several operators, including map, have a counterpart with a try prefix that takes a throwing closure. If you throw an error, the operator will emit that error downstream.

To try tryMap add this example to the playground:

```
example(of: "tryMap") {
  // 1
  Just("Directory name that does not exist")
    // 2
    .tryMap { try
FileManager.default.contentsOfDirectory(atPath: $0) }
    // 3
    .sink(receiveCompletion: { print($0) },
          receiveValue: { print($0) })
    .store(in: &subscriptions)
}
```

Here's what you just did, or at least tried to!

1. Create a publisher of a string representing a directory name that does not exist.

2. Use tryMap to attempt to get the contents of that nonexistent directory.

3. Receive and print out any values or completion events.

Notice that you still need to use the try keyword when calling a throwing method.

Run the playground and observe that tryMap outputs a failure completion event with the appropriate "folder doesn't exist" error (output abbreviated):

```
——— Example of: tryMap ———
failure(..."The folder "Directory name that does not exist"
doesn't exist."...)
```

Flattening publishers

Though somewhat mysterious at first, the concept of flattening isn't too complex to understand. You'll learn everything about it by working through few select examples.

flatMap(maxPublishers:_:)

The `flatMap` operator flattens multiple upstream publishers into a single downstream publisher — or more specifically, flatten the emissions from those publishers.

The publisher returned by `flatMap` does not — and often will not — be of the same type as the upstream publishers it receives.

A common use case for `flatMap` in Combine is when you want to pass elements emitted by one publisher to a method that itself returns a publisher, and ultimately subscribe to the elements emitted by that second publisher.

Time to implement an example to see this in action. Add this new example:

```
example(of: "flatMap") {
  // 1
  func decode(_ codes: [Int]) -> AnyPublisher<String, Never> {
    // 2
    Just(
      codes
        .compactMap { code in
          guard (32...255).contains(code) else { return nil }
          return String(UnicodeScalar(code) ?? " ")
        }
        // 3
        .joined()
    )
    // 4
    .eraseToAnyPublisher()
  }
}
```

From the top, you:

1. Define a function that takes an array of integers, each representing an ASCII code, and returns a type-erased publisher of strings that never emits errors.

2. Create a `Just` publisher that converts the character code into a string if it's within the range of 0.255, which includes standard and extended printable ASCII characters.

3. Join the strings together.

4. Type erase the publisher to match the return type for the fuction.

> **Note**: For more information about ASCII character codes, you can visit www.asciitable.com.

With that handiwork completed, add this code to your current example to put that function and the `flatMap` operator to work:

```
// 5
[72, 101, 108, 108, 111, 44, 32, 87, 111, 114, 108, 100, 33]
  .publisher
  .collect()
// 6
  .flatMap(decode)
// 7
  .sink(receiveValue: { print($0) })
  .store(in: &subscriptions)
```

With this code, you:

5. Create a secret message as an array of ASCII character codes, convert it to a publisher, and collect its emitted elements into a single array.

6. Use `flatMap` to pass the array element to your decoder function.

7. Subscribe to the elements emitted by the pubisher returned by `decode(_:)` and print out the values.

Run the playground, and you'll see the following:

```
——— Example of: flatMap ———
Hello, World!
```

Recall the definition from earlier: `flatMap` flattens the output from all received publishers into a single publisher. This can pose a memory concern, because it will buffer as many publishers as you send it to update the single publisher it emits downstream.

To understand how to manage this, take a look at this marble diagram of `flatMap`:

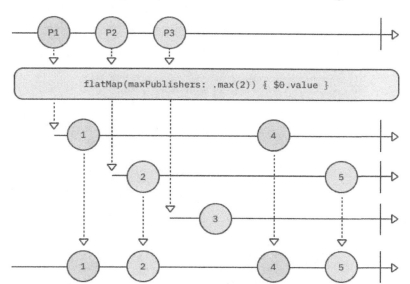

In the diagram, `flatMap` receives three publishers: P1, P2, and P3. Each of these publishers has a `value` property that is also a publisher. `flatMap` emits the `value` publishers' values from P1 and P2, but ignores P3 because `maxPublishers` is set to 2. You'll get more practice working with `flatMap` and its `maxPublishers` parameter in Chapter 19, "Testing."

You now have a handle on one of the most powerful operators in Combine. However, `flatMap` is not the only way to swap input with a different output. So, before wrapping up this chapter, you'll learn a couple more useful operating for doing the ol' switcheroo.

Replacing upstream output

Earlier in the `map` example, you worked with `Foundation`'s `Formatter.string(for:)` method. It produces an optional string, and you used the nil-coalescing operator (`??`) to replace a `nil` value with a non-`nil` value. Combine also includes an operator that you can use when you want to *always* deliver a value.

replaceNil(with:)

As depicted in the following marble diagram, `replaceNil` will receive optional values and replace `nil`s with the value you specify:

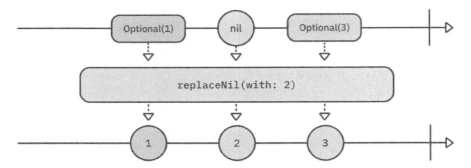

Add this new example to your playground:

```
example(of: "replaceNil") {
  // 1
  ["A", nil, "C"].publisher
    .eraseToAnyPublisher()
    .replaceNil(with: "-") // 2
    .sink(receiveValue: { print($0) }) // 3
    .store(in: &subscriptions)
}
```

What you just did:

1. Create a publisher from an array of optional strings.

2. Use `replaceNil(with:)` to replace `nil` values received from the upstream publisher with a new non-nil value.

3. Print out the value.

> **Note**: `replaceNil(with:)` has overloads which can confuse Swift into picking the wrong one for your use case. This results in the type remaining as `Optional<String>` instead of being fully unwrapped. The code above uses `eraseToAnyPublisher()` to work around that bug. You can learn more about this issue in the Swift forums: https://bit.ly/30M5Qv7

Run the playground, and you will see the following:

```
——— Example of: replaceNil ———
A
-
C
```

There is a subtle but important difference between using the nil-coalescing operator ?? and replaceNil. The ?? operator can still result in an nil result, while replaceNil cannot. Change the usage of replaceNil to the following, and you will see the error caused by the wrong operator overload:

```
.replaceNil(with: "-" as String?)
```

Revert that change before moving on. This example also demonstrates how you can chain together multiple operators in a compositional way. This allows you to manipulate the values coming from the origin publisher to the subscriber in a wide variety of ways.

replaceEmpty(with:)

You can use the replaceEmpty(with:) operator to replace — or really, *insert* — a value if a publisher completes without emitting a value.

In the following marble diagram, the publisher completes without emitting anything, and at that point the replaceEmpty(with:) operator inserts a value and publishes it downstream:

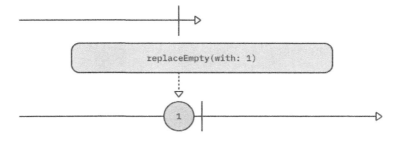

Add this new example to see it in action:

```
example(of: "replaceEmpty(with:)") {
  // 1
  let empty = Empty<Int, Never>()

  // 2
  empty
    .sink(receiveCompletion: { print($0) },
          receiveValue: { print($0) })
    .store(in: &subscriptions)
}
```

What you're doing here:

1. Create an empty publisher that immediately emits a completion event.

2. Subscribe to it, and print received events.

Use the `Empty` publisher type to create a publisher that immediately emits a `.finished` completion event. You could also configure it to *never* emit anything by passing `false` to its `completeImmediately` parameter, which is `true` by default. This publisher is useful for demo or testing purposes, or when all you want to do is signal completion of some task to a subscriber. Run the playground and you'll see it successfully completes:

```
——— Example of: replaceEmpty ———
finished
```

Now, insert this line of code before calling `sink`:

```
.replaceEmpty(with: 1)
```

Run the playground again, and this time you get a 1 before the completion:

```
1
finished
```

Incrementally transforming output

You've seen how Combine includes operators such as map that correspond and work similarly to higher-order functions found in the Swift standard library. However, Combine has a few more tricks up its sleeve that let you manipulate values received from an upstream publisher.

scan(_:_:)

A great example of this in the transforming category is scan. It will provide the current value emitted by an upstream publisher to a closure, along with the last value returned by that closure.

In the following marble diagram, scan begins by storing a starting value of 0. As it receives each value from the publisher, it adds it to the previously stored value, and then stores *and* emits the result:

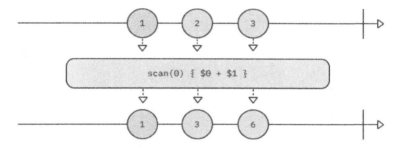

> **Note**: If you are using the full project to enter and run this code, there's no straightforward way to plot the output — as is possible in a playground. Instead, you can print the output by changing the sink code in the example below to .sink(receiveValue: { print($0) }).

For a practical example of how to use scan, add this new example to your playground:

```
example(of: "scan") {
  // 1
  var dailyGainLoss: Int { .random(in: -10...10) }

  // 2
  let august2019 = (0..<22)
    .map { _ in dailyGainLoss }
```

```
    .publisher
// 3
august2019
  .scan(50) { latest, current in
    max(0, latest + current)
  }
  .sink(receiveValue: { _ in })
  .store(in: &subscriptions)
}
```

In this example, you:

1. Create a computed property that generates a random integer between −10 and 10.

2. Use that generator to create a publisher from an array of random integers representing fictitious daily stock price changes for a month.

3. Use `scan` with a starting value of 50, and then add each daily change to the running stock price. The use of `max` keeps the price non-negative — thankfully stock prices can't fall below zero!

This time, you did not print anything in the subscription. Run the playground, and then click the square **Show Results** button in the right results sidebar.

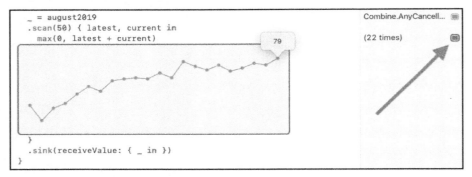

Talk about a bull run! How'd your stock do?

There's also an error-throwing `tryScan` operator that works similarly. If the closure throws an error, `tryScan` fails with that error.

Challenge

Practice makes *permanent*. Complete this challenge to ensure you're good to go with transforming operators before moving on.

Challenge: Create a phone number lookup using transforming operators

Your goal for this challenge is to create a publisher that does two things:

1. Receives a string of ten numbers or letters.

2. Looks up that number in a contacts data structure.

The starter playground, in the **challenge** folder, includes a `contacts` dictionary and three functions. You'll need to create a subscription to the `input` publisher using transforming operators and those functions. Insert your code right below the `Add your code here` placeholder, before the `forEach` blocks that will test your implementation.

> **Tip**: You can pass a function or closure directly to an operator as a parameter if the function signature matches. For example, `map(convert)`.

Breaking down this challenge, you'll need to:

1. Convert the input to numbers — use the `convert` function, which will return `nil` if it cannot convert the input to an integer.

2. If the previous operator returns `nil`, replace it with a `0`.

3. Collect ten values at a time, which correspond to the three-digit area code and seven-digit phone number format used in the United States.

4. Format the collected string value to match the format of the phone numbers in the contacts dictionary — use the provided `format` function.

5. "Dial" the input received from the previous operator — use the provided `dial` function.

Solution

Did your code produce the expected results? Starting with a subscription to `input`, first you needed to convert the string input one character at a time into integers:

```
input
  .map(convert)
```

Next you needed to replace `nil` values returned from `convert` with `0`s:

```
.replaceNil(with: 0)
```

To look up the result of the previous operations, you needed to collect those values, and then format them to match the phone number format used in the `contacts` dictionary:

```
.collect(10)
.map(format)
```

Finally, you needed to use the `dial` function to look up the formatted string input, and then subscribe:

```
.map(dial)
.sink(receiveValue: { print($0) })
```

Running the playground will produce the following:

```
——— Example of: Create a phone number lookup ———
Contact not found for 000-123-4567
Dialing Marin (408-555-4321)...
Dialing Shai (212-555-3434)...
```

Bonus points if you hook this up to a VoIP service!

Key points

- You call methods that perform operations on output from publishers "operators".
- Operators are also publishers.
- Transforming operators convert input from an upstream publisher into output that is suitable for use downstream.
- Marble diagrams are a great way to visualize how each Combine operators work.
- Be careful when using any operators that buffer values such as `collect` or `flatMap` to avoid memory problems.
- Be mindful when applying existing knowledge of functions from Swift standard library. Some similarly-named Combine operators work the same while others work entirely differently.
- It's common chaining multiple operators together in a subscription to create complex and compound transformations on events emitted by a publisher.

Where to go from here?

Way to go! You just transformed yourself into a transforming titan.

Now it's time to learn how to use another essential collection of operators to filter what you get from an upstream publisher.

Chapter 4: Filtering Operators

By Shai Mishali

As you might have realized by now, operators are basically the vocabulary that you use to manipulate Combine publishers. The more "words" you know, the better your control of your data will be.

In the previous chapter, you learned how to consume values and transform them into *other* values — definitely one of the most useful operator categories for your daily work.

But what happens when you want to limit the values or events emitted by the publisher, and only consume *some* of them? This chapter is all about how to do this with a special group of operators: **Filtering operators**!

Luckily, many of these operators have parallels with the same names in the Swift standard library, so don't be surprised if you're able to *filter* some of this chapter's content. :]

It's time to dive right in.

Getting started

You can find the starter playground for this chapter, **Starter.playground**, in the **projects** folder. As you progress through this chapter, you'll write code in the playground and then run the playground. This will help you understand how different operators manipulate events emitted by your publisher.

> **Note**: Most operators in this chapter have parallels with a `try` prefix, for example, `filter` vs. `tryFilter`. The only difference between them is that the latter provides a *throwing* closure. Any error you throw from within the closure will terminate the publisher with the thrown error. For brevity's sake, this chapter will only cover the non-throwing variations, since they are virtually identical.

Filtering basics

This first section will deal with the basics of filtering — consuming a publisher of values and conditionally deciding which of them to pass to the consumer.

The easiest way to do this is the aptly-named operator — `filter`, which takes a closure expectd to return a `Bool`. It'll only pass down values that match the provided predicate:

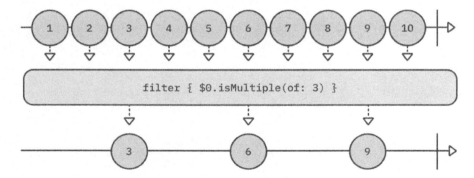

Add this new example to your playground:

```
example(of: "filter") {
  // 1
  let numbers = (1...10).publisher

  // 2
  numbers
    .filter { $0.isMultiple(of: 3) }
    .sink(receiveValue: { n in
      print("\(n) is a multiple of 3!")
    })
    .store(in: &subscriptions)
}
```

In the above example, you:

1. Create a new publisher, which will emit a finite number of values — 1 through 10, and then complete, using the publisher property on Sequence types.

2. Use the filter operator, passing in a predicate where you only allow through numbers that are multiples of three.

Run your playground. You should see the following in your console:

```
——— Example of: filter ———
3 is a multiple of 3!
6 is a multiple of 3!
9 is a multiple of 3!
```

Such an elegant way to cheat on your math homework, isn't it? :]

Many times in the lifetime of your app, you'll have publishers that emit identical values in a row that you might want to ignore. For example, if a user types "*a*" five times in a row and then types "*b*", you might want to disregard the excessive "*a*"s.

Combine provides the perfect operator for the task: removeDuplicates:

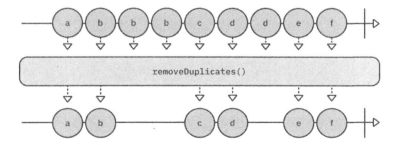

Notice how you don't have to provide any arguments to this operator. `removeDuplicates` automatically works for any values conforming to `Equatable`, including `String`.

Add the following example of `removeDuplicates()` to your playground — and be sure to include a space before the `?` in the `words` variable:

```
example(of: "removeDuplicates") {
  // 1
  let words = "hey hey there! want to listen to mister mister ?"
              .components(separatedBy: " ")
              .publisher
  // 2
  words
    .removeDuplicates()
    .sink(receiveValue: { print($0) })
    .store(in: &subscriptions)
}
```

This code isn't too different from the last one. You:

1. Separate a sentence into an array of words (e.g., `[String]`) and then create a new publisher to emit these words.

2. Apply `removeDuplicates()` to your `words` publisher.

Run your playground and take a look at the debug console:

```
——— Example of: removeDuplicates ———
hey
there!
want
to
listen
to
mister
?
```

As you can see, you've skipped the second "hey" and the second "mister". Awesome!

> **Note**: What about values that don't conform to `Equatable`? Well, `removeDuplicates` has another overload that takes a closure with two values, from which you'll return a `Bool` to indicate whether the values are equal or not.

Compacting and ignoring

Quite often, you'll find yourself dealing with a publisher emitting `Optional` values. Or even more commonly, you'll want to perform some operation on your values that might return `nil`, but who wants to handle all those `nil`s ?!

If your spidey sense is tingling, thinking of a very well-known method on `Sequence` from the Swift standard library called `compactMap` that does that job, good news – there's also an operator with the same name!

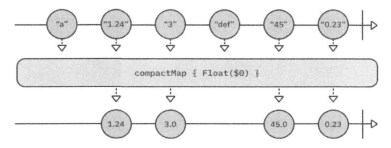

Add the following to your playground:

```
example(of: "compactMap") {
  // 1
  let strings = ["a", "1.24", "3",
                 "def", "45", "0.23"].publisher

  // 2
  strings
    .compactMap { Float($0) }
    .sink(receiveValue: {
      // 3
      print($0)
    })
    .store(in: &subscriptions)
}
```

Just as the diagram outlines, you:

1. Create a publisher that emits a finite list of strings.

2. Use `compactMap` to attempt to initialize a `Float` from each individual string. If `Float`'s initializer doesn't know how to convert the provided string, it returns `nil`. Those `nil` values are automatically filtered out by the `compactMap` operator.

3. Only print strings that have been successfully converted to `Float`s.

Run the above example in your playground and you should see output similar to the diagram above:

```
——— Example of: compactMap ———
1.24
3.0
45.0
0.23
```

All right, why don't you take a quick break from all these values… who cares about those, right? Sometimes, all you want to know is that the publisher has finished emitting values, disregarding the actual values. When such a scenario occurs, you can use the `ignoreOutput` operator:

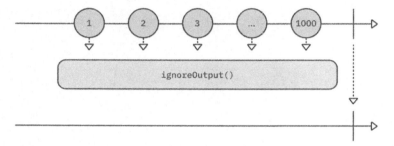

As the diagram above shows, it doesn't matter which values are emitted or how many of them, as they're all ignored; you only push the completion event through to the consumer.

Experiment with this example by adding the following code to your playground:

```
example(of: "ignoreOutput") {
  // 1
  let numbers = (1...10_000).publisher
  
  // 2
  numbers
    .ignoreOutput()
    .sink(receiveCompletion: { print("Completed with: \($0)") },
          receiveValue: { print($0) })
    .store(in: &subscriptions)
}
```

In the above example, you:

1. Create a publisher emitting 10,000 values from `1` through `10,000`.

2. Add the `ignoreOutput` operator, which omits all values and emits only the completion event to the consumer.

Can you guess what the output of this code will be?

If you guessed that no values will be printed, you're right! Run your playground and check out the debug console:

```
——— Example of: ignoreOutput ———
Completed with: finished
```

Finding values

In this section, you'll learn about two operators that also have their origins in the Swift standard library: `first(where:)` and `last(where:)`. As their names imply, you use them to find and emit *only* the first *or* the last value matching the provided predicate, respectively.

Time to check out a few examples, starting with `first(where:)`.

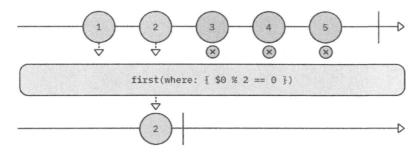

This operator is interesting because it's *lazy*, meaning: It only takes as many values as it needs until it finds one matching the predicate you provided. As soon as it finds a match, it cancels the subscription and completes.

Add the following piece of code to your playground to see how this works:

```
example(of: "first(where:)") {
  // 1
  let numbers = (1...9).publisher

  // 2
  numbers
    .first(where: { $0 % 2 == 0 })
    .sink(receiveCompletion: { print("Completed with: \($0)") },
          receiveValue: { print($0) })
    .store(in: &subscriptions)
}
```

Here's what the code you've just added does:

1. Creates a new publisher emitting numbers from 1 through 9.
2. Uses the `first(where:)` operator to find the first emitted *even* value.

Run this example in your playground and look at the console output:

```
——— Example of: first(where:) ———
2
Completed with: finished
```

It works exactly like you probably guessed it would. But wait, what about the subscription to the upstream, meaning the `numbers` publisher? Does it keep emitting its values even after it finds a matching even number? Test this theory by finding the following line:

```
numbers
```

Then add the `print("numbers")` operator immediately after that line, so it looks as follows:

```
numbers
  .print("numbers")
```

> **Note**: You can use the `print` operator anywhere in your operator chain to see exactly what events occur at that point.

Run your playground again, and take a look at the console. Your output should like similar to the following:

```
——— Example of: first(where:) ———
numbers: receive subscription: (1...9)
numbers: request unlimited
numbers: receive value: (1)
numbers: receive value: (2)
numbers: receive cancel
2
Completed with: finished
```

This is very interesting!

As you can see, as soon as `first(where:)` finds a matching value, it sends a cancellation through the subscription, causing the upstream to stop emitting values. Very handy!

Now, you can move on to the opposite of this operator — last(where:), whose purpose is to find the *last* value matching a provided predicate.

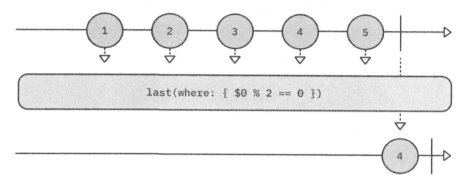

As opposed to first(where:), this operator is *greedy* since it must wait for the publisher to complete emitting values to know whether a matching value has been found. For that reason, the upstream must be finite.

Add the following code to your playground:

```
example(of: "last(where:)") {
  // 1
  let numbers = (1...9).publisher

  // 2
  numbers
    .last(where: { $0 % 2 == 0 })
    .sink(receiveCompletion: { print("Completed with: \($0)") },
          receiveValue: { print($0) })
    .store(in: &subscriptions)
}
```

Much like the previous code example, you:

1. Create a publisher that emits numbers between 1 and 9.

2. Use the last(where:) operator to find the *last* emitted even value.

Did you guess what the output will be? Run your playground and find out:

```
——— Example of: last(where:) ———
8
Completed with: finished
```

Remember I said earlier that the publisher must complete for this operator to work? Why is that?

Well, that's because there's no way for the operator to know if the publisher will emit a value that matches the criteria down the line, so the operator must know the full scope of the publisher before it can determine the last item matching the predicate.

To see this in action, replace the entire example with the following:

```
example(of: "last(where:)") {
  let numbers = PassthroughSubject<Int, Never>()

  numbers
    .last(where: { $0 % 2 == 0 })
    .sink(receiveCompletion: { print("Completed with: \($0)") },
          receiveValue: { print($0) })
    .store(in: &subscriptions)

  numbers.send(1)
  numbers.send(2)
  numbers.send(3)
  numbers.send(4)
  numbers.send(5)
}
```

In this example, you use a `PassthroughSubject` and manually send events through it.

Run your playground again, and you should see... absolutely nothing:

```
——— Example of: last(where:) ———
```

As expected, since the publisher never completes, there's no way to determine the last value matching the criteria.

To fix this, add the following as the last line of the example to send a completion through the subject:

```
numbers.send(completion: .finished)
```

Run your playground again, and everything should now work as expected:

```
——— Example of: last(where:) ———
4
Completed with: finished
```

I guess that everything must come to an end... or completion, in this case.

> **Note**: You can also use the `first()` and `last()` operators to simply get either the first or last value ever emitted by the publisher. These are also lazy and greedy, accordingly.

Dropping values

Dropping values is a useful capability you'll often need to leverage when working with publishers. For example, you can use it when you want to ignore values from one publisher until a second one starts publishing, or if you want to ignore a specific amount of values at the start of the stream.

Three operators fall into this category, and you'll start by learning about the simplest one first — `dropFirst`.

The `dropFirst` operator takes a `count` parameter — defaulting to 1 if omitted — and ignores the first `count` values emitted by the publisher. Only after skipping `count` values, the publisher will start passing values through.

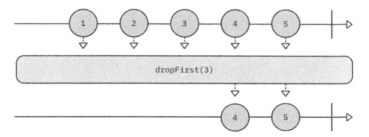

Add the following code to the end of your playground to try this operator:

```
example(of: "dropFirst") {
  // 1
  let numbers = (1...10).publisher
  
  // 2
  numbers
    .dropFirst(8)
    .sink(receiveValue: { print($0) })
    .store(in: &subscriptions)
}
```

As in the previous diagram, you:

1. Create a publisher that emits 10 numbers between 1 and 10.

2. Use `dropFirst(8)` to drop the first eight values, printing only 9 and 10.

Run your playground and you should see the following output:

```
——— Example of: dropFirst ———
9
10
```

Simple, right? Often, the most useful operators are!

Moving on to the next operator in the value dropping family – `drop(while:)`. This is another extremely useful variation that takes a predicate closure and ignores any values emitted by the publisher until the *first time* that predicate is met. As soon as the predicate is met, values begin to flow through the operator:

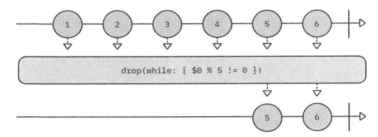

Add the following example to your playground to see this in action:

```
example(of: "drop(while:)") {
  // 1
  let numbers = (1...10).publisher

  // 2
  numbers
    .drop(while: { $0 % 5 != 0 })
    .sink(receiveValue: { print($0) })
    .store(in: &subscriptions)
}
```

In the following code, you:

1. Create a publisher that emits numbers between 1 and 10.

2. Use `drop(while:)` to wait for the first value that is divisible by five. As soon as the condition is met, values will start flowing through the operator and won't be dropped anymore.

Run your playground and look at the debug console:

```
——— Example of: drop(while:) ———
5
6
7
8
9
10
```

Excellent! As you can see, you've dropped the first four values. As soon as 5 arrives, the question "is this divisible by five?" is finally `true`, so it now emits 5 and all future values.

You might ask yourself – how is this operator different from `filter`? Both of them take a closure that controls which values are emitted based on the result of that closure.

The first difference is that `filter` lets values through if you return `true` in the closure, while `drop(while:)` *skips* values *as long* you return `true` from the closure.

The second, and more important difference is that `filter` never stops evaluating its condition for all values published by the upstream publisher. Even after the condition of `filter` evaluates to `true`, further values are still "questioned" and your closure must answer the question: "Do you want to let this value through?".

On the contrary, `drop(while:)`'s predicate closure will *never* be executed again after the condition is met. To confirm this, replace the following line:

```
.drop(while: { $0 % 5 != 0 })
```

With this piece of code:

```
.drop(while: {
  print("x")
  return $0 % 5 != 0
})
```

You added a `print` statement to print x to the debug console every time the closure is invoked. Run the playground and you should see the following output:

```
——— Example of: drop(while:) ———
x
x
x
x
x
```

```
5
6
7
8
9
10
```

As you might have noticed, x prints exactly five times. As soon as the condition is met (when 5 is emitted), the closure is never evaluated again.

Alrighty then. Two dropping operators down, one more to go.

The final and most elaborate operator of the filtering category is `drop(untilOutputFrom:)`.

Imagine a scenario where you have a user tapping a button, but you want to ignore all taps until your `isReady` publisher emits some result. This operator is perfect for this sort of condition.

It skips any values emitted by a publisher until a second publisher starts emitting values, creating a relationship between them:

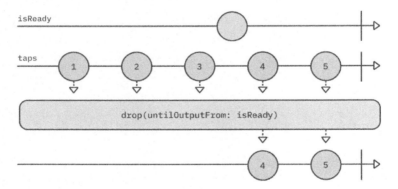

The top line represents the `isReady` stream and the second line represents taps by the user passing through `drop(untilOutputFrom:)`, which takes `isReady` as an argument.

At the end of your playground, add the following code that reproduces this diagram:

```
example(of: "drop(untilOutputFrom:)") {
  // 1
  let isReady = PassthroughSubject<Void, Never>()
  let taps = PassthroughSubject<Int, Never>()
  
  // 2
  taps
```

```
      .drop(untilOutputFrom: isReady)
      .sink(receiveValue: { print($0) })
      .store(in: &subscriptions)

  // 3
  (1...5).forEach { n in
    taps.send(n)

    if n == 3 {
      isReady.send()
    }
  }
}
```

In this code, you:

1. Create two `PassthroughSubjects` that you can manually send values through. The first is `isReady` while the second represents taps by the user.

2. Use `drop(untilOutputFrom: isReady)` to ignore any taps from the user until `isReady` emits at least one value.

3. Send five "taps" through the subject, just like in the diagram above. After the third tap, you send `isReady` a value.

Run your playground, then take a look at your debug console. You will see the following output:

```
——— Example of: drop(untilOutputFrom:) ———
4
5
```

This output is the same as the diagram above:

- There are five taps from the user. The first three are ignored.

- After the third tap, `isReady` emits a value.

- All future taps by the user are passed through.

You've gained quite a mastery of getting rid of unwanted values! Now, it's time for the final filtering operators group: Limiting values.

Limiting values

In the previous section, you've learned how to drop — or skip — values until a certain condition is met. That condition could be either matching some static value, a predicate closure, or a dependency on a different publisher.

This section tackles the opposite need: receiving values until some condition is met, and then forcing the publisher to complete. For example, consider a request that may emit an unknown amount of values, but you only want a single emission and don't care about the rest of them.

Combine solves this set of problems with the `prefix` family of operators. Even though the name isn't entirely intuitive, the abilities these operators provide are useful for many real-life situations.

The `prefix` family of operators is similar to the `drop` family and provides `prefix(_:)`, `prefix(while:)` and `prefix(untilOutputFrom:)`. However, instead of dropping values until some condition is met, the `prefix` operators *take* values until that condition is met.

Now, it's time for you to dive into the final set of operators for this chapter, starting with `prefix(_:)`.

As the opposite of `dropFirst`, `prefix(_:)` will take values only *up to* the provided amount and then complete:

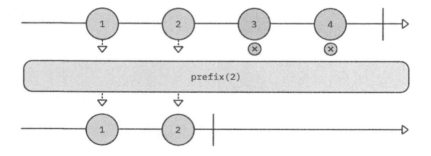

Add the following code to your playground to demonstrate this:

```
example(of: "prefix") {
  // 1
  let numbers = (1...10).publisher

  // 2
  numbers
    .prefix(2)
    .sink(receiveCompletion: { print("Completed with: \($0)") },
          receiveValue: { print($0) })
    .store(in: &subscriptions)
}
```

This code is quite similar to the `drop` code you used in the previous section. You:

1. Create a publisher that emits numbers from 1 through 10.

2. Use `prefix(2)` to allow the emission of only the first two values. As soon as two values are emitted, the publisher completes.

Run your playground and you'll see the following output:

```
——— Example of: prefix ———
1
2
Completed with: finished
```

Just like `first(where:)`, this operator is *lazy*, meaning it only takes up as many values as it needs and then terminates. This also prevents `numbers` from producing additional values beyond 1 and 2, since it also completes.

Next up is `prefix(while:)`, which takes a predicate closure and lets values from the upstream publisher through as long as the result of that closure is `true`. As soon as the result is `false`, the publisher will complete:

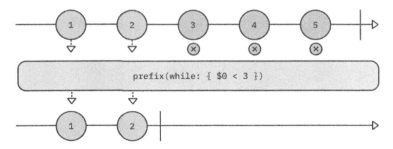

Add the following example to your playground to try this:

```
example(of: "prefix(while:)") {
  // 1
  let numbers = (1...10).publisher

  // 2
  numbers
    .prefix(while: { $0 < 3 })
    .sink(receiveCompletion: { print("Completed with: \($0)") },
          receiveValue: { print($0) })
    .store(in: &subscriptions)
}
```

This example is mostly identical to the previous one, aside from using a closure to evaluate the prefixing condition. You:

1. Create a publisher that emits values between 1 and 10.

2. Use `prefix(while:)` to let values through as long as they're smaller than 3. As soon as a value equal to or larger than 3 is emitted, the publisher completes.

Run the playground and check out the debug console; the output should be identical to the one from the previous operator:

```
——— Example of: prefix(while:) ———
1
2
Completed with: finished
```

With the first two `prefix` operators behind us, it's time for the most complex one: `prefix(untilOutputFrom:)`. Once again, as opposed to `drop(untilOutputFrom:)` which *skips* values until a second publisher emits, `prefix(untilOutputFrom:)` *takes* values until a second publisher emits.

Imagine a scenario where you have a button that the user can only tap twice. As soon as two taps occur, further tap events on the button should be omitted:

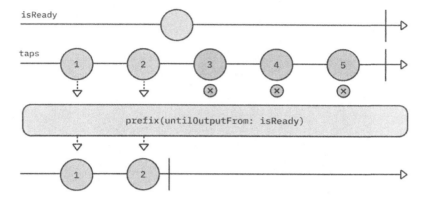

Add the final example for this chapter to the end of your playground:

```
example(of: "prefix(untilOutputFrom:)") {
  // 1
  let isReady = PassthroughSubject<Void, Never>()
  let taps = PassthroughSubject<Int, Never>()

  // 2
  taps
    .prefix(untilOutputFrom: isReady)
    .sink(receiveCompletion: { print("Completed with: \($0)") },
          receiveValue: { print($0) })
    .store(in: &subscriptions)

  // 3
  (1...5).forEach { n in
    taps.send(n)

    if n == 2 {
      isReady.send()
    }
  }
}
```

If you think back to the `drop(untilOutputFrom:)` example, you should find this easy to understand. You:

1. Create two `PassthroughSubject`s that you can manually send values through. The first is `isReady` while the second represents taps by the user.

2. Use `prefix(untilOutputFrom: isReady)` to let tap events through until `isReady` emits at least one value.

3. Send five "taps" through the subject, exactly as in the diagram above. After the second tap, you send `isReady` a value.

Run the playground. Looking at the console, you should see the following:

```
——— Example of: prefix(untilOutputFrom:) ———
1
2
Completed with: finished
```

Challenge

You have quite a lot of filtering knowledge at your disposal now. Why not try a short challenge?

Challenge: Filter all the things

Create an example that publishes a collection of numbers from 1 through 100, and use filtering operators to:

1. Skip the first 50 values emitted by the upstream publisher.

2. Take the next 20 values after those first 50 values.

3. Only take even numbers.

The output of your example should produce the following numbers, one per line:

52 54 56 58 60 62 64 66 68 70

> **Note**: In this challenge, you'll need to chain multiple operators together to produce the desired values.

You can find the full solution to this challenge in **projects/challenge/Final.playground**.

Key points

In this chapter, you learned that:

- Filtering operators let you control which values emitted by the upstream publisher are sent downstream, to another operator or to the consumer.

- When you don't care about the values themselves, and only want a completion event, `ignoreOutput` is your friend.

- Finding values is another sort of filtering, where you can find the first or last values to match a provided predicate using `first(where:)` and `last(where:)`, respectively.

- First-style operators are *lazy*; they take only as many values as needed and then complete. Last-style operators are *greedy* and must know the full scope of the values before deciding which of the values is the last to fulfill the condition.

- You can control how many values emitted by the upstream publisher are ignored before sending values downstream by using the `drop` family of operators.

- Similarly, you can control how many values the upstream publisher may emit *before* completing by using the `prefix` family of operators.

Where to go from here?

Wow, what a ride this chapter has been! You should rightfully feel like a master of filtering, ready to channel these upstream values in any way you desire.

With the knowledge of transforming and filtering operators already in your tool belt, it's time for you to move to the next chapter and learn another extremely useful group of operators: Combining operators.

Chapter 5: Combining Operators

By Shai Mishali

Now that the **transforming** and **filtering** operator categories are in your tool belt, you have a substantial amount of knowledge. You've learned how operators work, how they manipulate the upstream and how to use them to construct logical publisher chains from your data.

In this chapter, you'll learn about one of the more complex, yet useful, categories of operators: **Combining operators**. This set of operators lets you combine events emitted by different publishers and create meaningful combinations of data in your Combine code.

Why is combining useful? Think about a form with multiple inputs from the user — a username, a password and a checkbox. You'll need to *combine* these different pieces of data to compose a single publisher with all of the information you need.

As you learn more about how each operator functions and how to select the right one for your needs, your code will become substantially more capable and your skills will allow you to unlock new levels of publisher composition.

Getting started

You can find the starter playground for this chapter in the **projects/Starter.playground** folder. Throughout this chapter, you'll add code to your playground and run it to see how various operators create different combinations of publishers and their events.

Prepending

You'll start slowly here with a group of operators that are all about prepending values at the *beginning* of your publisher. In other words, you'll use them to add values that emit *before* any values from your original publisher.

In this section, you'll learn about prepend(Output...), prepend(Sequence) and prepend(Publisher).

prepend(Output...)

This variation of prepend takes a *variadic* list of values using the ... syntax. This means it can take **any number of values**, as long as they're of the same Output type as the original publisher.

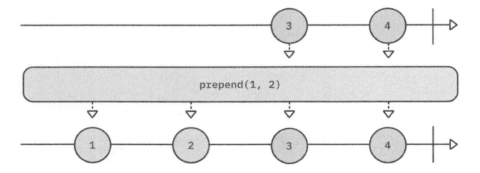

Add the following code to your playground to experiment with the above example:

```
example(of: "prepend(Output...)") {
  // 1
  let publisher = [3, 4].publisher

  // 2
  publisher
    .prepend(1, 2)
    .sink(receiveValue: { print($0) })
    .store(in: &subscriptions)
}
```

In the above code, you:

1. Create a publisher that emits the numbers 3 4.

2. Use `prepend` to add the numbers 1 and 2 before the publisher's own values.

Run your playground. You should see the following in your debug console:

```
——— Example of: prepend(Output...) ———
1
2
3
4
```

Pretty straightforward!

Hang on, do you remember how operators are chainable? That means you can easily add more than a single `prepend`, if you'd like.

Below the following line:

```
.prepend(1, 2)
```

Add the following:

```
.prepend(-1, 0)
```

Run your playground again. you should see the following output:

```
——— Example of: prepend(Output...) ———
-1
0
1
2
3
4
```

Notice that the order of operations is crucial here. The last prepend affects the upstream first, meaning -1 and 0 are prepended, then 1 and 2, and finally the original publisher's values.

prepend(Sequence)

This variation of `prepend` is similar to the previous one, with the difference that it takes any `Sequence`-conforming object as an input. For example, it could take an `Array` or a `Set`.

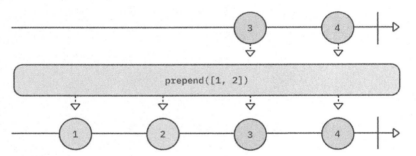

Add the following code to your playground to experiment with this operator:

```
example(of: "prepend(Sequence)") {
  // 1
  let publisher = [5, 6, 7].publisher
  
  // 2
  publisher
    .prepend([3, 4])
    .prepend(Set(1...2))
    .sink(receiveValue: { print($0) })
    .store(in: &subscriptions)
}
```

In this code, you:

1. Create a publisher that emits the numbers 5, 6 and 7.

2. Chain `prepend(Sequence)` twice to the original publisher. Once to prepend values from an `Array` and a second time to prepend values from a `Set`.

Run the playground. Your output should be similar to the following:

```
——— Example of: prepend(Sequence) ———
1
2
3
4
5
6
7
```

> **Note**: An important fact to remember about `Set`s, as opposed to `Array`s, is that they are **unordered**, so the order in which the items emit is not guaranteed. This means the first two values in the above example could be either 1 and 2, or 2 and 1.

But wait, there's more! Many types conform to `Sequence` in Swift, which lets you do some interesting things.

After the second prepend:

```
.prepend(Set(1...2))
```

Add the following line:

```
.prepend(stride(from: 6, to: 11, by: 2))
```

In this line of code, you create a `Strideable` which lets you *stride* between 6 and 11 in steps of 2. Since `Strideable` conforms to `Sequence`, you can use it in `prepend(Sequence)`.

Run your playground one more time and take a look at the debug console:

```
——— Example of: prepend(Sequence) ———
6
8
10
1
2
3
4
5
6
7
```

As you can see, three new values are now prepended to the publisher before the previous output – 6, 8 and 10, the result of striding between 6 and 11 in steps of 2.

prepend(Publisher)

The two previous operators prepended lists of values to an existing publisher. But what if you have two different publishers and you want to glue their values together? You can use prepend(Publisher) to add values emitted by a second publisher *before* the original publisher's values.

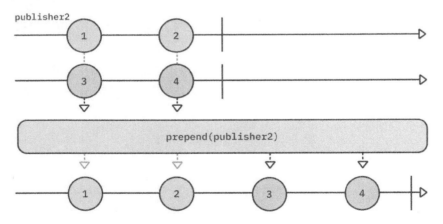

Try out the above example by adding the following to your playground:

```
example(of: "prepend(Publisher)") {
  // 1
  let publisher1 = [3, 4].publisher
  let publisher2 = [1, 2].publisher

  // 2
  publisher1
    .prepend(publisher2)
    .sink(receiveValue: { print($0) })
    .store(in: &subscriptions)
}
```

In this code, you:

1. Create two publishers. One emitting the numbers 3 and 4, and a second one emitting 1 and 2.

2. Prepend `publisher2` to the beginning of `publisher1`. `publisher1` will start performing its work and emit events only *after* `publisher2` sends a `.finished` completion event.

If you run your playground, your debug console should present the following output:

```
——— Example of: prepend(Publisher) ———
1
2
3
4
```

As expected, the values 1 and 2 are emitted first from `publisher2`; only then are 3 and 4 emitted by `publisher1`.

There's one more detail about this operator that you should be aware of, and it would be easiest to show with an example.

Add the following to the end of your playground:

```
example(of: "prepend(Publisher) #2") {
  // 1
  let publisher1 = [3, 4].publisher
  let publisher2 = PassthroughSubject<Int, Never>()

  // 2
  publisher1
    .prepend(publisher2)
    .sink(receiveValue: { print($0) })
    .store(in: &subscriptions)
```

```
  // 3
  publisher2.send(1)
  publisher2.send(2)
}
```

This example is similar to the previous one, except that `publisher2` is now a `PassthroughSubject` that you can push values to manually.

In the following example, you:

1. Create two publishers. The first emits values 3, and 4 while the second is a `PassthroughSubject` that can accept values dynamically.

2. Prepend the subject before `publisher1`.

3. Send the values 1 and 2 through the subject `publisher2`.

Take a second and run through this code inside your head. What do you expect the output to be?

Now, run the playground again and take a look at the debug console. You should see the following:

```
——— Example of: prepend(Publisher) #2 ———
1
2
```

Wait, what? Why are there only two numbers emitted here from `publisher2`? You must be thinking... hey there, Shai, didn't you just say values should *prepend* to the existing publisher?

Well, think about it — how can Combine know the prepended publisher, `publisher2`, has finished emitting values? It doesn't, since it has emitted values, but no completion event. For that reason, a prepended publisher **must complete** so Combine knows it's time to switch to the primary publisher.

After the following line:

```
publisher2.send(2)
```

Add this one:

```
publisher2.send(completion: .finished)
```

Combine now knows it can handle emissions from `publisher1` since `publisher2` has finished its work.

Run your playground again; you should see the expected output this time around:

```
——— Example of: prepend(Publisher) #2 ———
1
2
3
4
```

Appending

This next set of operators deals with concatenating events emitted by publishers with other values. But in this case, you'll deal with *appending* instead of prepending, using append(Output...), append(Sequence) and append(Publisher). These operators work similarly to their prepend counterparts.

append(Output...)

append(Output...) works similarly to its prepend counterpart: It also takes a variadic list of type Output but then *appends* its items after the *original* publisher has completed with a .finished event.

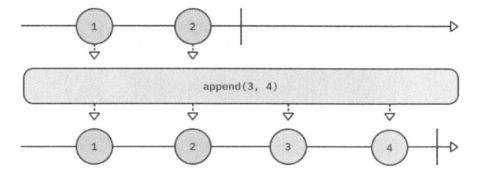

Add the following code to your playground to experiment with this operator:

```
example(of: "append(Output...)") {
  // 1
  let publisher = [1].publisher

  // 2
  publisher
    .append(2, 3)
    .append(4)
    .sink(receiveValue: { print($0) })
    .store(in: &subscriptions)
}
```

In the code above, you:

1. Create a publisher emitting only a single value: 1.

2. Use append twice, first to append 2 and 3 and then to append 4.

Think about this code for a minute — what do you think the output will be?

Run the playground and check out the output:

```
——— Example of: append(Output...) ———
1
2
3
4
```

Appending works exactly like you'd expect, where each append waits for the upstream to complete before adding its own work to it.

This means that the upstream **must complete** or appending would never occur since Combine couldn't know the previous publisher has finished emitting all of its values.

To verify this behavior, add the following example:

```
example(of: "append(Output...) #2") {
  // 1
  let publisher = PassthroughSubject<Int, Never>()

  publisher
    .append(3, 4)
    .append(5)
    .sink(receiveValue: { print($0) })
    .store(in: &subscriptions)

  // 2
  publisher.send(1)
  publisher.send(2)
}
```

This example is identical to the previous one, with two differences:

1. `publisher` is now a `PassthroughSubject`, which lets you manually send values to it.
2. You send 1 and 2 to the `PassthroughSubject`.

Run your playground again and you'll see that only the values sent to `publisher` are emitted:

```
——— Example of: append(Output...) #2 ———
1
2
```

Both append operators have no effect since they can't possibly work until `publisher` completes. Add the following line at the very end of the example:

```
publisher.send(completion: .finished)
```

Run your playground again and you should see all values, as expected:

```
——— Example of: append(Output...) #2 ———
1
2
3
4
5
```

This behavior is identical for the entire family of append operators; no appending occurs unless the previous publisher sends a `.finished` completion event.

append(Sequence)

This variation of append takes any Sequence-conforming object and appends its values after all values from the original publisher have emitted.

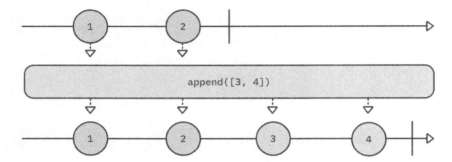

Add the following to your playground to experiment with this operator:

```
example(of: "append(Sequence)") {
  // 1
  let publisher = [1, 2, 3].publisher

  publisher
    .append([4, 5]) // 2
    .append(Set([6, 7])) // 3
    .append(stride(from: 8, to: 11, by: 2)) // 4
    .sink(receiveValue: { print($0) })
    .store(in: &subscriptions)
}
```

This code is similar to the prepend(Sequence) example from the previous section. You:

1. Create a publisher that emits 1, 2 and 3.

2. Append an Array with the values 4 and 5 (ordered).

3. Append a Set with the values 6 and 7 (unordered).

4. Append a Strideable that strides between 8 and 11 by steps of 2.

Run your playground and you should see the following output:

```
——— Example of: append(Sequence) ———
1
2
3
4
5
7
6
8
10
```

As you can see, the execution of the appends is sequential as the previous publisher must complete before the next append performs. Note that the set of 6 and 7 may be in a different order for you, as sets are unordered.

append(Publisher)

The last member of the append operators group is the variation that takes a Publisher and appends any values emitted by it to the end of the original publisher.

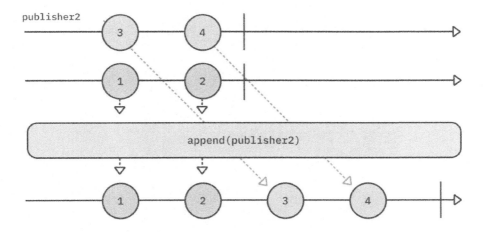

To try this example, add the following to your playground:

```
example(of: "append(Publisher)") {
  // 1
  let publisher1 = [1, 2].publisher
  let publisher2 = [3, 4].publisher

  // 2
  publisher1
    .append(publisher2)
    .sink(receiveValue: { print($0) })
    .store(in: &subscriptions)
}
```

In this code, you:

1. Create two publishers, where the first emits 1 and 2, and the second emits 3 and 4.

2. Append `publisher2` to `publisher1`, so all values from `publisher2` are appended at the end of `publisher1` once it completes.

Run the playground and you should see the following output:

```
——— Example of: append(Publisher) ———
1
2
3
4
```

Advanced combining

At this point, you know everything about appending and prepending values, sequences and even entire publishers.

This next section will dive into some of the more complex operators related to combining different publishers. Even though they're relatively complex, they're also some of the most useful operators for publisher composition. It's worth taking the time to get comfortable with how they work.

switchToLatest

Since this section includes some of the more complex combining operators in Combine, why not start with the most complex one of the bunch?!

Joking aside, `switchToLatest` is complex but highly useful. It lets you switch entire publisher subscriptions on the fly while canceling the pending publisher subscription, thus *switching* to the latest one.

You can only use it on publishers that *themselves* emit publishers.

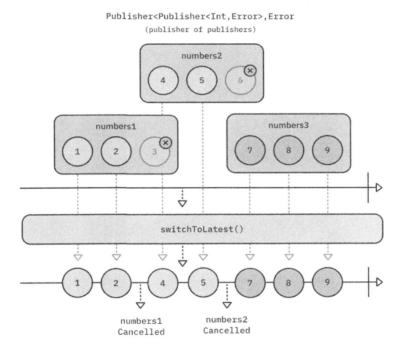

Add the following code to your playground to experiment with the example you see in the above diagram:

```
example(of: "switchToLatest") {
  // 1
  let publisher1 = PassthroughSubject<Int, Never>()
  let publisher2 = PassthroughSubject<Int, Never>()
  let publisher3 = PassthroughSubject<Int, Never>()

  // 2
  let publishers = PassthroughSubject<PassthroughSubject<Int, Never>, Never>()
```

```
// 3
publishers
  .switchToLatest()
  .sink(
    receiveCompletion: { _ in print("Completed!") },
    receiveValue: { print($0) }
  )
  .store(in: &subscriptions)

// 4
publishers.send(publisher1)
publisher1.send(1)
publisher1.send(2)

// 5
publishers.send(publisher2)
publisher1.send(3)
publisher2.send(4)
publisher2.send(5)

// 6
publishers.send(publisher3)
publisher2.send(6)
publisher3.send(7)
publisher3.send(8)
publisher3.send(9)

// 7
publisher3.send(completion: .finished)
publishers.send(completion: .finished)
}
```

Yikes, that's a lot of code! But don't worry, it's simpler than it looks. Breaking it down, you:

1. Create three `PassthroughSubjects` that accept integers and no errors.

2. Create a second `PassthroughSubject` that accepts *other* `PassthroughSubjects`. For example, you can send `publisher1`, `publisher2` or `publisher3` through it.

3. Use `switchToLatest` on your `publishers`. Now, every time you send a different publisher through the `publishers` subject, you switch to the new one and cancel the previous subscription.

4. Send `publisher1` to `publishers` and then send 1 and 2 to `publisher1`.

5. Send `publisher2`, which cancels the subscription to `publisher1`. You then send 3 to `publisher1`, but it's ignored, and send 4 and 5 to `publisher2`, which are pushed through because there is an active subscription to `publisher2`.

6. Send `publisher3`, which cancels the subscription to `publisher2`. As before, you send 6 to `publisher2` and it's ignored, and then send 7, 8 and 9, which are pushed through the subscription to `publisher3`.

7. Finally, you send a completion event to the current publisher, `publisher3`, and another completion event to `publishers`. This completes all active subscriptions.

If you followed the above diagram, you might have already guessed the output of this example.

Run the playground and look at the debug console:

```
––––––– Example of: switchToLatest –––––––
1
2
4
5
7
8
9
Completed!
```

If you're not sure why this is useful in a real-life app, consider the following scenario: Your user taps a button that triggers a network request. Immediately afterward, the user taps the button again, which triggers a second network request. But how do you get rid of the pending request, and only use the *latest* request? `switchToLatest` to the rescue!

Instead of just theorizing, why don't you try out this example?

Add the following code to your playground:

```
example(of: "switchToLatest - Network Request") {
  let url = URL(string: "https://source.unsplash.com/random")!

  // 1
  func getImage() -> AnyPublisher<UIImage?, Never> {
    URLSession.shared
      .dataTaskPublisher(for: url)
      .map { data, _ in UIImage(data: data) }
      .print("image")
      .replaceError(with: nil)
      .eraseToAnyPublisher()
  }

  // 2
  let taps = PassthroughSubject<Void, Never>()
```

```
taps
  .map { _ in getImage() } // 3
  .switchToLatest() // 4
  .sink(receiveValue: { _ in })
  .store(in: &subscriptions)

// 5
taps.send()

DispatchQueue.main.asyncAfter(deadline: .now() + 3) {
  taps.send()
}

DispatchQueue.main.asyncAfter(deadline: .now() + 3.1) {
  taps.send()
}
}
```

As in the previous example, this might look like a long and complicated piece of code, but it's simple once you break it down.

In this code, you:

1. Define a function, `getImage()`, which performs a network request to fetch a random image from Unsplash's public API. This uses `URLSession.dataTaskPublisher`, one of the many Combine extensions for Foundation. You'll learn much more about this and others in Section 3, "Combine in Action."

2. Create a `PassthroughSubject` to simulate user taps on a button.

3. Upon a button tap, map the tap to a new network request for a random image by calling `getImage()`. This essentially transforms `Publisher<Void, Never>` into `Publisher<Publisher<UIImage?, Never>, Never>` — a publisher of publishers.

4. Use `switchToLatest()` exactly like in the previous example, since you have a publisher of publishers. This guarantees only one publisher will emit values, and will automatically cancel any leftover subscriptions.

5. Simulate three delayed button taps using a `DispatchQueue`. The first tap is immediate, the second tap comes after three seconds, and the last tap comes just a tenth of a second after the second tap.

Run the playground and take a look at the output below:

```
—— Example of: switchToLatest - Network Request ——
image: receive subscription: (DataTaskPublisher)
image: request unlimited
image: receive value: (Optional(<UIImage:0x600000364120
anonymous {1080, 720}>))
image: receive finished
image: receive subscription: (DataTaskPublisher)
image: request unlimited
image: receive cancel
image: receive subscription: (DataTaskPublisher)
image: request unlimited
image: receive value: (Optional(<UIImage:0x600000378d80
anonymous {1080, 1620}>))
image: receive finished
```

You might notice that only two images are actually fetched; that's because only a tenth of a second passes between the second and third taps. The third tap switches to a new request before the second fetch returns, canceling the second subscription – hence the line that says `image: receive cancel`.

If you want to see a better visualization of this, tap the following button:

```
example(of: "switchToLatest - Network Request") {
  // 1
  func getImage() -> AnyPublisher<UIImage?, Never> {
    return URLSession.shared
      .dataTaskPublisher(for: URL(string: "https://source.unsplash.com/random")!)
      .map { data, _ in UIImage(data: data) }
      .print("image")
      .replaceError(with: nil)
      .eraseToAnyPublisher()
  }
}
```
(3 times)
(2 times)

Then run the playground again and wait a few seconds. You should see the last image loaded.

Right-click the image and select **Value History**:

You should see both loaded images — you may have to scroll to see both of them:

Before moving to the next operator, be sure to comment out this entire example to avoid running the asynchronous network requests every time you run your playground.

merge(with:)

Before you reach the end of this chapter, you'll wrap up with three operators that focus on combining the emissions of different publishers. You'll start with `merge(with:)`.

This operator **interleaves** emissions from different publishers of the same type, like so:

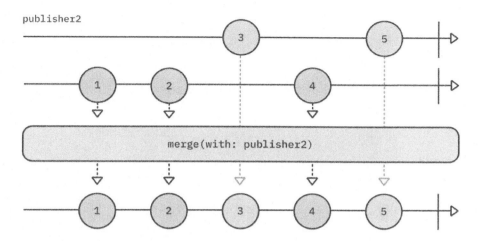

To try out this example, add the following code to your playground:

```
example(of: "merge(with:)") {
  // 1
  let publisher1 = PassthroughSubject<Int, Never>()
  let publisher2 = PassthroughSubject<Int, Never>()

  // 2
  publisher1
    .merge(with: publisher2)
    .sink(
      receiveCompletion: { _ in print("Completed") },
      receiveValue: { print($0) }
    )
    .store(in: &subscriptions)

  // 3
  publisher1.send(1)
  publisher1.send(2)

  publisher2.send(3)

  publisher1.send(4)

  publisher2.send(5)

  // 4
  publisher1.send(completion: .finished)
  publisher2.send(completion: .finished)
}
```

In this code, which correlates with the above diagram, you:

1. Create two `PassthroughSubjects` that accept and emit integer values and will not emit an error.

2. Merge `publisher1` with `publisher2`, interleaving the emitted values from both. Combine offers overloads that let you merge up to eight different publishers.

3. You add 1 and 2 to `publisher1`, then add 3 to `publisher2`, then add 4 to `publisher1` again and finally add 5 to `publisher2`.

4. You send a completion event to both `publisher1` and `publisher2`.

Run your playground and you should see the following output, as expected:

```
——— Example of: merge(with:) ———
1
2
3
4
5
Completed
```

combineLatest

`combineLatest` is another operator that lets you combine different publishers. It also lets you combine publishers of different value types, which can be extremely useful. However, instead of interleaving the emissions of all publishers, it emits **a tuple** with the latest values of *all* publishers whenever *any* of them emit a value.

One catch though: The origin publisher and every publisher passed to `combineLatest` must emit *at least* one value before `combineLatest` itself will emit anything.

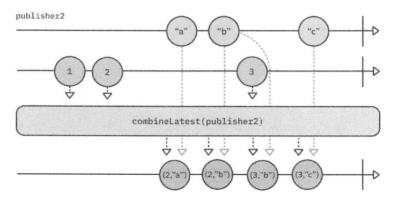

Add the following code to your playground to try out this operator:

```
example(of: "combineLatest") {
  // 1
  let publisher1 = PassthroughSubject<Int, Never>()
  let publisher2 = PassthroughSubject<String, Never>()

  // 2
  publisher1
    .combineLatest(publisher2)
    .sink(
      receiveCompletion: { _ in print("Completed") },
      receiveValue: { print("P1: \($0), P2: \($1)") }
    )
    .store(in: &subscriptions)

  // 3
  publisher1.send(1)
  publisher1.send(2)

  publisher2.send("a")
  publisher2.send("b")

  publisher1.send(3)

  publisher2.send("c")

  // 4
  publisher1.send(completion: .finished)
  publisher2.send(completion: .finished)
}
```

This code reproduces the above diagram. You:

1. Create two `PassthroughSubjects`. The first accepts integers with no errors, while the second accepts strings with no errors.

2. Combine the latest emissions of `publisher2` with `publisher1`. You may combine up to four different publishers using different overloads of `combineLatest`.

3. Send 1 and 2 to `publisher1`, then "a" and "b" to `publisher2`, then 3 to `publisher1` and finally "c" to `publisher2`.

4. Send a completion event to both `publisher1` and `publisher2`.

Run the playground and take a look at the output in your console:

```
——— Example of: combineLatest ———
P1: 2, P2: a
P1: 2, P2: b
```

```
P1: 3, P2: b
P1: 3, P2: c
Completed
```

You might notice that the 1 emitted from `publisher1` is never pushed through `combineLatest`. That's because `combineLatest` only starts emitting combinations once every publisher emits *at least* one value. Here, that condition is true only after "a" emits, at which point the latest emitted value from `publisher1` is 2. That's why the first emission is (2, "a").

zip

You'll finish with one final operator for this chapter: `zip`. You might recognize this one from the Swift standard library method with the same name on Sequence types.

This operator works similarly, emitting tuples of paired values in the same indexes. It waits for each publisher to emit an item, then emits a single tuple of items after all publishers have emitted an value at the current index.

This means that if you are zipping two publishers, you'll get a single tuple emitted every time both publishers emit a new value.

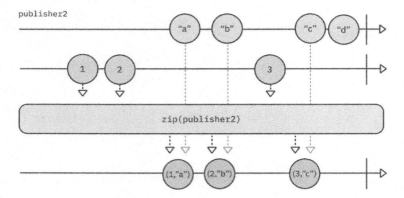

Add the following code to your playground to try this example:

```
example(of: "zip") {
  // 1
  let publisher1 = PassthroughSubject<Int, Never>()
  let publisher2 = PassthroughSubject<String, Never>()

  // 2
  publisher1
    .zip(publisher2)
```

```
    .sink(
      receiveCompletion: { _ in print("Completed") },
      receiveValue: { print("P1: \($0), P2: \($1)") }
    )
    .store(in: &subscriptions)
  // 3
  publisher1.send(1)
  publisher1.send(2)
  publisher2.send("a")
  publisher2.send("b")
  publisher1.send(3)
  publisher2.send("c")
  publisher2.send("d")

  // 4
  publisher1.send(completion: .finished)
  publisher2.send(completion: .finished)
}
```

In this final example, you:

1. Create two `PassthroughSubjects`, where the first accepts integers and the second accepts strings. Both cannot emit errors.

2. Zip `publisher1` with `publisher2`, pairing their emissions once they each emit a new value.

3. Send 1 and 2 to `publisher1`, then "a" and "b" to `publisher2`, then 3 to `publisher1` again, and finally "c" and "d" to `publisher2`.

4. Complete both `publisher1` and `publisher2`.

Run your playground a final time and take a look at the debug console:

```
——— Example of: zip ———
P1: 1, P2: a
P1: 2, P2: b
P1: 3, P2: c
Completed
```

Notice how each emitted value "waits" for the other zipped publisher to emit a value. 1 waits for the first emission from the second publisher, so you get (1, "a"). Likewise, 2 waits for the next emission from the second publisher, so you get (2, "b"). The last emitted value from the second publisher, "d", is ignored since there is no corresponding emission from the first publisher to pair with.

Key points

In this chapter, you learned how to take different publishers and create meaningful combinations from them. More specifically, you learned that:

- You can use the `prepend` and `append` families of operators to add emissions from one publisher before or after a different publisher.

- While `switchToLatest` is relatively complex, it's extremely useful. It takes a publisher that emits publishers, switches to the latest publisher and cancels the subscription to the previous publisher.

- `merge(with:)` lets you *interleave* values from multiple publishers.

- `combineLatest` emits the latest values of all combined publishers whenever *any* of them emit a value, once all of the combined publishers have emitted at least one value.

- `zip` pairs emissions from different publishers, emitting a tuple of pairs after all publishers have emitted an value.

- You can mix combination operators to create interesting and complex relationships between publishers and their emissions.

Where to go from here?

This has been quite a long chapter, but it includes some of the most useful and involved operators Combine has to offer. Kudos to you for making it this far!

No challenges this time. Try to experiment with all of the operators you've learned thus far, there are plenty of use cases to play with.

You have two more groups of operators to learn about in the next two chapters: "Time Manipulation Operators" and "Sequence Operators," so move on to the next chapter!

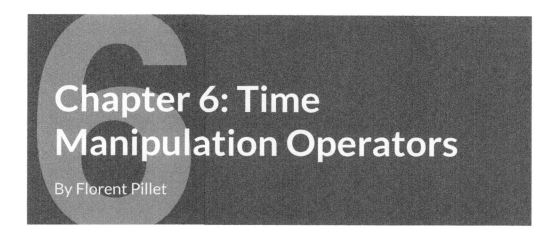

Chapter 6: Time Manipulation Operators
By Florent Pillet

Timing is everything. The core idea behind reactive programming is to model asynchronous event flow *over time*. In this respect, the Combine framework provides a range of operators that allow you to deal with time. In particular, how sequences react to and transform values over time.

As you'll see throughout this chapter, managing the time dimension of your sequence of values is easy and straightforward. It's one of the great benefits of using a framework like Combine.

Getting started

To learn about time manipulation operators, you'll practice with an animated Xcode Playground that visualizes how data flows over time. This chapter comes with a starter playground you'll find in the **projects** folder.

The playground is divided into several pages. You'll use each page to exercise one or more related operators. It also includes some ready-made classes, functions and sample data that'll come in handy to build the examples.

If you have the playground set to show rendered markup, at the bottom of each page there will be a **Next** link that you can click to go to the next page.

> **Note:** To toggle showing rendered markup on and off, select **Editor ▸ Show Rendered/Raw Markup** from the menu.

You can also select the page you want from the Project navigator in the left sidebar or even the jump bar at the top of the page. There are lots of ways to get around in Xcode!

Look at Xcode, and you'll see the sidebar control at the top-left part of the window:

1. Make sure the left sidebar button is toggled so you can see the list of Playground pages:

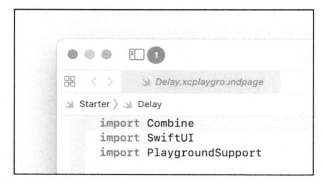

2. Next, look at the top-right side of the window. You'll see the view controls:

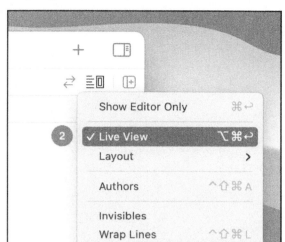

Show the editor with **Live View**. This will display a live view of the sequences you build in code. This is where the real action will happen!

3. Showing the Debug area is important for most of the examples in this chapter. Toggle the Debug area using the following icon at the bottom-right of the window, or using the keyboard shortcut **Command-Shift-Y**:

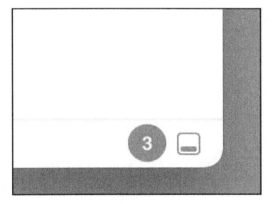

Playground not working?

From time to time Xcode may "act up" and not run properly your playground. If this happens to you, open the **Preferences** dialog in Xcode and select the **Locations** tab. Click the arrow next to the Derived Data location, depicted by the red circled **1** in the screenshot below. It shows the `DerivedData` folder in the Finder.

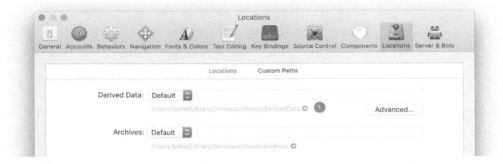

Quit Xcode, move the `DerivedData` folder to trash then launch Xcode again. Your playground should now work properly!

Shifting time

Every now and again you need time traveling. While Combine can't help with fixing your past relationship mistakes, it can freeze time for a little while to let you wait until self-cloning is available.

The most basic time manipulation operator delays values from a publisher so that you see them later than they actually occur.

The `delay(for:tolerance:scheduler:options)` operator time-shifts a whole sequence of values: Every time the upstream publisher emits a value, delay keeps it for a while then emits it after the delay you asked for, on the scheduler you specified.

Open the **Delay** playground page. The first thing you'll see is that you're not only importing the **Combine** framework but also **SwiftUI**! This animated playground is built with SwiftUI and Combine. When you feel in an adventurous mood, it'll be a good idea to peruse through the code in the **Sources** folder.

But first things first. Start by defining a couple of constants you'll be able to tweak later:

```
let valuesPerSecond = 1.0
let delayInSeconds = 1.5
```

You're going to create a publisher that emits one value every second, then delay it by 1.5 seconds and display both timelines simultaneously to compare them. Once you complete the code on this page, you'll be able to adjust the constants and watch results in the timelines.

Next, create the publishers you need:

```
// 1
let sourcePublisher = PassthroughSubject<Date, Never>()

// 2
let delayedPublisher =
sourcePublisher.delay(for: .seconds(delayInSeconds), scheduler: DispatchQueue.main)

// 3
let subscription = Timer
  .publish(every: 1.0 / valuesPerSecond, on: .main, in: .common)
  .autoconnect()
  .subscribe(sourcePublisher)
```

Breaking this code down:

1. `sourcePublisher` is a simple `Subject` which you'll feed dates a `Timer` emits. The type of values is of little importance here. You only care about imaging **when** a publisher emits a value, and when the value shows up after a delay.

2. `delayedPublisher` will delay values from a `sourcePublisher` and emit them on the main scheduler. You'll learn all about schedulers in Chapter 17, "Schedulers." For now, specify that values must end up on the main queue, ready for display to consume them.

3. Create a timer that delivers one value per second on the main thread. Start it immediately with `autoconnect()` and feed the values it emits through the `sourcePublisher` subject.

> **Note:** This particular timer is a Combine extension on the Foundation `Timer` class. It takes a `RunLoop` and `RunLoop.Mode`, and not a `DispatchQueue` as you may expect. You'll learn all about timers in Chapter 11, "Timers." Also, timers are part of a class of publishers that are **connectable**. This means they need to be connected to before they start emitting values. You use `autoconnect()` which immediately connects upon the first subscription.

You're getting to the part where you create the two views that will let you visualize events. Add this code to your playground:

```
// 4
let sourceTimeline = TimelineView(title: "Emitted values (\
(valuesPerSecond) per sec.):")

// 5
let delayedTimeline = TimelineView(title: "Delayed values (with
a \(delayInSeconds)s delay):")

// 6
let view = VStack(spacing: 50) {
  sourceTimeline
  delayedTimeline
}

// 7
PlaygroundPage.current.liveView = UIHostingController(rootView:
view.frame(width: 375, height: 600))
```

In this code, you:

4. Create a `TimelineView` that will display values from the timer. `TimelineView` is a SwiftUI view, its code can be found at **Sources/Views.swift**.

5. Create another `TimelineView` to display delayed values.

6. Create a simple SwiftUI vertical stack to display both timelines one above the other.

7. Set up the live view for this playground page. The additional `frame(widht:height:)` modifier is just there to help set a fixed frame for Xcode's previews.

At this stage, you see two empty timelines on the screen. You now need to feed them with the values from each publisher! Add this final code to the playground:

```
sourcePublisher.displayEvents(in: sourceTimeline)
delayedPublisher.displayEvents(in: delayedTimeline)
```

In this last piece of code, you connect the source and delayed publishers to their respective timelines to display events.

Once you save these source changes, Xcode will recompile the playground code and... look at the Live View pane! Finally!

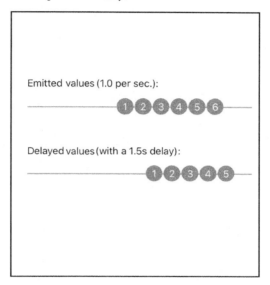

You'll see two timelines. The top timeline shows values the timer emitted. The bottom timeline shows the same values, delayed. The numbers inside the circles reflect the count of values emitted, not their actual content.

> **Note**: As exciting as it is to see a live observable diagram, it might confuse at first. Static timelines usually have their values aligned to the left. But, if you think twice about it, they also have the most recent ones on the right side just as the animated diagrams you observe right now.

Collecting values

In certain situations, you may need to collect values from a publisher at specified time intervals. This is a form of buffering that can be useful. For example, when you want to average a group of values over short periods of time and output the average.

Switch to the **Collect** page by clicking the **Next** link at the bottom, or by selecting it in the Project navigator or jump bar.

As in the previous example, you'll begin with some constants:

```
let valuesPerSecond = 1.0
let collectTimeStride = 4
```

Of course, reading these constants gives you an idea of where this is all going. Create your publishers now:

```
// 1
let sourcePublisher = PassthroughSubject<Date, Never>()

// 2
let collectedPublisher = sourcePublisher
  .collect(.byTime(DispatchQueue.main, .seconds(collectTimeStride)))
```

Like in the previous example, you:

1. Set up a source publisher — a subject that will relay the values a timer emits.

2. Create a `collectedPublisher` which collects values it receives during strides of `collectTimeStride` using the `collect` operator. The operator emits these groups of values as arrays on the specified scheduler: `DispatchQueue.main`.

> **Note**: You might remember learning about the `collect` operator in Chapter 3, "Transforming Operators," where you used a simple number to define how to group values together. This overload of `collect` accepts a strategy for grouping values; in this case, by time.

You'll use a `Timer` again to emit values at regular intervals as you did for the `delay` operator:

```
let subscription = Timer
  .publish(every: 1.0 / valuesPerSecond, on: .main, in: .common)
  .autoconnect()
  .subscribe(sourcePublisher)
```

Next, create the timeline views like in the previous example. Then, set the playground's live view to a vertical stack showing the source timeline and the timeline of collected values:

```
let sourceTimeline = TimelineView(title: "Emitted values:")
let collectedTimeline = TimelineView(title: "Collected values
(every \(collectTimeStride)s):")

let view = VStack(spacing: 40) {
  sourceTimeline
  collectedTimeline
}

PlaygroundPage.current.liveView = UIHostingController(rootView:
view.frame(width: 375, height: 600))
```

Finally, feed the timelines with events from both publishers:

```
sourcePublisher.displayEvents(in: sourceTimeline)
collectedPublisher.displayEvents(in: collectedTimeline)
```

You're done! Now look at the live view for a while:

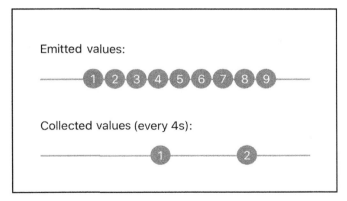

You see values appear at regular intervals on the **Emitted values** timeline. Below it, you see that every four seconds the **Collected values** timeline displays a single value. But what is it?

You may have guessed that the value is an array of values received during the last four seconds. You can improve the display to see what's actually in it! Go back to the line where you created the `collectedPublisher` object. Add the use of the `flatMap` operator just below it, so it looks like this:

```
let collectedPublisher = sourcePublisher
  .collect(.byTime(DispatchQueue.main, .seconds(collectTimeStrid
e)))
  .flatMap { dates in dates.publisher }
```

Do you remember your friend `flatMap` you learned about in Chapter 3, "Transforming Operators?" You're putting it to good use here: Every time `collect` emits a group of values it collected, `flatMap` breaks it down again to individual values but emitted **immediately one after the other**. To this end, it uses the `publisher` extension of `Collection` that turns a sequence of values into a Publisher, emitting immediately all values in the sequence as individual values.

Now, look at the effect it has on the timeline:

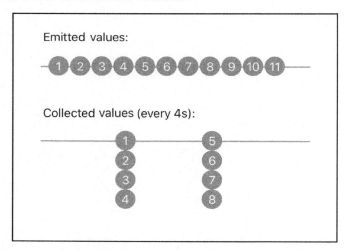

You can now see that, every four seconds, `collect` emits an array of values collected during the last time interval.

Collecting values (part 2)

The second option the `collect(_:options:)` operator offers allows you to keep collecting values at regular intervals. It also allows you to limit the number of values collected.

Staying on the same **Collect** page, and add a new constant right below `collectTimeStride` at the top:

```
let collectMaxCount = 2
```

Next, create a new publisher after `collectedPublisher`:

```
let collectedPublisher2 = sourcePublisher
  .collect(.byTimeOrCount(DispatchQueue.main,
                          .seconds(collectTimeStride),
                          collectMaxCount))
  .flatMap { dates in dates.publisher }
```

This time, you are using the `.byTimeOrCount(Context, Context.SchedulerTimeType.Stride, Int)` variant to collect up to `collectMaxCount` values at a time. What does this mean? Keep adding code and you'll find out!

Add a new `TimelineView` for the second collect publisher in between `collectedTimeline` and `let view = VStack...`:

```
let collectedTimeline2 = TimelineView(title: "Collected values (at most \(collectMaxCount) every \(collectTimeStride)s):")
```

And of course add it to the list of stacked views, so `view` looks like this:

```
let view = VStack(spacing: 40) {
  sourceTimeline
  collectedTimeline
  collectedTimeline2
}
```

Finally, make sure it displays the events it emits in the timeline by adding the following at the end of your playground:

```
collectedPublisher2.displayEvents(in: collectedTimeline2)
```

Now, let this timeline run for a while so you can witness the difference:

```
Emitted values:
─①②③④⑤⑥⑦⑧⑨⑩─

Collected values (every 4s):
        ①       ⑤
        ②       ⑥
        ③       ⑦
        ④       ⑧

Collected values (at most 2 every 4s):
─①  ③  ⑤  ⑦  ⑨─
 ②  ④  ⑥  ⑧  ⑩
```

You can see here that the second timeline is limiting its collection to two values at a time, as required by the `collectMaxCount` constant. It's a useful tool to know about!

Holding off on events

When coding user interfaces, you frequently deal with text fields. Wiring up text field contents to an action using Combine is a common task. For example, you may want to send a search URL request that returns a list of items matching what's typed in the text field.

But of course, you don't want to send a request every time your user types a single letter! You need some kind of mechanism to help pick up on typed text only when the user is done typing for a while.

Combine offers two operators that can help you here: `debounce` and `throttle`. Let's explore them!

Debounce

Switch to the playground page named **Debounce**. Make sure that the Debug area is visible — **View ▸ Debug Area ▸ Activate Console** — so you can see the printouts of values debounce emits.

Start by creating a couple of publishers:

```
// 1
let subject = PassthroughSubject<String, Never>()
// 2
let debounced = subject
  .debounce(for: .seconds(1.0), scheduler: DispatchQueue.main)
  // 3
  .share()
```

In this code, you:

1. Create a source publisher which will emit strings.

2. Use debounce to wait for one second on emissions from `subject`. Then, it will send the last value sent in that one-second interval, if any. This has the effect of allowing a max of one value per second to be sent.

3. You are going to subscribe multiple times to debounced. To guarantee consistency of the results, you use `share()` to create a single subscription point to debounce that will show the same results at the same time to all subscribers.

> **Note:** Diving into the `share()` operator is out of the scope of this chapter. Just remember that it is helpful when a single subscription to a publisher is required to deliver the same results to multiple subscribers. You'll learn more about `share()` in Chapter 13, "Resource Management."

For these next few examples, you will use a set of data to simulate a user typing text in a text field. Don't type this in — it's already been implemented in **Sources/ Data.swift** for you:

```
public let typingHelloWorld: [(TimeInterval, String)] = [
  (0.0, "H"),
  (0.1, "He"),
  (0.2, "Hel"),
  (0.3, "Hell"),
  (0.5, "Hello"),
```

```
    (0.6, "Hello "),
    (2.0, "Hello W"),
    (2.1, "Hello Wo"),
    (2.2, "Hello Wor"),
    (2.4, "Hello Worl"),
    (2.5, "Hello World")
]
```

The simulated user starts typing at `0.0` seconds, pauses after `0.6` seconds, and resumes typing at `2.0` seconds.

> **Note:** The time values you'll see in the Debug area may be offset by one or two tenth of a second. Since you'll be emitting values on the main queue using `DispatchQueue.asyncAfter()`, you are guaranteed a *minimum* time interval between values but maybe not *exactly* what you requested.

In the playground's **Debounce** page, create two timelines to visualize events, and wire them up to the two publishers:

```
let subjectTimeline = TimelineView(title: "Emitted values")
let debouncedTimeline = TimelineView(title: "Debounced values")

let view = VStack(spacing: 100) {
    subjectTimeline
    debouncedTimeline
}

PlaygroundPage.current.liveView = UIHostingController(rootView:
view.frame(width: 375, height: 600))

subject.displayEvents(in: subjectTimeline)
debounced.displayEvents(in: debouncedTimeline)
```

You are now familiar with this playground structure where you stack timelines on the screen and connect them to the publishers for event display.

This time, you're going to do something more: Print values each publisher emits, along with the time (since start) at which they show up. This will help you figure out what's happening.

Add this code:

```
let subscription1 = subject
  .sink { string in
    print("+\(deltaTime)s: Subject emitted: \(string)")
  }

let subscription2 = debounced
  .sink { string in
    print("+\(deltaTime)s: Debounced emitted: \(string)")
  }
```

Each subscription prints the values it receives, along with the time since start. `deltaTime` is a dynamic global variable defined in **Sources/DeltaTime.swift** which formats the time difference since the playground started running.

Now you need to feed your subject with data. This time you're going to use a pre-made data source that simulates a user typing text. It's all defined in **Sources/Data.swift** and you can modify it at will. Take a look, you'll see that it's a simulation of a user typing the words "Hello World".

Add this code to the end of the playground page:

```
subject.feed(with: typingHelloWorld)
```

The `feed(with:)` method takes a data set and sends data to the given `subject` at pre-defined time intervals. A handy tool for simulations and mocking data input! You may want to keep this around when you write tests for your code because you **will** write tests, won't you?

Now look at the result:

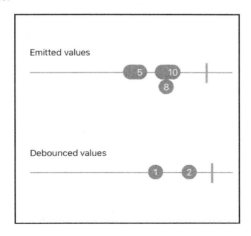

You see the emitted values at the top, there are 11 strings total being pushed to the sourcePublisher. You can see that the user *paused* between the two words. This is the time where debounce emitted the captured input.

You can confirm this by looking at the debug area where the prints show up:

```
+0.0s: Subject emitted: H
+0.1s: Subject emitted: He
+0.2s: Subject emitted: Hel
+0.3s: Subject emitted: Hell
+0.5s: Subject emitted: Hello
+0.6s: Subject emitted: Hello
+1.6s: Debounced emitted: Hello
+2.1s: Subject emitted: Hello W
+2.1s: Subject emitted: Hello Wo
+2.4s: Subject emitted: Hello Wor
+2.4s: Subject emitted: Hello Worl
+2.7s: Subject emitted: Hello World
+3.7s: Debounced emitted: Hello World
```

As you can see, at `0.6` seconds the user pauses and resumes typing only at `2.1` seconds. Meanwhile, you configured debounce to wait for a one-second pause. It obliges (at `1.6` seconds) and emits the latest received value.

Same around the end where typing ends at `2.7` seconds and debounce kicks in one second later at `3.7` seconds. Cool!

> **Note**: One thing to watch out for is the publisher's completion. If your publisher completes right after the last value was emitted, but before the time configured for debounce elapses, you will never see the last value in the debounced publisher!

Throttle

The kind of holding-off pattern that debounce allows is so useful that Combine provides a close relative: `throttle(for:scheduler:latest:)`. It's very close to debounce, but the differences justify the need for two operators.

Switch to the **Throttle** page in the playground and get coding. First, you need a constant, as usual:

```
let throttleDelay = 1.0
// 1
```

```
  let subject = PassthroughSubject<String, Never>()
// 2
  let throttled = subject
    .throttle(for: .seconds(throttleDelay), scheduler:
DispatchQueue.main, latest: false)
// 3
    .share()
```

Breaking down this code:

1. The source publisher will emit strings.

2. Your throttled subject will now only emit the first value it received from `subject` during each one-second interval because you set `latest` to `false`.

3. Like in the previous operator, debounce, adding the `share()` operator here guarantees that all subscribers see the same output at the same time from the throttled subject.

Create timelines to visualize events, and wire them up to the two publishers:

```
  let subjectTimeline = TimelineView(title: "Emitted values")
  let throttledTimeline = TimelineView(title: "Throttled values")

  let view = VStack(spacing: 100) {
    subjectTimeline
    throttledTimeline
  }

  PlaygroundPage.current.liveView = UIHostingController(rootView:
view.frame(width: 375, height: 600))

  subject.displayEvents(in: subjectTimeline)
  throttled.displayEvents(in: throttledTimeline)
```

Now you also want to print the values each publisher emits, to better understand what's going on. Add this code:

```
  let subscription1 = subject
    .sink { string in
      print("+\(deltaTime)s: Subject emitted: \(string)")
    }

  let subscription2 = throttled
    .sink { string in
      print("+\(deltaTime)s: Throttled emitted: \(string)")
    }
```

Again, you're going to feed your source publisher with a simulated "Hello World" user input. Add this final line to your playground page:

```
subject.feed(with: typingHelloWorld)
```

Your playground is ready! You can now see what's happening in the live view:

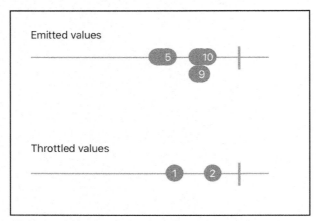

Isn't this puzzling? It doesn't look *that much* different from the previous debounce output! Well, it actually is.

First, look closely at both. You can see that the values emitted by `throttle` have slightly different timing.

Second, to get a better picture of what's happening, look at the debug console:

```
+0.0s: Subject emitted: H
+0.0s: Throttled emitted: H
+0.1s: Subject emitted: He
+0.2s: Subject emitted: Hel
+0.3s: Subject emitted: Hell
+0.5s: Subject emitted: Hello
+0.6s: Subject emitted: Hello
+1.0s: Throttled emitted: He
+2.2s: Subject emitted: Hello W
+2.2s: Subject emitted: Hello Wo
+2.2s: Subject emitted: Hello Wor
+2.4s: Subject emitted: Hello Worl
+2.7s: Subject emitted: Hello World
+3.0s: Throttled emitted: Hello W
```

This is clearly different! You can see a few interesting things here:

- When the subject emits its first value, `throttle` immediately relays it. Then, it starts *throttling* the output.

- At `1.0` second, `throttle` emits "He". Remember you asked it to send you the first value (since the last) after one second.

- At `2.2` seconds, typing resumes. You can see that at this time, `throttle` didn't emit anything. This is because no new value had been received from the source publisher.

- At `3.0` seconds, after typing completes, `throttle` kicks in again and outputs the first value again, i.e., the value at `2.2` seconds.

There you have the fundamental difference between `debounce` and `throttle`:

- `debounce` waits for a pause in values it receives, then emits the latest one after the specified interval.

- `throttle` waits for the specified interval, then emits either the first or the latest of the values it received during that interval. It doesn't care about pauses.

To see what happens when you change `latest` to `true`, change your setup of the throttled publisher to the following:

```
let throttled = subject
  .throttle(for: .seconds(throttleDelay), scheduler: DispatchQueue.main, latest: true)
  .share()
```

Now, observe the resulting output in the debug area:

```
+0.0s: Subject emitted: H
+0.0s: Throttled emitted: H
+0.1s: Subject emitted: He
+0.2s: Subject emitted: Hel
+0.3s: Subject emitted: Hell
+0.5s: Subject emitted: Hello
+0.6s: Subject emitted: Hello
+1.0s: Throttled emitted: Hello
+2.0s: Subject emitted: Hello W
+2.3s: Subject emitted: Hello Wo
+2.3s: Subject emitted: Hello Wor
+2.6s: Subject emitted: Hello Worl
+2.6s: Subject emitted: Hello World
+3.0s: Throttled emitted: Hello World
```

The throttled output occurs at precisely `1.0` second and `3.0` seconds with the latest value in the time window instead of the earliest one. Compare this with the output from debounce from the earlier example:

```
...
+1.6s: Debounced emitted: Hello
...
+3.7s: Debounced emitted: Hello World
```

The output is the same, but `debounce` is delayed from the pause.

Timing out

Next in this roundup of time manipulation operators is a special one: **timeout**. Its primary purpose is to semantically distinguish an actual timer from a timeout condition. Therefore, when a timeout operator fires, it either completes the publisher or emits an error you specify. In both cases, the publisher terminates.

Switch to the **Timeout** playground page. Begin by adding this code:

```
let subject = PassthroughSubject<Void, Never>()

// 1
let timedOutSubject = subject.timeout(.seconds(5), scheduler: DispatchQueue.main)
```

1. The `timedOutSubject` publisher will time-out after five seconds without the upstream publisher emitting any value. This form of `timeout` forces a publisher completion without any failure.

You now need to add your timeline, as well as a button to let you trigger events:

```
let timeline = TimelineView(title: "Button taps")

let view = VStack(spacing: 100) {
  // 1
  Button(action: { subject.send() }) {
    Text("Press me within 5 seconds")
  }
  timeline
}

PlaygroundPage.current.liveView = UIHostingController(rootView: view.frame(width: 375, height: 600))

timedOutSubject.displayEvents(in: timeline)
```

1. This is a new one! You add a button above the timeline, which sends a new value through the source subject when pressed. The `action` closure will execute every time you press the button.

> **Note**: Have you noticed you're using a subject that emits `Void` values? Yes, this is totally legitimate! It signals that *something* happened. But, there is no particular value to carry. So, you simply use `Void` as the value type. This is such a common case that `Subject` has an extension with a `send()` function that takes no parameter in case the `Output` type is `Void`. This saves you from writing the awkward `subject.send(())` statement!

Your playground page is now complete. Watch it run and do nothing: the `timeout` will trigger after five seconds and complete the publisher.

Now, run it again. This time, keep pressing the button at less-than-five-seconds intervals. The publisher never completes because `timeout` doesn't kick in.

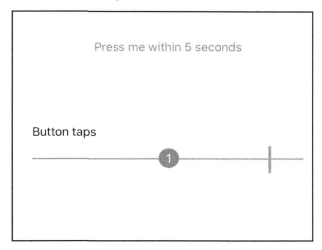

Of course, the simple completion of a publisher is not what you want in many cases. Instead, you need the `timeout` publisher to send a failure so you can accurately take action in this case.

Go to the top of the playground page and define the error type you want:

```
enum TimeoutError: Error {
  case timedOut
}
```

Next, modify the definition of `subject` to change the error type from `Never` to `TimeoutError`. Your code should look like this:

```
let subject = PassthroughSubject<Void, TimeoutError>()
```

Now you need to modify the call to `timeout`. The complete signature for this operator is `timeout(_:scheduler:options:customError:)`. Here is your chance to provide your custom error type!

Modify the line that creates the `timedOutSubject` to this:

```
let timedOutSubject = subject.timeout(.seconds(5),
                                      scheduler: DispatchQueue.main,
                                      customError: { .timedOut })
```

Now when you run the playground and don't press the button for five seconds, you can see that the `timedOutSubject` emits a failure.

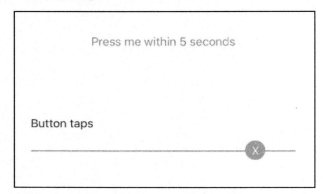

Now that the time allocated to this operator ran out, let's move to the last one in this section.

Measuring time

To complete this roundup of time manipulation operators, you'll look at one particular operator which doesn't manipulate time but just *measures* it. The `measureInterval(using:)` operator is your tool when you need to find out the time that elapsed between two consecutive values a publisher emitted.

Switch to the **MeasureInterval** playground page. Begin by creating a pair of publishers:

```
let subject = PassthroughSubject<String, Never>()

// 1
let measureSubject = subject.measureInterval(using: DispatchQueue.main)
```

The `measureSubject` will emit measurements on the scheduler you specify. Here, the main queue.

Now as usual, add a couple of timelines:

```
let subjectTimeline = TimelineView(title: "Emitted values")
let measureTimeline = TimelineView(title: "Measured values")

let view = VStack(spacing: 100) {
  subjectTimeline
  measureTimeline
}

PlaygroundPage.current.liveView = UIHostingController(rootView: view.frame(width: 375, height: 600))

subject.displayEvents(in: subjectTimeline)
measureSubject.displayEvents(in: measureTimeline)
```

Finally, here comes the interesting part. Print out values both publishers emit, and then feed the subject:

```
let subscription1 = subject.sink {
  print("+\(deltaTime)s: Subject emitted: \($0)")
}

let subscription2 = measureSubject.sink {
  print("+\(deltaTime)s: Measure emitted: \($0)")
}

subject.feed(with: typingHelloWorld)
```

Run your playground and have a look at the debug area! This is where you see what `measureInterval(using:)` emits:

```
+0.0s: Subject emitted: H
+0.0s: Measure emitted: Stride(magnitude: 16818353)
+0.1s: Subject emitted: He
+0.1s: Measure emitted: Stride(magnitude: 87377323)
+0.2s: Subject emitted: Hel
+0.2s: Measure emitted: Stride(magnitude: 111515697)
+0.3s: Subject emitted: Hell
+0.3s: Measure emitted: Stride(magnitude: 105128640)
+0.5s: Subject emitted: Hello
+0.5s: Measure emitted: Stride(magnitude: 228804831)
+0.6s: Subject emitted: Hello
+0.6s: Measure emitted: Stride(magnitude: 104349343)
+2.2s: Subject emitted: Hello W
+2.2s: Measure emitted: Stride(magnitude: 1533804859)
+2.2s: Subject emitted: Hello Wo
+2.2s: Measure emitted: Stride(magnitude: 154602)
+2.4s: Subject emitted: Hello Wor
+2.4s: Measure emitted: Stride(magnitude: 228888306)
+2.4s: Subject emitted: Hello Worl
+2.4s: Measure emitted: Stride(magnitude: 138241)
+2.7s: Subject emitted: Hello World
+2.7s: Measure emitted: Stride(magnitude: 333195273)
```

The values are a bit puzzling, aren't they? It turns out that, as per the documentation, the type of the value `measureInterval` emits is "*the time interval of the provided scheduler*". In the case of `DispatchQueue`, the `TimeInterval` is defined as "*A DispatchTimeInterval created with the value of this type in nanoseconds.*".

What you are seeing here is a count, in nanoseconds, **between each consecutive value** received from the source subject. You can now fix the display to show more readable values. Modify the code that prints values from `measureSubject` like so:

```
let subscription2 = measureSubject.sink {
  print("+\(deltaTime)s: Measure emitted: \(Double($0.magnitude) / 1_000_000_000.0)")
}
```

Now, you'll see values in seconds.

But what happens if you use a different scheduler? You can try it using a `RunLoop` instead of a `DispatchQueue`!

> **Note**: You will explore the `RunLoop` and `DispatchQueue` schedulers in depth in Chapter 17, "Schedulers."

Back to the top of the file, create a second subject that uses a `RunLoop`:

```
let measureSubject2 = subject.measureInterval(using:
RunLoop.main)
```

You don't need to bother wiring up a new timeline view, because what's interesting is the debug output. Add this third subscription to your code:

```
let subscription3 = measureSubject2.sink {
  print("+\(deltaTime)s: Measure2 emitted: \($0)")
}
```

Now, you'll see the output from the `RunLoop` scheduler as well, with magnitudes directly expressed in seconds:

```
+0.0s: Subject emitted: H
+0.0s: Measure emitted: 0.016503769
+0.0s: Measure2 emitted: Stride(magnitude: 0.015684008598327637)
+0.1s: Subject emitted: He
+0.1s: Measure emitted: 0.087991755
+0.1s: Measure2 emitted: Stride(magnitude: 0.08793699741363525)
+0.2s: Subject emitted: Hel
+0.2s: Measure emitted: 0.115842671
+0.2s: Measure2 emitted: Stride(magnitude: 0.11583995819091797)
...
```

The scheduler you use for measurement is really up to your personal taste. It is generally a good idea to stick with `DispatchQueue` for everything. But that's your personal choice!

Challenge

Challenge: Data

If time allows, you may want to try a little challenge to put this new knowledge to good use!

Open the starter challenge playground in the **projects/challenge** folder. You see some code waiting for you:

- A subject that emits integers.
- A function call that feeds the subject with mysterious data.

In between those parts, your challenge is to:

- Group data by batches of `0.5` seconds.
- Turn the grouped data into a string.
- If there is a pause longer than `0.9` seconds in the feed, print the 👏 emoji. Hint: Create a second publisher for this step and merge it with the first publisher in your subscription.
- Print it.

> **Note**: To convert an `Int` to a `Character`, you can do something like `Character(Unicode.Scalar(value)!)`.

If you code this challenge correctly, you'll see a sentence printed in the Debug area. What is it?

Solution

You'll find the solution to this challenge in the **challenge/Final.playground** Xcode playground.

Here's the solution code:

```
// 1
let strings = subject
  // 2
  .collect(.byTime(DispatchQueue.main, .seconds(0.5)))
  // 3
  .map { array in
    String(array.map { Character(Unicode.Scalar($0)!) })
  }

// 4
let spaces = subject.measureInterval(using: DispatchQueue.main)
  .map { interval in
    // 5
    interval > 0.9 ? "👏" : ""
  }

// 6
let subscription = strings
  .merge(with: spaces)
  // 7
  .filter { !$0.isEmpty }
```

```
.sink {
  // 8
  print($0)
}
```

From the top, you:

1. Create a first publisher derived from the subject which emits the strings.

2. Use `collect()` using the `.byTime` strategy to group data in `0.5` seconds batches.

3. Map each integer value to a Unicode scalar, then to a character and then turn the whole lot into a string using `map`.

4. Create a second publisher derived from the subject, which measures the intervals between each character.

5. If the interval is greater than `0.9` seconds, map the value to the 👏 emoji. Otherwise, map it to an empty string.

6. The final publisher is a merge of both strings and the 👏 emoji.

7. Filter out empty strings for better display.

8. Print the result!

Your solution might have been subtly different, and that's OK. As long as you met the requirements, you get the W!

Running the playground with this solution will print the following output to the console:

Key points

In this chapter, you looked at time from a different perspective. In particular, you learned that:

- Combine's handling of asynchronous events extends to manipulating time itself.
- Even though it doesn't provide time-traveling options, the framework has operators that let you abstract work over long periods of time, rather than just handling discrete events.
- Time can be shifted using the `delay` operator.
- You can manage the flow of values over time like a dam and release them by chunks using `collect`.
- Picking individual values over time is easy with `debounce` and `throttle`.
- Not letting time run out is the job of `timeout`.
- Time can be measured with `measureInterval`.

Where to go from here?

This was a lot to learn. To put events in their right order, move along to the next chapter and learn about sequence operators!

Chapter 7: Sequence Operators

By Shai Mishali

At this point, you know most of the operators that Combine has to offer! How great is that? There's still one more category for you to dig into, though: **Sequence Operators**.

Sequence operators are easiest to understand when you realize that publishers are just sequences themselves. Sequence operators work with a publisher's values, much like an array or a set — which, of course, are just finite sequences!

With that in mind, sequence operators mostly deal with the publisher as a whole and not with individual values, as other operator categories do.

Many of the operators in this category have nearly identical names and behaviors as their counterparts in the Swift standard library.

Getting started

You can find the starter playground for this chapter in **projects/Starter.playground**. Throughout this chapter, you'll add code to your playground and run it to see how these different sequence operators manipulate your publisher. You'll use the `print` operator to log all publishing events.

Finding values

The first section of this chapter consists of operators that locate specific values the publisher emits based on different criteria. These are similar to the collection methods in the Swift standard library.

min

The `min` operator lets you find the minimum value emitted by a publisher. It's *greedy*, which means it must wait for the publisher to send a `.finished` completion event. Once the publisher completes, only the minimum value is emitted by the operator:

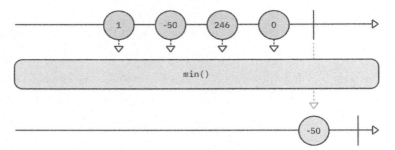

Add the following example to your playground to try `min`:

```
example(of: "min") {
  // 1
  let publisher = [1, -50, 246, 0].publisher

  // 2
  publisher
    .print("publisher")
    .min()
    .sink(receiveValue: { print("Lowest value is \($0)") })
    .store(in: &subscriptions)
}
```

In this code, you:

1. Create a publisher emitting four different numbers.

2. Use the `min` operator to find the minimum number emitted by the publisher and print that value.

Run your playground and you'll see the following output in the console:

```
——— Example of: min ———
publisher: receive subscription: ([1, -50, 246, 0])
publisher: request unlimited
publisher: receive value: (1)
publisher: receive value: (-50)
publisher: receive value: (246)
publisher: receive value: (0)
publisher: receive finished
Lowest value is -50
```

As you can see, the publisher emits all its values and finishes, then `min` finds the minimum and sends it downstream to `sink` to print it out.

But wait, how does Combine know which of these numbers is the minimum? Well, that's thanks to the fact numeric values conform to the `Comparable` protocol. You can use `min()` directly, without any arguments, on publishers that emit `Comparable`-conforming types.

But what happens if your values don't conform to `Comparable`? Luckily, you can provide your own comparator closure using the `min(by:)` operator.

Consider the following example, where your publisher emits many pieces of `Data` and you'd like to find the smallest one.

Add the following code to your playground:

```
example(of: "min non-Comparable") {
  // 1
  let publisher = ["12345",
                   "ab",
                   "hello world"]
    .map { Data($0.utf8) } // [Data]
    .publisher // Publisher<Data, Never>

  // 2
  publisher
    .print("publisher")
    .min(by: { $0.count < $1.count })
    .sink(receiveValue: { data in
      // 3
```

```
            let string = String(data: data, encoding: .utf8)!
            print("Smallest data is \(string), \(data.count) bytes")
        })
        .store(in: &subscriptions)
}
```

In the above code:

1. You create a publisher that emits three `Data` objects created from various strings.

2. Since `Data` doesn't conform to `Comparable`, you use the `min(by:)` operator to find the `Data` object with the smallest number of bytes.

3. You convert the smallest `Data` object back to a string and print it out.

Run your playground and you'll see the following in your console:

```
——— Example of: min non-Comparable ———
publisher: receive subscription: ([5 bytes, 2 bytes, 11 bytes])
publisher: request unlimited
publisher: receive value: (5 bytes)
publisher: receive value: (2 bytes)
publisher: receive value: (11 bytes)
publisher: receive finished
Smallest data is ab, 2 bytes
```

Like the previous example, the publisher emits all its `Data` objects and finishes, then `min(by:)` finds and emits the data with the smallest byte size and `sink` prints it out.

max

As you'd guess, `max` works exactly like `min`, except that it finds the *maximum* value emitted by a publisher:

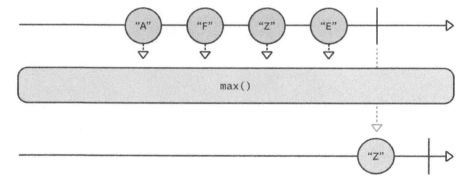

Add the following code to your playground to try this example:

```
example(of: "max") {
  // 1
  let publisher = ["A", "F", "Z", "E"].publisher

  // 2
  publisher
    .print("publisher")
    .max()
    .sink(receiveValue: { print("Highest value is \($0)") })
    .store(in: &subscriptions)
}
```

In the following code, you:

1. Create a publisher that emits four different letters.

2. Use the max operator to find the letter with the highest value and print it.

Run your playground. You'll see the following output in your playground:

```
——— Example of: max ———
publisher: receive subscription: (["A", "F", "Z", "E"])
publisher: request unlimited
publisher: receive value: (A)
publisher: receive value: (F)
publisher: receive value: (Z)
publisher: receive value: (E)
publisher: receive finished
Highest value is Z
```

Exactly like min, max is *greedy* and must wait for the upstream publisher to finish emitting its values before it determines the maximum value. In this case, that value is Z.

> **Note**: Exactly like min, max also has a companion max(by:) operator that accepts a predicate to determine the maximum value emitted among non-Comparable values.

first

While the `min` and `max` operators deal with finding a published value at some unknown index, the rest of the operators in this section deal with finding emitted values at *specific* places, starting with the `first` operator.

The `first` operator is similar to Swift's `first` property on collections, except that it lets the first emitted value through and then completes. It's *lazy*, meaning it doesn't wait for the upstream publisher to finish, but instead will cancel the subscription when it receives the first value emitted.

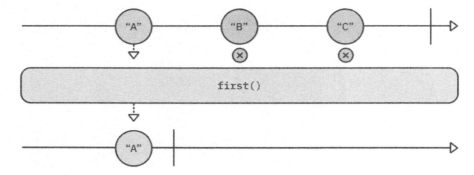

Add the above example to your playground:

```
example(of: "first") {
  // 1
  let publisher = ["A", "B", "C"].publisher

  // 2
  publisher
    .print("publisher")
    .first()
    .sink(receiveValue: { print("First value is \($0)") })
    .store(in: &subscriptions)
}
```

In the above code, you:

1. Create a publisher emitting three letters.

2. Use `first()` to let only the first emitted value through and print it out.

Run your playground and take a look at the console:

```
––––– Example of: first –––––
publisher: receive subscription: (["A", "B", "C"])
publisher: request unlimited
publisher: receive value: (A)
publisher: receive cancel
First value is A
```

As soon as `first()` gets the publisher's first value, it cancels the subscription to the upstream publisher.

If you're looking for more granular control, you can also use `first(where:)`. Just like its counterpart in the Swift standard library, it will emit the first value that matches a provided predicate — if there is one.

Add the following example to your playground:

```
example(of: "first(where:)") {
  // 1
  let publisher = ["J", "O", "H", "N"].publisher
  
  // 2
  publisher
    .print("publisher")
    .first(where: { "Hello World".contains($0) })
    .sink(receiveValue: { print("First match is \($0)") })
    .store(in: &subscriptions)
}
```

In this code, you:

1. Create a publisher that emits four letters.

2. Use the `first(where:)` operator to find the first letter contained in `Hello World` and then print it out.

Run the playground and you'll see the following output:

```
——— Example of: first(where:) ———
publisher: receive subscription: (["J", "O", "H", "N"])
publisher: request unlimited
publisher: receive value: (J)
publisher: receive value: (O)
publisher: receive value: (H)
publisher: receive cancel
First match is H
```

In the above example, the operator checks if `Hello World` contains the emitted letter until it finds the first match: H. Upon finding that much, it cancels the subscription and emits the letter for `sink` to print out.

last

Just as `min` has an opposite, `max`, `first` also has an opposite: `last`!

`last` works exactly like `first`, except it emits the *last* value that the publisher emits. This means it's also *greedy* and must wait for the upstream publisher to finish:

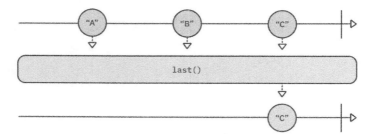

Add this example to your playground:

```
example(of: "last") {
  // 1
  let publisher = ["A", "B", "C"].publisher
  
  // 2
  publisher
    .print("publisher")
    .last()
    .sink(receiveValue: { print("Last value is \($0)") })
    .store(in: &subscriptions)
}
```

In this code, you:

1. Create a publisher that will emit three letters and finish.

2. Use the `last` operator to only emit the last value published and print it out.

Run the playground and you'll see the following output:

```
——— Example of: last ———
publisher: receive subscription: (["A", "B", "C"])
publisher: request unlimited
publisher: receive value: (A)
publisher: receive value: (B)
publisher: receive value: (C)
publisher: receive finished
Last value is C
```

`last` waits for the upstream publisher to send a `.finished` completion event, at which point it sends the last emitted value downstream to be printed out in `sink`.

> **Note**: Exactly like `first`, `last` also has a `last(where:)` overload, which emits the last value emitted by a publisher that matches a specified predicate.

output(at:)

The last two operators in this section don't have counterparts in the Swift standard library. The `output` operators will look for a value emitted by the upstream publisher at the specified index.

You'll start with `output(at:)`, which emits only the value emitted at the specified index:

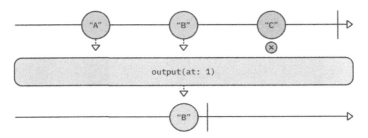

Add the following code to your playground to try this example:

```
example(of: "output(at:)") {
  // 1
  let publisher = ["A", "B", "C"].publisher

  // 2
  publisher
    .print("publisher")
    .output(at: 1)
    .sink(receiveValue: { print("Value at index 1 is \($0)") })
    .store(in: &subscriptions)
}
```

In the above code, you:

1. Create a publisher which emits three letters.

2. Use output(at:) to only let through the value emitted at index 1 — i.e., the second value.

Run the example in your playground and peek at your console:

```
——— Example of: output(at:) ———
publisher: receive subscription: (["A", "B", "C"])
publisher: request unlimited
publisher: receive value: (A)
publisher: request max: (1) (synchronous)
publisher: receive value: (B)
Value at index 1 is B
publisher: receive cancel
```

Here, the output indicates the value at index 1 is B. However, you might've noticed an additional interesting fact: The operator *demands* one more value after every emitted value, since it knows it's only looking for a single item. While this is an implementation detail of the specific operator, it provides interesting insight into how Apple designs some of their own built-in Combine operators to leverage backpressure.

output(in:)

You'll wrap up this section with the second overload of the output operator: output(in:).

While output(at:) emits a *single* value emitted at a specified index, output(in:) emits values whose indices are within a provided *range*:

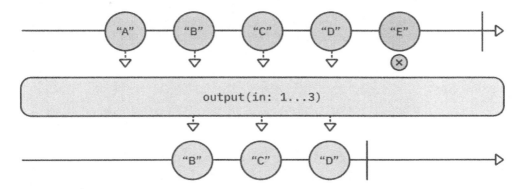

To try this out, add the following example to your playground:

```
example(of: "output(in:)") {
  // 1
  let publisher = ["A", "B", "C", "D", "E"].publisher

  // 2
  publisher
    .output(in: 1...3)
    .sink(receiveCompletion: { print($0) },
          receiveValue: { print("Value in range: \($0)") })
    .store(in: &subscriptions)
}
```

In the previous code, you:

1. Create a publisher that emits five different letters.

2. Use the output(in:) operator to only let through values emitted in indices 1 through 3, then print out those values.

Can you guess what the output of this example will be? Run your playground and find out:

```
——— Example of: output(in:) ———
Value in range: B
Value in range: C
Value in range: D
finished
```

Well, did you guess correctly? The operator emits **individual values** within the range of indices, not a collection of them. The operator prints the values B, C and D as they're in indices 1, 2 and 3, respectively. Then, since all items within the range have been emitted, it cancels the subscription as soon as it receives all values within the provided range.

Querying the publisher

The following operators also deal with the entire set of values emitted by a publisher, but they don't produce any specific value that it emits. Instead, these operators emit a different value representing some query on the publisher as a whole. A good example of this is the count operator.

count

The count operator will emit a single value - the number of values were emitted by the upstream publisher, once the publisher sends a .finished completion event:

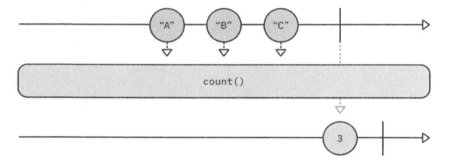

Add the following code to try this example:

```
example(of: "count") {
  // 1
  let publisher = ["A", "B", "C"].publisher

  // 2
  publisher
    .print("publisher")
    .count()
    .sink(receiveValue: { print("I have \($0) items") })
    .store(in: &subscriptions)
}
```

In the above code, you:

1. Create a publisher that emits three letters.

2. Use `count()` to emit a single value indicating the number of values emitted by the upstream publisher.

Run your playground and check your console. You'll see the following output:

```
——— Example of: count ———
publisher: receive subscription: (["A", "B", "C"])
publisher: request unlimited
publisher: receive value: (A)
publisher: receive value: (B)
publisher: receive value: (C)
publisher: receive finished
I have 3 items
```

As expected, the value 3 is only printed out once the upstream publisher sends a `.finished` completion event.

contains

Another useful operator is `contains`. You've probably used its counterpart in the Swift standard library more than once.

The `contains` operator will emit `true` and cancel the subscription if the specified value is emitted by the upstream publisher, or `false` if none of the emitted values are equal to the specified one:

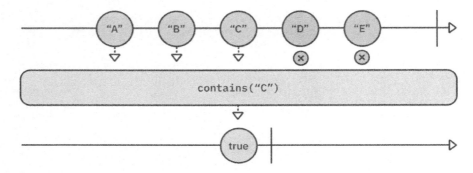

Add the following to your playground to try `contains`:

```
example(of: "contains") {
  // 1
  let publisher = ["A", "B", "C", "D", "E"].publisher
  let letter = "C"

  // 2
  publisher
    .print("publisher")
    .contains(letter)
    .sink(receiveValue: { contains in
      // 3
      print(contains ? "Publisher emitted \(letter)!"
                     : "Publisher never emitted \(letter)!")
    })
    .store(in: &subscriptions)
}
```

In the previous code, you:

1. Create a publisher emitting five different letters — A through E — and create a `letter` value to use with `contains`.

2. Use `contains` to check if the upstream publisher emitted the value of `letter`: C.

3. Print an appropriate message based on whether or not the value was emitted.

Run your playground and check the console:

```
——— Example of: contains ———
publisher: receive subscription: (["A", "B", "C", "D", "E"])
publisher: request unlimited
publisher: receive value: (A)
publisher: receive value: (B)
publisher: receive value: (C)
publisher: receive cancel
Publisher emitted C!
```

Huzzah! You got a message indicating C was emitted by the publisher. You might have also noticed `contains` is lazy, as it only consumes as many upstream values as it needs to perform its work. Once C is found, it cancels the subscription and doesn't produce any further values.

Why don't you try another variation? Replace the following line:

```
let letter = "C"
```

With:

```
let letter = "F"
```

Next, run your playground again. You'll see the following output:

```
——— Example of: contains ———
publisher: receive subscription: (["A", "B", "C", "D", "E"])
publisher: request unlimited
publisher: receive value: (A)
publisher: receive value: (B)
publisher: receive value: (C)
publisher: receive value: (D)
publisher: receive value: (E)
publisher: receive finished
Publisher never emitted F!
```

In this case, `contains` waits for the publisher to emit F. However, the publisher finishes without emitting F, so `contains` emits `false` and you see the appropriate message printed out.

Finally, sometimes you want to look for a match for a predicate that you provide or check for the existence of an emitted value that doesn't conform to `Comparable`. For these specific cases, you have `contains(where:)`.

Add the following example to your playground:

```
example(of: "contains(where:)") {
  // 1
  struct Person {
    let id: Int
    let name: String
  }

  // 2
  let people = [
    (123, "Shai Mishali"),
    (777, "Marin Todorov"),
    (214, "Florent Pillet")
  ]
    .map(Person.init)
    .publisher

  // 3
  people
    .contains(where: { $0.id == 800 })
    .sink(receiveValue: { contains in
      // 4
      print(contains ? "Criteria matches."
                     : "Couldn't find a match for the criteria")
    })
    .store(in: &subscriptions)
}
```

The previous code is a bit more complex, but not by much. You:

1. Define a `Person` struct with an `id` and a `name`.

2. Create a publisher that emits three different instances of `People`.

3. Use `contains` to see if the `id` of any of them is `800`.

4. Print an appropriate message based on the emitted result.

Run your playground and you'll see the following output:

```
——— Example of: contains(where:) ———
Couldn't find a match for the criteria
```

It didn't find any matches, as expected, because none of the emitted people have an id of 800.

Next, change the implementation of `contains(where:)`:

```
.contains(where: { $0.id == 800 })
```

To the following:

```
.contains(where: { $0.id == 800 || $0.name == "Marin Todorov" })
```

Run the playground again and look at the console:

```
——— Example of: contains(where:) ———
Criteria matches!
```

This time it found a value matching the predicate, since Marin is indeed one of the people in your list. Awesome! :]

allSatisfy

A bunch of operators down, and only two to go! Both of them have counterpart collection methods in the Swift standard library.

You'll start with `allSatisfy`, which takes a closure predicate and emits a Boolean indicating whether *all* values emitted by the upstream publisher match that predicate. It's greedy and will, therefore, wait until the upstream publisher emits a `.finished` completion event:

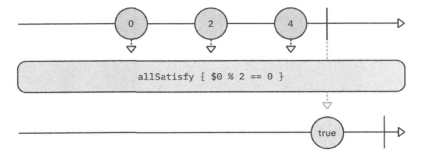

Add the following example to your playground to try this:

```
example(of: "allSatisfy") {
  // 1
  let publisher = stride(from: 0, to: 5, by: 2).publisher

  // 2
  publisher
    .print("publisher")
    .allSatisfy { $0 % 2 == 0 }
    .sink(receiveValue: { allEven in
      print(allEven ? "All numbers are even"
                    : "Something is odd...")
    })
    .store(in: &subscriptions)
}
```

In the above code, you:

1. Create a publisher that emits numbers between 0 to 5 in steps of 2 (i.e., 0, 2 and 4).

2. Use allSatisfy to check if all emitted values are even, then print an appropriate message based on the emitted result.

Run the code and check the console output:

```
——— Example of: allSatisfy ———
publisher: receive subscription: (Sequence)
publisher: request unlimited
publisher: receive value: (0)
publisher: receive value: (2)
publisher: receive value: (4)
publisher: receive finished
All numbers are even
```

Since all values are indeed even, the operator emits true after the upstream publisher sends a .finished completion, and the appropriate message is printed out.

However, if even a single value doesn't pass the predicate condition, the operator will emit false immediately and will cancel the subscription.

Replace the following line:

```
let publisher = stride(from: 0, to: 5, by: 2).publisher
```

With:

```
let publisher = stride(from: 0, to: 5, by: 1).publisher
```

You simply changed the `stride` to step between 0 and 5 by 1, instead of 2. Run the playground once again and take a look at the console:

```
——— Example of: allSatisfy ———
publisher: receive subscription: (Sequence)
publisher: request unlimited
publisher: receive value: (0)
publisher: receive value: (1)
publisher: receive cancel
Something is odd...
```

In this case, as soon as 1 is emitted, the predicate doesn't pass anymore, so `allSatisfy` emits `false` and cancels the subscription.

reduce

Well, here we are! The final operator for this rather packed chapter: `reduce`.

The `reduce` operator is a bit different from the rest of the operators covered in this chapter. It doesn't look for a specific value or query the publisher as a whole. Instead, it lets you iteratively accumulate a *new* value based on the emissions of the upstream publisher.

This might sound confusing at first, but you'll get it in a moment. The easiest way to start is with a diagram:

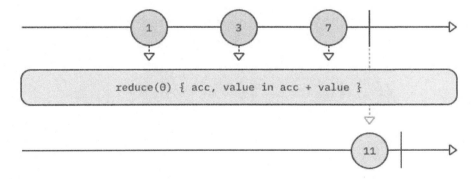

Combine's `reduce` operator works like its counterparts in the Swift standard library: `reduce(_:_)` and `reduce(into:_:)`.

It lets you provide a seed value and an accumulator closure. That closure receives the accumulated value — starting with the seed value — and the current value. From that closure, you return *a new* accumulated value. Once the operator receives a `.finished` completion event, it emits the final accumulated value.

In the case of the above diagram, you can think of it this way :

```
Seed value is 0
Receives 1, 0 + 1 = 1
Receives 3, 1 + 3 = 4
Receives 7, 4 + 7 = 11
Emits 11
```

Time for you to try a quick example to get a better sense of this operator. Add the following to your playground:

```swift
example(of: "reduce") {
  // 1
  let publisher = ["Hel", "lo", " ", "Wor", "ld", "!"].publisher

  publisher
    .print("publisher")
    .reduce("") { accumulator, value in
      // 2
      accumulator + value
    }
    .sink(receiveValue: { print("Reduced into: \($0)") })
    .store(in: &subscriptions)
}
```

In this code, you:

1. Create a publisher that emits six `String`s.

2. Use `reduce` with a seed of an empty string, appending the emitted values to it to create the final string result.

Run the playground and take a look at the console output:

```
——— Example of: reduce ———
publisher: receive subscription: (["Hel", "lo", " ", "Wor", "ld", "!"])
publisher: request unlimited
publisher: receive value: (Hel)
publisher: receive value: (lo)
publisher: receive value: ( )
publisher: receive value: (Wor)
publisher: receive value: (ld)
publisher: receive value: (!)
publisher: receive finished
Reduced into: Hello World!
```

Notice how the accumulated result — Hello World! — is only printed once the upstream publisher sent a .finished completion event.

The second argument for reduce is a closure that takes two values of some type and returns a value of that same type. In Swift, + is an *also* a function that matches that signature.

So as a final neat trick, you can *reduce* the syntax above. Replace the following code:

```
.reduce("") { accumulator, value in
  // 3
  return accumulator + value
}
```

With simply:

```
.reduce("", +)
```

If you run your playground again, it will work exactly the same as before, with a bit of a fancier syntax. ;]

> **Note**: Does this operator feel a bit familiar? Well, that might be because you learned about scan in Chapter 3, "Transforming Operators." scan and reduce have the same functionality, with the main difference being that scan emits the accumulated value for *every* emitted value, while reduce emits *a single* accumulated value once the upstream publisher sends a .finished completion event. Feel free to change reduce to scan in the above example and try it out for yourself.

Key points

- Publishers are actually sequences, as they produce values much like collections and sequences do.
- You can use `min` and `max` to emit the minimum or maximum value emitted by a publisher, respectively.
- `first`, `last` and `output(at:)` are useful when you want to find a value emitted at a specific index. Use `output(in:)` to find values emitted within a *range* of indices.
- `first(where:)` and `last(where:)` each take a predicate to determine which values it should let through.
- Operators such as `count`, `contains` and `allSatisfy` don't emit values emitted by the publisher. Rather, they emit a different value based on the emitted values.
- `contains(where:)` takes a predicate to determine if the publisher contains the given value.
- Use `reduce` to accumulate emitted values into a single value.

Where to go from here?

Congrats on completing the last chapter on operators for this book! give yourself a quick pat on the back and high-five yourself while you're at it. :]

You'll wrap up this section by working on your first practical project, where you'll build a Collage app using Combine and many of the operators you've learned. Take a few deep breaths, grab a cup of coffee, and move on to the next chapter.

Chapter 8: In Practice: Project "Collage Neue"

By Marin Todorov

In the past few chapters, you learned a lot about using publishers, subscribers and all kinds of different operators in the "safety" of a Swift playground. But now, it's time to put those new skills to work and get your hands dirty with a real iOS app.

To wrap up this section, you'll work on a project that includes real-life scenarios where you can apply your newly acquired Combine knowledge.

This project will take you through:

- Using Combine publishers in tandem with system frameworks like Photos.

- Handling user events with Combine.

- Using a variety of operators to create different subscriptions to drive your app's logic.

- Wrapping existing Cocoa APIs so you can conveniently use them in your Combine code.

The project is called **Collage Neue** and it's an iOS app which allows the user to create simple collages out of their photos, like this:

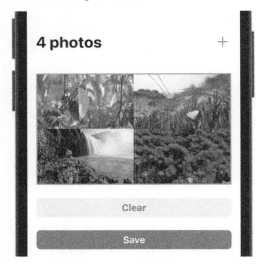

This project will get you some practical experience with Combine before you move on to learning about more operators, and is a nice break from theory-heavy chapters.

You will work through a number of loosely connected tasks where you will use techniques based on the materials you have covered so far in this book.

Additionally, you will get to use a few operators that will be introduced later on to help you power some of the advanced features of the app.

Without further ado — it's time to get coding!

Getting started with "Collage Neue"

To get started with Collage Neue, open the starter project provided with this chapter's materials. The app's structure is rather simple — there is a main view to create and preview collages and an additional view where users select photos to add to their in-progress collage:

> **Note**: In this chapter, you will specifically excercise working with Combine. You'll get to try various ways of binding data but will not focus on working with Combine and SwiftUI specifically; you will look into how to use these two frameworks together in Chapter 15, In Practice: Combine & SwiftUI.

Currently, the project doesn't implement any logic. But, it does include some code you can leverage so you can focus only on Combine related code. Let's start by fleshing out the user interaction that adds photos to the current collage.

Open **CollageNeueModel.swift** and import the Combine framework at the top of the file:

```
import Combine
```

This will allow you to use Combine types in your model file. To get started, add two new private properties to the `CollageNeueModel` class:

```
private var subscriptions = Set<AnyCancellable>()
private let images = CurrentValueSubject<[UIImage], Never>([])
```

`subscriptions` is the collection where you will store any subscriptions tied to the lifecycle of the main view or the model itself. In case the model is released, or you manually reset `subscriptions`, all the ongoing subscriptions will be conveniently canceled.

> **Note**: As mentioned in Chapter 1, "Hello, Combine!," subscribers return a `Cancellable` token to allow controlling the lifecycle of a subscription. `AnyCancellable` is a type-erased type to allow storing cancelables of different types in the same collection like in your code above.

You will use `images` to emit the user's currently selected photos for the current collage. When you bind data to UI controls, it's most often suitable to use a `CurrentValueSubject` instead of a `PassthroughSubject`. The former always guarantees that upon subscription at least one value will be sent and your UI will never have an undefined state.

Generally speaking, a `CurrentValueSubject` is a perfect fit to represent **state**, such as an array of photos or a loading state, while `PassthroughSubject` is more fitting to represent **events**, for example a user tapping a button, or simply indicating something has happened.

Next, to get some images added to the collage and test your code, append the following line to `add()`:

```
images.value.append(UIImage(named: "IMG_1907")!)
```

Whenever the user taps the + button in the top-right navigation item, which is bound to `CollageNeueModel.add()`, you will add **IMG_1907.jpg** to the current `images` array and send that value through the subject.

You can find **IMG_1907.jpg** in the project's Asset Catalog — it's a nice photo I took near Barcelona some years ago.

Conveniently, `CurrentValueSubject` allows you to mutate its `value` directly, instead of emitting the new value with `send(_:)`. The two are identical so you can use whichever syntax feels better - you can try `send(_:)` in the next paragraph.

To also be able to clear the currently selected photos, move over to `clear()`, in the same file, and add there:

```
images.send([])
```

This line sends an empty array as the latest value of `images`.

Lastly, you need to bind the `images` subject to a view on screen. There are different ways to do that but, to cover more ground in this practical chapter, you are going to use a `@Published` property for that.

Add a new property to your model like so:

```
@Published var imagePreview: UIImage?
```

`@Published` is a property wrapper that wraps a "vanilla" property into a publisher - how cool is that? Since your model conforms to `ObservableObject`, binding `imagePreview` to a view on screen becomes super simple.

Scroll to `bindMainView()` and add this code to bind the `images` subject to the image preview on-screen.

```
// 1
images
  // 2
  .map { photos in
    UIImage.collage(images: photos, size: Self.collageSize)
  }
  // 3
  .assign(to: &$imagePreview)
```

The play-by-play for this subscription is as follows:

1. You begin a subscription to the current collection of photos.

2. You use map to convert them to a single collage by calling into `UIImage.collage(images:size:)`, a helper method defined in **UIImage+Collage.swift**.

3. You use the `assign(to:)` subscriber to bind the resulting collage image to `imagePreview`, which is the center screen image view. Using the `assign(to:)` subscriber automatically manages the subscription lifecycle.

Last, but not least, you need to display `imagePreview` in your view. Open **MainView.swift** and find the line `Image(uiImage: UIImage())`. Replace it with:

```
Image(uiImage: model.imagePreview ?? UIImage())
```

You use the latest preview, or an empty `UIImage` if a preview doesn't exist.

Time to test that new subscription! Build and run the app and click the + button few times. You should see a collage preview, featuring one more copy of the same photo each time you click +:

You get the photos collection, convert it to a collage and assign it to an image view in a single subscription!

In a typical scenario, however, you will need to update not one UI control but several. Creating separate subscriptions for each of the bindings *might* be overkill. So, let's see how we can perform a number of updates as a single batch.

There is already a method included in `MainView` called `updateUI(photosCount:)`, which does various UI updates: it'll disables the **Save** button when the current selection contains an odd number of photos, enable the **Clear** button whenever there is a collage in progress and more.

To call `upateUI(photosCount:)` every time the user adds a photo to the collage, you will use the `handleEvents(...)` operator. This is, as previously mentioned, the operator to use whenever you'd like to perform side effects like logging or others.

Usually, it's recommended to update UI from a `sink(...)` or `assign(to:on:)` but, in order to give it a try, in this section you'll do that in `handleEvents`.

Go back to **CollageNeueModel.swift** and add a new property:

```
let updateUISubject = PassthroughSubject<Int, Never>()
```

To exercise using subjects to communicate between different types (e.g. in this case you're using it so your model can "talk back" to your view) you add a new subject called the `updateUISubject`.

Via this new subject you will emit the number of currently selected photos so the view can observe the count and update its state accordingly.

In `bindMainView()`, insert this operator just before the line where you use `map`:

```
.handleEvents(receiveOutput: { [weak self] photos in
  self?.updateUISubject.send(photos.count)
})
```

> **Note:** The `handleEvents` operator enables you to perform side effects when a publisher emits an event. You'll learn a lot more about it in Chapter 10, "Debugging."

This will feed the current selection to `updateUI(photosCount:)` just before they are converted into a single collage image inside the `map` operator.

Now, to observe `updateUISubject` in `MainView`, open **MainView.swift** and a new modifier directly below `.onAppear(...)`:

```
.onReceive(model.updateUISubject, perform: updateUI)
```

This modifier observes the given publisher and calls `updateUI(photosCount:)` for the lifetime of the view. If you're curious, scroll down to `updateUI(photosCount:)` and peak into the code.

Build and run the project and you will notice the two buttons below the preview are disabled, which is the correct initial state:

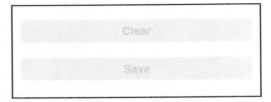

The buttons will keep changing state as you add more photos to the current collage. For example, when you select one or three photos the **Save** button will be disabled but **Clear** will be enabled, like so:

Presenting views

You saw how easy it is to route your UI's data through a subject and bind it to some controls on-screen. Next, you'll tackle another common task: Presenting a new view and getting some data back when the user is done using it.

The general idea of binding data remains the same. You just need more publishers, or subjects, to define the correct data flow.

Open `PhotosView` and you will see it already contains the code to load photos from the Camera Roll and display them in a collection view.

Your next task is to add the necessary Combine code to your model to allow the user to select some Camera Roll photos and add them to their collage.

Add the following subject in **CollageNeueModel.swift**:

```
private(set) var selectedPhotosSubject =
  PassthroughSubject<UIImage, Never>()
```

This code allows `CollageNeueModel` to replace the subject with a new one after the subject has completed but other types only have access to send or subscribe to receive events.

Speaking of that, let's hook up the collection view delegate method to that subject.

Scroll down to `selectImage(asset:)`. The already-provided code fetches the given photo asset from the device library. Once the photo is ready, you should use the subject to send out the image to any subscribers.

Replace the `// Send the selected image` comment with:

```
self.selectedPhotosSubject.send(image)
```

Well, that was easy! However, since you're exposing the subject to other types, you'd like to explicitly send a completion event in case the view is being dismissed to tear down any external subscriptions.

Again, you can achieve this in a couple of different ways, but for this chapter, open **PhotosView.swift** and find the `.onDisappear(...)` modifier.

Add inside `.onDisappear(...)`:

```
model.selectedPhotosSubject.send(completion: .finished)
```

This code will send a `finished` event when you navigate back from the presented view. To wrap up the current task, you still need to subscribe to the selected photos and display those in your main view.

Open **CollageNeueModel.swift**, find `add()`, and replace its body with:

```
let newPhotos = selectedPhotos

newPhotos
  .map { [unowned self] newImage in
  // 1
    return self.images.value + [newImage]
  }
  // 2
```

```
  .assign(to: \.value, on: images)
// 3
  .store(in: &subscriptions)
```

In the code above, you:

1. Get the current list of selected images and append any new images to it.

2. Use `assign` to send the updated images array through the `images` subject.

3. You store the new subscription in `subscriptions`. However, the subscription will end whenever the user dismisses the presented view controller.

With your new binding ready to test, the last step is to lift the flag that presents the photo picker view.

Open **MainView.swift** and find the + button action closure where you call `model.add()`. Add one more line to that closure:

```
isDisplayingPhotoPicker = true
```

The `isDisplayingPhotoPicker` state property is already wired to present `PhotosView` when set to `true` so you're ready to test!

Run the app and try out the newly added code. Tap on the + button and you will see the system photos access dialogue pop-up on-screen. Since this is your own app it's safe to tap **Allow Access to All Photos** to allow accessing the complete photo library on your Simulator from the Collage Neue app:

This will reload the collection view with the default photos included with the iOS Simulator, or your own photos if you're testing on your device:

Tap a few of those. They'll flash to indicate they've been added to the collage. Then, tap to go back to the main screen where you will see your new collage in full glory:

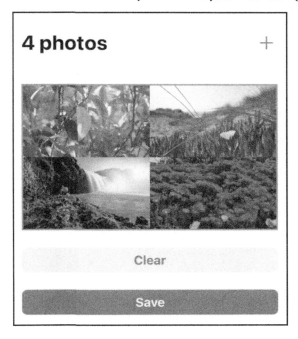

There is one loose end to take care of before moving on. If you navigate few times between the photo picker and the main view you will notice that you cannot add any more photos after the very first time.

Why is this happening?

The issue stems from how you're reusing `selectedPhotosSubject` each time you present the photo picker. The first time you close that view, you send a `finished` completion event and the subject is completed.

You can still you use it to create new subscriptions but those subscriptions complete as soon as you create them.

To fix this, create a new subject each time you present the photo picker. Scroll to `add()` and insert to its top:

```
selectedPhotosSubject = PassthroughSubject<UIImage, Never>()
```

This will create a new subject each time you present the photo picker. You should now be free to navigate back and forth between the views while still being able to add more photos to the collage.

Wrapping a callback function as a future

In a playground, you might play with subjects and publishers and be able to design everything exactly as you like it, but in real apps, you will interact with various Cocoa APIs, such as accessing the Camera Roll, reading the device's sensors or interacting with some database.

Later in this book, you will learn how to create your own custom publishers. However, in many cases simply adding a subject to an existing Cocoa class is enough to plug its functionality in your Combine workflow.

In this part of the chapter, you will work on a new custom type called `PhotoWriter` which will allow you to save the user's collage to disk. You will use the callback-based Photos API to do the saving and use a Combine `Future` to allow other types to subscribe to the operation result.

> **Note**: If you need to refresh your knowledge on `Future`, revisit the "Hello Future" section in Chapter 2: Publishers & Subscribers.

Open **Utility/PhotoWriter.swift**, which contains an empty `PhotoWriter` class, and add the following static function to it:

```
static func save(_ image: UIImage) -> Future<String,
PhotoWriter.Error> {
  Future { resolve in

  }
}
```

This function will try to asynchronously store the given image on disk and return a future that this API's consumers will subscribe to.

You'll use the closure-based `Future` initializer to return a ready-to-go future which will execute the code in the provided closure once initialized.

Let's start fleshing out the future's logic by inserting the following code inside the closure:

```
do {

} catch {
  resolve(.failure(.generic(error)))
}
```

This is a pretty good start. You will perform the saving inside the do block and, should it throw an error, you'll resolve the future with a failure.

Since you don't know the exact errors that could be thrown while saving the photo, you just take the thrown error and wrap it as a `PhotoWriter.Error.generic` error.

Now, for the real "meat" of the function: Insert the following inside the do body:

```
try PHPhotoLibrary.shared().performChangesAndWait {
  // 1
  let request =
PHAssetChangeRequest.creationRequestForAsset(from: image)

  // 2
  guard let savedAssetID =
    request.placeholderForCreatedAsset?.localIdentifier else {
    // 3
    return resolve(.failure(.couldNotSavePhoto))
  }

  // 4
  resolve(.success(savedAssetID))
}
```

Here, you use `PHPhotoLibrary.performChangesAncWait(_)` to access the Photos library synchronously. The future's closure is itself executed asynchronously, so don't worry about blocking the main thread. With this, you'll perform the following changes from within the closure:

1. First, you create a request to store `image`.

2. Then, you attempt to get the newly-created asset's identifier via `request.placeholderForCreatedAsset?.localIdentifier`.

3. If the creation has failed and you didn't get an identifier back, you resolve the future with a `PhotoWriter.Error.couldNotSavePhoto` error.

4. Finally, in case you got back a `savedAssetID`, you resolve the future with success.

That's everything you need to wrap a callback function, resolve with a failure if you get back an error or resolve with success in case you have some result to return!

Now, you can use `PhotoWriter.save(_:)` to save the current collage when the user taps **Save**. Open **CollageNeueModel.swift** and inside `save()` append:

```swift
guard let image = imagePreview else { return }
// 1
PhotoWriter.save(image)
  .sink(
    receiveCompletion: { [unowned self] completion in
      // 2
      if case .failure(let error) = completion {
        lastErrorMessage = error.localizedDescription
      }
      clear()
    },
    receiveValue: { [unowned self] id in
      // 3
      lastSavedPhotoID = id
    }
  )
  .store(in: &subscriptions)
```

In this code, you:

1. Subscribe the `PhotoWriter.save(_:)` future by using `sink(receiveCompletion:receiveValue:)`.

2. In case of completion with a failure, you save the error message to `lastErrorMessage`.

3. In case you get back a value — the new asset identifier — you store it in `lastSavedPhotoID`.

`lastErrorMessage` and `lastSavedPhotoID` are already wired in the SwiftUI code to present the user with the respective messages.

Run the app one more time, pick a couple of photos and tap **Save**. This will call into your shiny new publisher and, upon saving the collage, will display an alert like so:

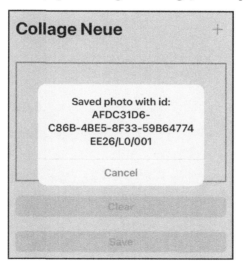

A note on memory management

Here is a good place for a quick side-note on memory management with Combine. As mentioned earlier, Combine code has to deal with a lot of asynchronously executed pieces of work and those are always a bit cumbersome to manage when dealing with classes.

When you write your own custom Combine code, you might be dealing predominantly with structs, so you won't need to explicitly specify capturing semantics in the closures you use with `map`, `flatMap`, `filter`, etc.

However, when you're dealing with UI code with UIKit/AppKit code (i.e. you have subclasses of `UIViewController`, `UICollectionController`, etc.) or when you have `ObservableObjects` for your SwiftUI views, you will need to pay attention to your memory management for all these classes.

When writing Combine code, standard rules apply, so you should use the same Swift capture semantics as always:

- If you're capturing an object that could be released from memory, like the presented photos view controller earlier, you should use `[weak self]` or another variable than `self` if you capture another object.

- If you're capturing an object that could not be released, like the main view controller in that Collage app, you can safely use `[unowned self]`. For example, one that you never pop-out of the navigation stack and is therefore always present.

Sharing subscriptions

Looking back to the code in `CollageNeueModel.add()`, you could do a few more things with the images being selected by the user in `PhotosView`.

This poses an uneasy question: Should you subscribe multiple times to the same `selectedPhotos` publisher, or do something else?

Turns out, subscribing to the same publisher might have unwanted side effects. If you think about it, you don't know what the publisher is doing upon subscription, do you? It might be creating new resources, making network requests or other unexpected work.

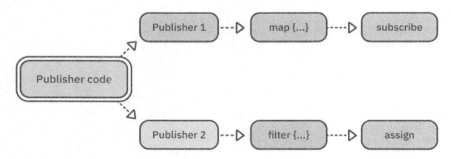

The correct way to go when creating multiple subscriptions to the same publisher is to *share* the original publisher using the `share()` operator. This wraps the publisher in a class and therefore it can safely emit to multiple subscribers without performing its underlying work again.

Still in **CollageNeueModel.swift**, find the line `let newPhotos = selectedPhotos` and replace it with:

```
let newPhotos = selectedPhotos.share()
```

Now, it's safe to create multiple subscriptions to `newPhotos` without being afraid that the publisher is performing side effects multiple times for each new subscriber:

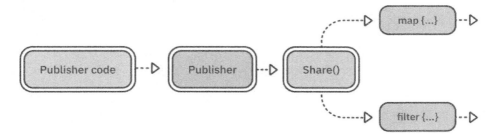

A caveat to keep in mind is that `share()` does not re-emit any values from the shared subscription, so you only get values that occur *after* you subscribe.

For example, if you have two subscriptions on a `share()`d publisher and the source publisher emits synchronously upon subscribing, only the first subscriber will get the value, since the second one wasn't subscribed when the value was actually emitted. If the source publisher emits asynchronously, that's less often an issue.

A reliable solution to that problem is building your own sharing operator which re-emits, or *replays*, past values when a new subscriber subscribes. Building your own operators is not complicated at all - you will, in fact, build one called `shareReplay()` in Chapter 18, "Custom Publishers & Handling Backpressure," which will allow you to use share in the way described above.

Operators in practice

Now that you learned about a few useful reactive patterns, it's time to practice some of the operators you covered in previous chapters and see them in action.

Open **CollageNeueModel.swift** and replace the line where you share the selectedPhotos subscription `let newPhotos = selectedPhotos.share()` with:

```
let newPhotos = selectedPhotos
  .prefix(while: { [unowned self] _ in
    self.images.value.count < 6
  })
  .share()
```

You already learned about `prefix(while:)` as one of the powerful Combine filtering operators and here you get to use it in practice. The code above will keep the subscription to `selectedPhotos` alive as long as the total count of images selected is less than six. This will effectively allow the user to select up to six photos for their collage.

Adding `prefix(while:)` just before the call to `share()` allows you to filter the incoming values, not only on one subscription, but on all subscriptions that subscribe to `newPhotos`.

Run the app and try adding more than six photos. You will see that after the first six that the main view controller doesn't accept more.

In the same way, you can implement any logic you need by combining all the operators you already know and love like `filter`, `dropFirst`, `map` and so on.

And that's a wrap for this chapter! You did well and deserve a nice pat on the shoulder!

Challenges

Congratulations on working through this tutorial-style chapter! If you'd like to work through one more optional task before moving on to more theory in the next chapter, keep reading below.

Open **Utility/PHPhotoLibrary+Combine.swift** and read the code that gets the Photos library authorization for the Collage Neue app from the user. You will certainly notice that the logic is quite straightforward and is based on a "standard" callback API.

This provides you with a great opportunity to wrap a Cocoa API as a future on your own. For this challenge, add a new static property to `PHPhotoLibrary` called `isAuthorized`, which is of type `Future<Bool, Never>` and allows other types to subscribe to the Photos library authorization status.

You've already done this a couple of times in this chapter and the existing `fetchAuthorizationStatus(callback:)` function should be pretty straight forward to use. Good luck! Should you experience any difficulties along the way, don't forget that you can always peak into the **challenge** folder provided for this chapter and have a look at the example solution.

Finally, don't forget to use the new `isAuthorized` publisher in `PhotosView`!

For bonus points, display an error message in case the user doesn't grant access to their photos and navigate back to the main view controller when they tap **Close**.

To play with different authorization states and test your code, open the Settings app on your Simulator or device and navigate to Privacy/Photos.

Change the authorization status of Collage to either "None" or "All Photos" to test how your code behaves in those states:

If you made it successfully on your own so far into the challenges, you really deserve an extra round of applause! Either way, one possible solution you can consult with at any time is provided in the challenges folder for this chapter.

Key points

- In your day-to-day tasks, you'll most likely have to deal with callback or delegate-based APIs. Luckily, those are easily wrapped as futures or publishers by using a subject.

- Moving from various patterns like delegation and callbacks to a single Publisher/Subscriber pattern makes mundane tasks like presenting views and fetching back values a breeze.

- To avoid unwanted side-effects when subscribing a publisher multiple times, use a shared publisher via the `share()` operator.

Where to go from here?

That's a wrap for Section II: "Operators" Starting with the next chapter, you will start looking more into the ways Combine integrates with the existing Foundation and UIKit/AppKit APIs.

Section III: Combine in Action

You now know most of Combine's basics. You learned how publishers, subscribers and subscriptions work and the intertwined relationship between these pieces, as well as how you can use operators to manipulate publishers and their emissions.

While theory is great and definitely useful, practical real-life knowledge is king!

This section is divided into five mini-chapters, each with its own focus on practical approaches for leveraging Combine for specific use-cases. You'll learn how to leverage Combine for networking, how to debug your combine publishers, how to use timers and observe KVO-compliant objects, as well as learn how resources work in Combine.

To wrap up this section, you'll get your hands dirty and build an entire Combine-backed network layer — how exciting!

Chapter 9: Networking

By Florent Pillet

As programmers, a lot of what we do revolves around networking. Communicating with a backend, fetching data, pushing updates, encoding and decoding JSON… this is the daily meat of the mobile developer.

Combine offers a few select APIs to help perform common tasks declaratively. These APIs revolve around two key components of modern applications:

- Use `URLSession` to perform network requests.
- Use the `Codable` protocol to encode and decode JSON data.

URLSession extensions

`URLSession` is the standard way to perform network data transfer tasks. It offers a modern asynchronous API with powerful configuration options and fully transparent backgrounding support. It supports a variety of operations such as:

- Data transfer tasks to retrieve the content of a URL.
- Download tasks to retrieve the content of a URL and save it to a file.
- Upload tasks to upload files and data to a URL.
- Stream tasks to stream data between two parties.
- Websocket tasks to connect to websockets.

Out of these, only the first one, data transfer tasks, exposes a Combine publisher. Combine handles these tasks using a single API with two variants, taking a `URLRequest` or just a URL.

Here's a look at how you can use this API:

```swift
guard let url = URL(string: "https://mysite.com/mydata.json")
else {
  return
}

// 1
let subscription = URLSession.shared
  // 2
  .dataTaskPublisher(for: url)
  .sink(receiveCompletion: { completion in
    // 3
    if case .failure(let err) = completion {
      print("Retrieving data failed with error \(err)")
    }
  }, receiveValue: { data, response in
    // 4
    print("Retrieved data of size \(data.count), response = \(response)")
  })
```

Here's what's happening with this code:

1. It's crucial that you keep the resulting subscription; otherwise, it gets immediately canceled and the request never executes.

2. You're using the overload of `dataTaskPublisher(for:)` that takes a URL as a parameter.

3. Make sure you always handle errors! Network connections are prone to failure.

4. The result is a tuple with both a `Data` object and a `URLResponse`.

As you can see, Combine provides a transparent bare-bones publisher abstraction on top of `URLSession.dataTask`, only exposing a publisher instead of a closure.

Codable support

The `Codable` protocol is a modern, powerful and Swift-only encoding and decoding mechanism that you absolutely should know about. If you don't, please do yourself a favor and learn about it from Apple's documentation and tutorials on raywenderlich.com!

Foundation supports encoding to and decoding from JSON through `JSONEncoder` and `JSONDecoder`. You can also use `PropertyListEncoder` and `PropertyListDecoder`, but these are less useful in the context of network requests.

In the previous example, you downloaded some JSON. Of course, you could decode it with a `JSONDecoder`:

```
let subscription = URLSession.shared
  .dataTaskPublisher(for: url)
  .tryMap { data, _ in
    try JSONDecoder().decode(MyType.self, from: data)
  }
  .sink(receiveCompletion: { completion in
    if case .failure(let err) = completion {
      print("Retrieving data failed with error \(err)")
    }
  }, receiveValue: { object in
    print("Retrieved object \(object)")
  })
```

You decode the JSON inside a `tryMap`, which works, but Combine provides an operator to help reduce the boilerplate: `decode(type:decoder:)`.

In the example above, replace the `tryMap` operator with the following lines:

```
.map(\.data)
.decode(type: MyType.self, decoder: JSONDecoder())
```

Unfortunately, since `dataTaskPublisher(for:)` emits a tuple, you can't directly use `decode(type:decoder:)` without first using a `map(_:)` that only emits the `Data` part of the result.

The only advantage is that you instantiate the `JSONDecoder` only once, when setting up the publisher, versus creating it every time in the `tryMap(_:)` closure.

Publishing network data to multiple subscribers

Every time you subscribe to a publisher, it starts doing work. In the case of network requests, this means sending the same request multiple times if multiple subscribers need the result.

Combine, surprisingly, lacks operators to make this easy, as other frameworks have. You could use the `share()` operator, but that's tricky because you need to subscribe all your subscribers before the result comes back.

Besides using a caching mechanism, one solution is to use the `multicast()` operator, which creates a `ConnectablePublisher` that publishes values through a `Subject`. It allows you to subscribe multiple times to the subject, then call the publisher's `connect()` method when you're ready:

```
let url = URL(string: "https://www.raywenderlich.com")!
let publisher = URLSession.shared
// 1
  .dataTaskPublisher(for: url)
  .map(\.data)
  .multicast { PassthroughSubject<Data, URLError>() }

// 2
let subscription1 = publisher
  .sink(receiveCompletion: { completion in
    if case .failure(let err) = completion {
      print("Sink1 Retrieving data failed with error \(err)")
    }
  }, receiveValue: { object in
    print("Sink1 Retrieved object \(object)")
  })
```

```
// 3
let subscription2 = publisher
  .sink(receiveCompletion: { completion in
    if case .failure(let err) = completion {
      print("Sink2 Retrieving data failed with error \(err)")
    }
  }, receiveValue: { object in
    print("Sink2 Retrieved object \(object)")
  })
// 4
let subscription = publisher.connect()
```

In this code, you:

1. Create your `DataTaskPublisher`, map to its data and then `multicast` it. The closure you pass must return a subject of the appropriate type. Alternately, you can pass an existing subject to `multicast(subject:)`. You'll learn more about `multicast` in Chapter 13, "Resource Management."

2. Subscribe a first time to the publisher. Since it's a `ConnectablePublisher` it won't start working right away.

3. Subscribe a second time.

4. Connect the publisher, when you're ready. It will start working and pushing values to all of its subscribers.

With this code, you send the request one time and share the outcome with the two subscribers.

> **Note**: Make sure to store all of your `Cancellables`; otherwise, they would be deallocated and canceled when leaving the current code scope, which would be immediate in this specific case.

This process remains a bit convoluted, as Combine does not offer operators for this kind of scenario like other reactive frameworks do. In Chapter 18, "Custom Publishers & Handling Backpressure," you'll explore crafting a better solution.

Key points

- Combine offers a publisher-based abstraction for its `dataTask(with:completionHandler:)` method called `dataTaskPublisher(for:)`.

- You can decode `Codable`-conforming models using the built-in `decode` operator on a publisher that emits `Data` values.

- While there's no operator to share a replay of a subscription with multiple subscribers, you can recreate this behavior using a `ConnectablePublisher` and the `multicast` operator.

Where to go from here?

Great job on going through this chapter!

If you want to learn more about using `Codable`, you can check out the following resources:

- *"Encoding and Decoding in Swift"* at raywenderlich.com: https://www.raywenderlich.com/3418439-encoding-and-decoding-in-swift

- *"Encoding and Decoding Custom Types"* on Apple's official documentation: https://developer.apple.com/documentation/foundation/archives_and_serialization/encoding_and_decoding_custom_types

Chapter 10: Debugging

By Florent Pillet

Understanding the event flow in asynchronous code has always been a challenge. It is particularly the case in the context of Combine, as chains of operators in a publisher may not immediately emit events. For example, operators like throttle(for:scheduler:latest:) will not emit all events they receive, so you need to understand what's going on. Combine provides a few operators to help with debugging your reactive flows. Knowing them will help you troubleshoot puzzling situations.

Printing events

The `print(_:to:)` operator is the first one you should use when you're unsure whether anything is going through your publishers. It's a passthrough publisher which prints a lot of information about what's happening.

Even with simple cases like this one:

```
let subscription = (1...3).publisher
  .print("publisher")
  .sink { _ in }
```

The output is very detailed:

```
publisher: receive subscription: (1...3)
publisher: request unlimited
publisher: receive value: (1)
publisher: receive value: (2)
publisher: receive value: (3)
publisher: receive finished
```

Here you see that the `print(_:to:)` operators shows a lot of information, as it:

- Prints when it receives a subscription and shows the description of its upstream publisher.

- Prints the subscriber's demand requests so you can see how many items are being requested.

- Prints every value the upstream publisher emits.

- Finally, prints the completion event.

There is an additional parameter that takes a `TextOutputStream` object. You can use this to redirect strings to print to a logger. You can also add information to the log, like the current date and time, etc. The possibilities are endless!

For example, you can create a simple logger that displays the time interval between each string so you can get a sense of how fast your publisher emits values:

```swift
class TimeLogger: TextOutputStream {
  private var previous = Date()
  private let formatter = NumberFormatter()

  init() {
    formatter.maximumFractionDigits = 5
    formatter.minimumFractionDigits = 5
  }

  func write(_ string: String) {
    let trimmed = string.trimmingCharacters(in: .whitespacesAndNewlines)
    guard !trimmed.isEmpty else { return }
    let now = Date()
    print("+\(formatter.string(for: now.timeIntervalSince(previous))!)s: \(string)")
    previous = now
  }
}
```

It's very simple to use in your code:

```swift
let subscription = (1...3).publisher
  .print("publisher", to: TimeLogger())
  .sink { _ in }
```

And the result displays the time between each printed line:

```
+0.00111s: publisher: receive subscription: (1...3)
+0.03485s: publisher: request unlimited
+0.00035s: publisher: receive value: (1)
+0.00025s: publisher: receive value: (2)
+0.00027s: publisher: receive value: (3)
+0.00024s: publisher: receive finished
```

As mentioned above, the possibilities are quite endless here.

> **Note**: Depending on the computer and the version of Xcode you're running this code on, the interval printed above may vary slightly.

Acting on events — performing side effects

Besides printing out information, it is often useful to perform actions upon specific events. We call this **performing side effects**, as actions you take "on the side" don't directly impact further publishers down the stream, but can have an effect like modifying an external variable.

The `handleEvents(receiveSubscription:receiveOutput:receiveCompletion:receiveCancel:receiveRequest:)` (wow, what a signature!) lets you intercept any and all events in the lifecycle of a publisher and then take action at each step.

Imagine you're tracking an issue where a publisher must perform a network request, then emit some data. When you run it, it never receives any data. What's happening? Is the request really working? Do you even listen to what comes back?

Consider this code:

```
let request = URLSession.shared
  .dataTaskPublisher(for: URL(string: "https://
www.raywenderlich.com/")!)

request
  .sink(receiveCompletion: { completion in
    print("Sink received completion: \(completion)")
  }) { (data, _) in
    print("Sink received data: \(data)")
  }
```

You run it and never see anything print. Can you see the issue by looking at the code?

If not, use `handleEvents` to track what's happening. You can insert this operator between the publisher and `sink`:

```
.handleEvents(receiveSubscription: { _ in
  print("Network request will start")
}, receiveOutput: { _ in
  print("Network request data received")
}, receiveCancel: {
  print("Network request cancelled")
})
```

Then, run the code again. This time you see some debugging output:

```
Network request will start
Network request cancelled
```

There! You found it: You forgot to keep the `Cancellable` around. So, the subscription starts but gets canceled immediately. Now, you can fix your code by retaining the `Cancellable`:

```
let subscription = request
  .handleEvents...
```

Then, running your code again, you'll now see it behaving correctly:

```
Network request will start
Network request data received
Sink received data: 303094 bytes
Sink received completion: finished
```

Using the debugger as a last resort

The last resort operator is one you pull in situations where you really need to introspect things at certain times in the debugger, because nothing else helped you figure out what's wrong.

The first simple operator is `breakpointOnError()`. As the name suggests, when you use this operator, if any of the upstream publishers emits an error, Xcode will break in the debugger to let you look at the stack and, hopefully, find why and where your publisher errors out.

A more complete variant is `breakpoint(receiveSubscription:receiveOutput:receiveCompletion:)`. It allows you to intercept all events and decide on a case-by-case basis whether you want to pause the debugger.

For example, you could break only if certain values pass through the publisher:

```
.breakpoint(receiveOutput: { value in
  return value > 10 && value < 15
})
```

Assuming the upstream publisher emits integer values, but values 11 to 14 should never happen, you can configure `breakpoint` to break only in this case and let you investigate! You can also conditionally break subscription and completion times, but cannot intercept cancelations like the `handleEvents` operator.

> **Note**: None of the breakpoint publishers will work in Xcode playgrounds. You will see an error stating that execution was interrupted, but it won't drop into the debugger since playgrounds generally don't support breakpoint debugging.

Key points

- Track the lifecycle of a publisher with the `print` operator,
- Create your own `TextOutputStream` to customize the output strings,
- Use the `handleEvents` operator to intercept lifecycle events and perform actions,
- Use the `breakpointOnError` and `breakpoint` operators to break on specific events.

Where to go from here?

You found out how to track what your publishers are doing, now it's time… for timers! Move on to the next chapter to learn how to trigger events at regular intervals with Combine.

Chapter 11: Timers

By Florent Pillet

Repeating and non-repeating timers are always useful when coding. Besides executing code asynchronously, you often need to control *when* and *how often* a task should repeat.

Before the `Dispatch` framework was available, developers relied on `RunLoop` to asynchronously perform tasks and implement concurrency. You could use `Timer` to create repeating and non-repeating timers. Then, Apple released the `Dispatch` framework, including `DispatchSourceTimer`.

Although all of the above are capable of creating timers, not all timers are equal in Combine. Read on!

Using RunLoop

The main thread and any thread you create, preferably using the Thread class, can have its own RunLoop. Just invoke RunLoop.current from the current thread: Foundation would create one for you if needed. Beware, unless you understand how run loops operate — in particular, that you need a loop that runs the run loop — you'll be better off simply using the main RunLoop that runs the main thread of your application.

> **Note**: One important note and a red light warning in Apple's documentation is that the RunLoop class is not thread-safe. You should only call RunLoop methods for the run loop of the current thread.

RunLoop implements the Scheduler protocol you'll learn about in Chapter 17, "Schedulers." It defines several methods which are relatively low-level, and the only one that lets you create cancellable timers:

```
let runLoop = RunLoop.main

let subscription = runLoop.schedule(
  after: runLoop.now,
  interval: .seconds(1),
  tolerance: .milliseconds(100)
) {
  print("Timer fired")
}
```

This timer does not pass any value and does not create a publisher. It starts at the date specified in the after: parameter with the specified interval and tolerance, and that's about it. Its only usefulness in relation to Combine is that the Cancellable it returns lets you stop the timer after a while.

An example of this could be:

```
runLoop.schedule(after: .init(Date(timeIntervalSinceNow: 3.0)))
{
  subscription.cancel()
}
```

But all things considered, RunLoop is not the best way to create a timer. You'll be better off using the Timer class!

Using the Timer class

`Timer` is the oldest timer that was available in the original Mac OS X, long before Apple renamed it "macOS." It has always been tricky to use because of its delegation pattern and tight relationship with `RunLoop`. Combine brings a modern variant you can directly use as a publisher without all the setup boilerplate.

You can create a repeating timer publisher this way:

```
let publisher = Timer.publish(every: 1.0, on: .main,
  in: .common)
```

The two parameters `on` and `in` determine:

- **On** which `RunLoop` your timer attaches to. Here, the main thread's `RunLoop`.
- **In** which run loop mode(s) the timer runs. Here, the default run loop mode.

Unless you understand how a run loop operates, you should stick with these default values. Run loops are the basic mechanism for asynchronous event source processing in macOS, but their API is a bit cumbersome. You can get a `RunLoop` for any `Thread` that you create yourself or obtain from Foundation by calling `RunLoop.current`, so you could write the following as well:

```
let publisher = Timer.publish(every: 1.0, on: .current,
  in: .common)
```

> **Note**: Running this code on a Dispatch queue other than `DispatchQueue.main` may lead to unpredictable results. The Dispatch framework manages its threads without using run loops. Since a run loop requires one of its `run` methods to be called to process events, you would never see the timer fire on any queue other than the main one. Stay safe and target `RunLoop.main` for your Timers.

The publisher the timer returns is a `ConnectablePublisher`. It's a special variant of `Publisher` that won't start firing upon subscription until you explicitly call its `connect()` method. You can also use the `autoconnect()` operator which automatically connects when the first subscriber subscribes.

> **Note**: You'll learn more about connectable publishers in Chapter 13, "Resource Management."

Therefore, the best way to create a publisher that will start a timer upon subscription is to write:

```
let publisher = Timer
  .publish(every: 1.0, on: .main, in: .common)
  .autoconnect()
```

The timer repeatedly emits the current date, its `Publisher.Output` type being a `Date`. You can make a timer that emits increasing values by using the `scan` operator:

```
let subscription = Timer
  .publish(every: 1.0, on: .main, in: .common)
  .autoconnect()
  .scan(0) { counter, _ in counter + 1 }
  .sink { counter in
    print("Counter is \(counter)")
  }
```

There is an additional `Timer.publish()` parameter you didn't see here: `tolerance`. It specifies the acceptable deviation from the duration you asked for, as a `TimeInterval`. But note that using a value lower than your `RunLoop`'s `minimumTolerance` value may not produce the expected results.

Using DispatchQueue

You can use a dispatch queue to generate timer events. While the Dispatch framework has a `DispatchTimerSource` event source, Combine surprisingly doesn't provide a timer interface to it. Instead, you're going to use an alternative method to generate timer events in your queue. This can be a bit convoluted, though:

```
let queue = DispatchQueue.main

// 1
let source = PassthroughSubject<Int, Never>()

// 2
var counter = 0

// 3
let cancellable = queue.schedule(
```

```
    after: queue.now,
    interval: .seconds(1)
) {
    source.send(counter)
    counter += 1
}

// 4
let subscription = source.sink {
    print("Timer emitted \($0)")
}
```

In the previous code, you:

1. Create a Subject you will send timer values to.

2. Prepare a counter. You'll increment it every time the timer fires.

3. Schedule a repeating action on the selected queue every second. The action starts immediately.

4. Subscribe to the subject to get the timer values.

As you can see, this is not pretty. It would help to move this code to a function and pass both the interval and the start time.

Key points

- Create timers using good old `RunLoop` class if you have Objective-C code nostalgia.
- Use `Timer.publish` to obtain a publisher which generates values at given intervals on the specified `RunLoop`.
- Use `DispatchQueue.schedule` for modern timers emitting events on a dispatch queue.

Where to go from here?

In Chapter 18, "Custom Publishers & Handling Backpressure," you'll learn how to write your own publishers, and you'll create an alternative timer publisher using `DispatchSourceTimer`.

But don't hurry! There is plenty to learn before that, starting with Key-Value Observing in the next chapter.

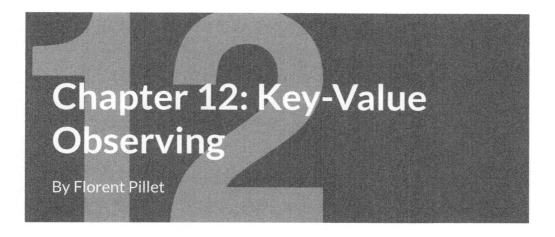

Chapter 12: Key-Value Observing

By Florent Pillet

Dealing with change is at the core of Combine. Publishers let you subscribe to them to handle asynchronous events. In earlier chapters, you learned about `assign(to:on:)` which enables you to update the value of an object's property every time a publisher emits a new value.

But, what about a mechanism to observe changes to single variables?

Combine ships with a few options around this:

- It provides a publisher for any property of an object that is **KVO (Key-Value Observing)**-compliant.
- The `ObservableObject` protocol handles cases where multiple variables could change.

Introducing publisher(for:options:)

KVO has always been an essential component of Objective-C. A large number of properties from Foundation, UIKit and AppKit classes are KVO-compliant. Therefore, you can observe their changes using the KVO machinery.

It's easy to observe KVO-compliant properties. Here is an example using an `OperationQueue` (a class from Foundation):

```
let queue = OperationQueue()

let subscription = queue.publisher(for: \.operationCount)
  .sink {
    print("Outstanding operations in queue: \($0)")
  }
```

Every time you add a new operation to the queue, its `operationCount` increments, and your sink receives the new count. When the queue has consumed an operation, the count decrements and again, your sink receives the updated count.

There are many other framework classes exposing KVO-compliant properties. Just use `publisher(for:)` with a key path to a KVO-compliant property, and *voilà*! You get a publisher capable of emitting value changes. You'll learn more about this and available options later in this chapter.

> **Note**: Apple does not provide a central list of KVO-compliant properties throughout its frameworks. The documentation for each class usually indicates which properties are KVO-compliant. But sometimes the documentation can be sparse, and you'll only find a quick note in the documentation for some of the properties, or even in the system headers themselves.

Preparing and subscribing to your own KVO-compliant properties

You can also use Key-Value Observing in your own code, provided that:

- Your objects are classes (not structs) and conform to `NSObject`,
- You mark the properties to make observable with the `@objc dynamic` attributes.

Once you have done this, the objects and properties you marked become KVO-compliant and can be observed with Combine!

> **Note:** While the Swift language doesn't directly support KVO, marking your properties `@objc dynamic` forces the compiler to generate hidden methods that trigger the KVO machinery. Describing this machinery is out of the scope of this book. Suffice to say the machinery heavily relies on specific methods from the `NSObject` protocol, which explains why your objects need to conform to it.

Try an example in a playground:

```
// 1
class TestObject: NSObject {
  // 2
  @objc dynamic var integerProperty: Int = 0
}

let obj = TestObject()

// 3
let subscription = obj.publisher(for: \.integerProperty)
  .sink {
    print("integerProperty changes to \($0)")
  }

// 4
obj.integerProperty = 100
obj.integerProperty = 200
```

In the above code, you:

1. Create a class that conforms to the `NSObject` protocol. This is required for KVO.

2. Mark any property you want to make observable as `@objc dynamic`.

3. Create and subscribe to a publisher observing the `integerProperty` property of `obj`.

4. Update the property a couple times.

When running this code in a playground, can you guess what the debug console displays?

You may be surprised, but here is the display you obtain:

```
integerProperty changes to 0
integerProperty changes to 100
integerProperty changes to 200
```

You first get the initial value of `integerProperty`, which is 0, then you receive the two changes. You can avoid this initial value if you're not interested in it — read on to find out how!

Did you notice that in `TestObject` you are using a plain Swift type (`Int`) and that KVO, which is an Objective-C feature, still works? KVO will work fine with any Objective-C type and with any Swift type *bridged to Objective-C*. This includes all the native Swift types as well as arrays and dictionaries, provided their values are all bridgeable to Objective-C.

Try it! Add a couple more properties to `TestObject`:

```
@objc dynamic var stringProperty: String = ""
@objc dynamic var arrayProperty: [Float] = []
```

As well as subscriptions to their publishers:

```
let subscription2 = obj.publisher(for: \.stringProperty)
  .sink {
    print("stringProperty changes to \($0)")
  }

let subscription3 = obj.publisher(for: \.arrayProperty)
  .sink {
    print("arrayProperty changes to \($0)")
  }
```

And finally, some property changes:

```
obj.stringProperty = "Hello"
obj.arrayProperty = [1.0]
obj.stringProperty = "World"
obj.arrayProperty = [1.0, 2.0]
```

You'll see both initial values and changes appear in your debug area. Nice!

If you ever use a pure-Swift type that isn't bridged to Objective-C though, you'll start running into trouble:

```
struct PureSwift {
  let a: (Int, Bool)
}
```

Then, add a property to `TestObject`:

```
@objc dynamic var structProperty: PureSwift = .init(a:
(0,false))
```

You'll immediately see an error in Xcode, stating that "Property cannot be marked @objc because its type cannot be represented in Objective-C." Here, you reached the limits of Key-Value Observing.

> **Note**: Be careful when observing changes to system frameworks objects. Make sure the documentation mentions the property is observable because you can't have a clue by just looking at a system object's property list. This is true for Foundation, UIKit, AppKit, etc. Historically, properties had to be made "KVO-aware" to be observable.

Observation options

The full signature of the method you are calling to observe changes is `publisher(for:options:)`. The `options` parameter is an option set with four values: `.initial`, `.prior`, `.old` and `.new`. The default is `[.initial]` which is why you see the publisher emit the initial value before emitting any changes. Here is a breakdown of the options:

- `.initial` emits the initial value.
- `.prior` emits both the *previous* and the *new* value when a change occurs.
- `.old` and `.new` are unused in this publisher, they both do nothing (just let the new value through).

If you don't want the initial value, you can simply write:

```
obj.publisher(for: \.stringProperty, options: [])
```

If you specify `.prior`, you'll get two separate values every time a change occurs. Modifying the `integerProperty` example:

```
let subscription = obj.publisher(for: \.integerProperty,
  options: [.prior])
```

You would now see the following in the debug console for the `integerProperty` subscription:

```
integerProperty changes to 0
integerProperty changes to 100
integerProperty changes to 100
integerProperty changes to 200
```

The property first changes from `0` to `100`, so you get two values: `0` and `100`. Then, it changes from `100` to `200` so you again get two values: `100` and `200`.

ObservableObject

Combine's `ObservableObject` protocol works on Swift objects, not just on objects deriving from `NSObject`. It teams up with the `@Published` property wrapper to help you create classes with a compiler-generated `objectWillChange` publisher.

It saves you from writing a lot of boilerplate and allows creating objects which self-monitor their own properties and notify when any of them will change.

Here is an example:

```
class MonitorObject: ObservableObject {
  @Published var someProperty = false
  @Published var someOtherProperty = ""
}

let object = MonitorObject()
let subscription = object.objectWillChange.sink {
  print("object will change")
}

object.someProperty = true
object.someOtherProperty = "Hello world"
```

The `ObservableObject` protocol conformance makes the compiler automatically generate the `objectWillChange` property. It's an `ObservableObjectPublisher` which emits `Void` items and `Never` fails.

You'll get `objectWillChange` firing every time one of the object's `@Published` variables change. Unfortunately, you can't know *which* property actually changed. This is designed to work very well with SwiftUI which coalesces events to streamline screen updates.

Key points

- Key-Value Observing mostly relies on the Objective-C runtime and methods of the `NSObject` protocol.
- Many Objective-C classes in Apple frameworks offer some KVO-compliant properties.
- You can make your own properties observable, provided they are classes conforming to `NSObject`, and marked with the `@objc dynamic` attributes.
- You can also conform to `ObservableObject` and use `@Published` for your properties. The compiler-generated `objectWillChange` publisher triggers every time one of the `@Published` properties changes (but doesn't tell you which one changed).

Where to go from here?

Observing is a lot of fun, but sharing is caring! Keep reading to learn about Resources in Combine, and how you can save them by sharing them!

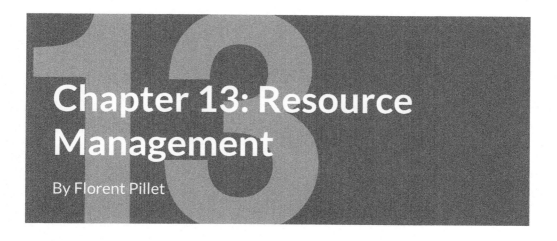

Chapter 13: Resource Management

By Florent Pillet

In previous chapters, you discovered that rather than duplicate your efforts, you sometimes want to share resources like network requests, image processing and file decoding. Anything resource-intensive that you can avoid repeating multiple times is worth looking into. In other words, you should *share* the outcome of a single resource – the values a publisher's work produces – between multiple subscribers rather than duplicate that outcome.

Combine offers two operators for you to manage resources: The `share()` operator and the `multicast(_:)` operator.

The share() operator

The purpose of this operator is to let you obtain a publisher by **reference** rather than by **value**. Publishers are usually structs: When you pass a publisher to a function or store it in several properties, Swift copies it several times. When you subscribe to each of the copies, the publisher can only do one thing: Start the work it's designed to do and deliver the values.

The `share()` operator returns an instance of the `Publishers.Share` **class**. Often, publishers are implemented as `struct`s, but in `share()`s case, as mentioned before, the operator obtains a **reference** to the `Share` publisher instead of using value semantics, which allows it to share the underlying publisher.

This new publisher "shares" the upstream publisher. It will subscribe to the upstream publisher once, with the first incoming subscriber. It will then relay the values it receives from the upstream publisher to this subscriber and to all those that subscribe after it.

> **Note**: New subscribers will only receive values the upstream publisher emits *after* they subscribe. There's no buffering or replay involved. If a subscriber subscribes to a shared publisher after the upstream publisher has completed, that new subscriber only receives the completion event.

To put this concept into practice, imagine you're performing a network request, like you learned how to do in Chapter 9, "Networking." You want multiple subscribers to receive the result without requesting multiple times. Your code would look something like this:

```
let shared = URLSession.shared
  .dataTaskPublisher(for: URL(string: "https://
www.raywenderlich.com")!)
  .map(\.data)
  .print("shared")
  .share()

print("subscribing first")

let subscription1 = shared.sink(
  receiveCompletion: { _ in },
  receiveValue: { print("subscription1 received: '\($0)'") }
)

print("subscribing second")
```

```
let subscription2 = shared.sink(
  receiveCompletion: { _ in },
  receiveValue: { print("subscription2 received: '\($0)'") }
)
```

The first subscriber triggers the "work" (in this case, performing the network request) of share()'s upstream publisher. The second subscriber will simply "connect" to it and receive values at the same time as the first.

Running this code in a playground, you'd see an output similar to:

```
subscribing first
shared: receive subscription: (DataTaskPublisher)
shared: request unlimited
subscribing second
shared: receive value: (303425 bytes)
subscription1 received: '303425 bytes'
subscription2 received: '303425 bytes'
shared: receive finished
```

Using the print(_:to:) operator's output, you can see that:

- The first subscription triggers a subscription to the DataTaskPublisher.

- The second subscription doesn't change anything: The publisher keeps running. No second request goes out.

- When the request completes, the publisher emits the resulting data to both subscribers then completes.

To verify that the request is only sent once, you could comment out the share() line and the output would look similar to this:

```
subscribing first
shared: receive subscription: (DataTaskPublisher)
shared: request unlimited
subscribing second
shared: receive subscription: (DataTaskPublisher)
shared: request unlimited
shared: receive value: (303425 bytes)
subscription1 received: '303425 bytes'
shared: receive finished
shared: receive value: (303425 bytes)
subscription2 received: '303425 bytes'
shared: receive finished
```

You can clearly see that when the DataTaskPublisher is not shared, it receives two subscriptions! And in this case, the request runs twice, once for each subscription.

But there's a problem: What if the second subscriber comes after the shared request has completed? You could simulate this case by delaying the second subscription.

Don't forget to uncomment `share()` if you're following along in a playground. Then, replace the `subscription2` code with the following:

```swift
var subscription2: AnyCancellable? = nil

DispatchQueue.main.asyncAfter(deadline: .now() + 5) {
  print("subscribing second")

  subscription2 = shared.sink(
    receiveCompletion: { print("subscription2 completion \($0)")
  },
    receiveValue: { print("subscription2 received: '\($0)'") }
  )
}
```

Running this, you'd see that `subscription2` receives nothing if the delay is longer than the time it takes for the request to complete:

```
subscribing first
shared: receive subscription: (DataTaskPublisher)
shared: request unlimited
subscribing second
shared: receive value: (303425 bytes)
subscription1 received: '303425 bytes'
shared: receive finished
subscribing second
subscription2 completion finished
```

By the time `subscription2` is created, the request has already completed and the resulting data has been emitted. How can you make sure *both* subscriptions receive the request result?

The multicast(_:) operator

To share a single subscription to a publisher and *replay* the values to new subscribers even after the upstream publisher has completed, you need something like a `shareReplay()` operator. Unfortunately, this operator is not part of Combine. However, you'll learn how to create one in Chapter 18, "Custom Publishers & Handling Backpressure."

In Chapter 9, "Networking," you used `multicast(_:)`. This operator builds on `share()` and uses a `Subject` of your choice to publish values to subscribers. The unique characteristic of `multicast(_:)` is that the publisher it returns is a `ConnectablePublisher`. What this means is it won't subscribe to the upstream publisher until you call its `connect()` method. This leaves you ample time to set up all the subscribers you need before letting it connect to the upstream publisher and start the work.

To adjust the previous example to use `multicast(_:)` you could write:

```swift
// 1
let subject = PassthroughSubject<Data, URLError>()

// 2
let multicasted = URLSession.shared
  .dataTaskPublisher(for: URL(string: "https://
www.raywenderlich.com")!)
  .map(\.data)
  .print("multicast")
  .multicast(subject: subject)

// 3
let subscription1 = multicasted
  .sink(
    receiveCompletion: { _ in },
    receiveValue: { print("subscription1 received: '\($0)'") }
  )

let subscription2 = multicasted
  .sink(
    receiveCompletion: { _ in },
    receiveValue: { print("subscription2 received: '\($0)'") }
  )

// 4
let cancellable = multicasted.connect()
```

Here's what this code does:

1. Prepares a subject, which relays the values and completion event the upstream publisher emits.

2. Prepares the multicasted publisher, using the above `subject`.

3. Subscribes to the shared — i.e., *multicasted* — publisher, like earlier in this chapter.

4. Instructs the publisher to **connect** to the upstream publisher.

This effectively starts the work, but only after you've had time to set up all your subscriptions. This way, you make sure no subscriber will miss the downloaded data.

The resulting output, if you run this in a playground, would be:

```
multicast: receive subscription: (DataTaskPublisher)
multicast: request unlimited
multicast: receive value: (303425 bytes)
subscription1 received: '303425 bytes'
subscription2 received: '303425 bytes'
multicast: receive finished
```

> **Note**: A multicast publisher, like all `ConnectablePublishers`, also provides an `autoconnect()` method, which makes it work like `share()`: The first time you subscribe to it, it connects to the upstream publisher and starts the work immediately. This is useful in scenarios where the upstream publisher emits a single value and you can use a `CurrentValueSubject` to share it with subscribers.

Sharing subscription work, in particular for resource-heavy processes such as networking, is a must for most modern apps. Not keeping an eye on this could result not only in memory issues, but also possibly bombarding your server with a ton of unnecessary network requests.

Future

While `share()` and `multicast(_:)` give you full-blown publishers, Combine comes with one more way to let you share the result of a computation: `Future`, which you learned about in Chapter 2, "Publishers & Subscribers."

You create a `Future` by handing it a closure which receives a `Promise` argument. You further *fulfill* the promise whenever you have a result available, either successful or failed. Look at an example to refresh your memory:

```
// 1
func performSomeWork() throws -> Int {
  print("Performing some work and returning a result")
  return 5
}

// 2
let future = Future<Int, Error> { fulfill in
```

```
    do {
      let result = try performSomeWork()
      // 3
      fulfill(.success(result))
    } catch {
      // 4
      fulfill(.failure(error))
    }
  }

  print("Subscribing to future...")

  // 5
  let subscription1 = future
    .sink(
      receiveCompletion: { _ in print("subscription1 completed") },
      receiveValue: { print("subscription1 received: '\($0)'") }
    )

  // 6
  let subscription2 = future
    .sink(
      receiveCompletion: { _ in print("subscription2 completed") },
      receiveValue: { print("subscription2 received: '\($0)'") }
    )
```

This code:

1. Provides a function simulating work (possibly asynchronous) performed by the `Future`.

2. Creates a new `Future`. Note that the work starts **immediately** without waiting for subscribers.

3. In case the work succeeds, it fulfills the `Promise` with the result.

4. If the work fails, it passes the error to the `Promise`.

5. Subscribes once to show that we receive the result.

6. Subscribes a second time to show that we receive the result too without performing the work twice.

What's interesting from a resource perspective is that:

- `Future` is a **class**, not a struct.

- Upon creation, it **immediately** invokes your closure to start computing the result and fulfill the promise as soon as possible.

- It stores the result of the fulfilled `Promise` and delivers it to **current and future** subscribers.

In practice, it means that `Future` is a convenient way to immediately start performing some work (without waiting for subscriptions) while performing work only once and delivering the result to any amount of subscribers. But it performs work and returns a single result, not a stream of results, so the use cases are narrower than full-blown publishers.

It's a good candidate to use for when you need to share the single result a network request produces!

> **Note**: Even if you never subscribe to a `Future`, creating it will call your closure and perform the work. You cannot rely on `Deferred` to defer closure execution until a subscriber comes in, because `Deferred` is a struct and would cause a new `Future` to be created every time there is a new subscriber!

Key points

- Sharing subscription work is critical when dealing with resource-heavy processes, such as networking.
- Use `share()` when you simply need to share a publisher with multiple subscribers.
- Use `multicast(_:)` when you need fine control over when the upstream publisher starts to work and how values propagate to subscribers.
- Use `Future` to share the single result of a computation to multiple subscribers.

Where to go from here?

Congratulations for finishing the last theoretical mini-chapter for this section!

You'll wrap up this section by working on a hands-on project, where you'll build a API client to interact with the Hacker News API. Time to move along!

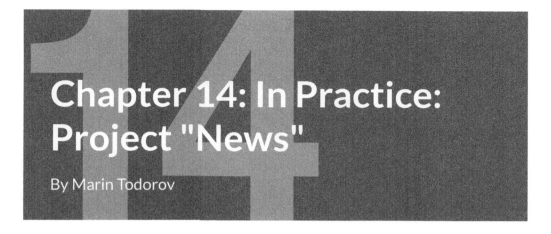

Chapter 14: In Practice: Project "News"

By Marin Todorov

In the past few chapters, you learned about quite a few practical applications of the Combine integration in Foundation types. You learned how to use URLSession's data task publisher to make network calls, you saw how to observe KVO-compatible objects with Combine and more.

In this chapter, you will *combine* your solid knowledge about operators with some of the Foundation integrations you just discovered and will work through a series of tasks like in the previous "In Practice" chapter. This time around, you will work on building a Hacker News API client.

"Hacker News," whose API you are going to be using in this chapter, is a social news website focused on computers and entrepreneurship. If you haven't already, you can check them out at: https://news.ycombinator.com.

In this chapter, you will work in an Xcode playground focusing only on the API client itself.

In Chapter 15, "In Practice: Combine & SwiftUI," you will take the completed API and use it to build a real Hacker News reader app by plugging the network layer into a SwiftUI-based user interface. Along the way, you will learn the basics of SwiftUI and how to make your Combine code work with the new declarative Apple framework for building amazing, reactive app UIs.

Without further ado, let's get started!

Getting started with the Hacker News API

Open the included starter playground **API.playground** in **projects/starter** and peek inside. You will find some simple starter code included to help you hit the ground running and let you focus on Combine code only:

Inside the `API` type, you will find two nested helper types:

- An enum called `Error` which features two custom errors your API will throw in case it cannot reach the server or it cannot decode the server response.

- A second enum called `EndPoint` which contains the URLs of the two API endpoints your type is going to be connecting to.

Further down, you will find the `maxStories` property. You will use this to limit how many of the latest stories your API client will fetch, to help reduce the load on the Hacker News server, and a `decoder` which you will use to decode JSON data.

Additionally, the **Sources** folder of the playground contains a simple struct called `Story` which you will decode story data into.

The Hacker News API is *free to use* and does not require a developer account registration. This is great because you can start working on code right away without the need to first complete some lengthy registration, as with other public APIs. The Hacker News team wins a ton of karma points!

Getting a single story

Your first task is to add a method to `API` which will contact the server using the `EndPoint` type to get the correct endpoint URL and will fetch the data about a single story. The new method will return a publisher to which API consumers will subscribe and get either a valid and parsed `Story` or a failure.

Scroll down the playground source code and find the comment saying `// Add your API code here`. Just below that line, insert a new method declaration:

```
func story(id: Int) -> AnyPublisher<Story, Error> {
  return Empty().eraseToAnyPublisher()
}
```

To avoid compilation errors in your playground, you return an `Empty` publisher which completes immediately. As you'll finish building the method body, you'll remove the expression and return your new subscription, instead.

As mentioned, this publisher's output is a `Story` and its failure is the custom `API.Error` type. As you will see later on, in case there are network errors or other mishaps, you will need to convert those into one of the `API.Error` cases to match the expected return type.

Start modeling the subscription by creating a network request to the single-story endpoint of the Hacker News API. Inside the new method, above the `return` statement, insert:

```
URLSession.shared
  .dataTaskPublisher(for: EndPoint.story(id).url)
```

You start by making a request to `Endpoint.story(id).url`. The `url` property of the endpoint contains the complete HTTP URL to request. The single story URL looks like this (with a matching ID): https://hacker-news.firebaseio.com/v0/item/12345.json (Visit https://bit.ly/2nL2ojS if you'd like to preview the API response.)

Next, to parse JSON on a background thread and keep the rest of the app responsive, let's create a new custom dispatch queue. Add a new property to `API` above the `story(id:)` method like so:

```
private let apiQueue = DispatchQueue(label: "API",
                                    qos: .default,
                                    attributes: .concurrent)
```

You will use this queue to process JSON responses and, therefore, you need to switch your network subscription to that queue. Back in `story(id:)`, add the line **below** calling `dataTaskPublisher(for:)`:

```
.receive(on: apiQueue)
```

Once you've switched to the background queue, you need to fetch the JSON data out of the response. The `dataTaskPublisher(for:)` publisher returns an output of type (`Data`, `URLResponse`) as a tuple but for your subscription, you need only the data.

Add another line to the method to map the current output to only the data from the resulting tuple:

```
.map(\.data)
```

The output type of this operator is `Data`, which you can feed to a decode operator and try converting the response to a `Story`.

Append to the subscription:

```
.decode(type: Story.self, decoder: decoder)
```

In case it receives anything but a valid story JSON, `decode(...)` will throw an error and the publisher will complete with a failure.

You will learn about error handling in detail in Chapter 16, "Error Handling." In the current chapter, you will use few operators and get a taste of a few different ways to handle errors but you will not go into the nitty-gritty of how things work.

For the current `story(id:)` method, you will return an empty publisher in case things go south for any reason. This is easy to do by using the `catch` operator. Add to the subscription:

```
.catch { _ in Empty<Story, Error>() }
```

You ignore the thrown error and return `Empty()`. This, as you hopefully still remember, is a publisher that completes immediately without emitting any output values like so:

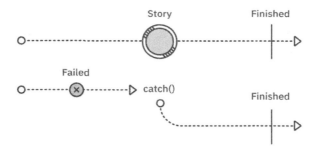

Handling the upstream errors this way via `catch(_)` allows you to:

- Emit the value and complete if you get back a `Story`.
- Return an `Empty` publisher which completes successfully without emitting any values, in case of a failure.

Next, to wrap up the method code and return your neatly designed publisher, you need to replace the current subscription at the end. Add:

```
.eraseToAnyPublisher()
```

You can now remove the temporary `Empty` you've added before. Find the following line and remove it:

```
return Empty().eraseToAnyPublisher()
```

Your code should now compile with no issues, but just to make sure you haven't missed a step in all the excitement, review your progress so far and make sure your completed code looks like this:

```
func story(id: Int) -> AnyPublisher<Story, Error> {
  URLSession.shared
    .dataTaskPublisher(for: EndPoint.story(id).url)
    .receive(on: apiQueue)
    .map(\.data)
    .decode(type: Story.self, decoder: decoder)
    .catch { _ in Empty<Story, Error>() }
    .eraseToAnyPublisher()
}
```

Even though your code compiles, this method still won't produce any output just yet. You're about to take care of that next.

Now you can instantiate `API` and try calling into the Hacker News server.

Scroll down just a bit and find the comment line `// Call the API here`. This is a good spot to make a test API call. Insert the following code:

```
let api = API()
var subscriptions = [AnyCancellable]()
```

Fetch a story by providing a random ID to test with by adding:

```
api.story(id: 1000)
  .sink(receiveCompletion: { print($0) },
        receiveValue: { print($0) })
  .store(in: &subscriptions)
```

You create a new publisher by calling `api.story(id: 1000)` and subscribe to it via `sink(...)` which prints any output values or completion event. To keep the subscription alive until the request has completed you store it in `subscriptions`.

As soon as the playground runs again, it will make a network call to hacker-news.firebaseio.com and print the result in the console:

```
61    api.story(id: 1000)
62      .sink(receiveCompletion: { print($0) }) { print($0) }
63      .store(in: &subscriptions)
```

```
How Important is the .com TLD?
by python_kiss
http://www.netbusinessblog.com/2007/02/19/how-important-is-the-dot-com/
-----
finished
```

The returned JSON data from the server is a rather simple structure like this:

```
{
  "by":"python_kiss",
  "descendants":0,
  "id":1000,
  "score":4,
  "time":1172394646,
  "title":"How Important is the .com TLD?",
  "type":"story",
  "url":"http://www.netbusinessblog.com/2007/02/19/how-important-is-the-dot-com/"
}
```

The `Codable` conformance of `Story` parses and stores the values of the following properties: `by`, `id`, `time`, `title` and `url`.

Once the request completes successfully, you'll see the following output, or a similar output in case you changed the 1000 value in the request, in the console:

```
How Important is the .com TLD?
by python_kiss
http://www.netbusinessblog.com/2007/02/19/how-important-is-the-dot-com/
-----
finished
```

The `Story` type conforms to `CustomDebugStringConvertible` and it has a custom `debugDescription` that returns the title, author name and story URL neatly ordered, like above.

The output ends with a `finished` completion event. To try what happens in case of an error, replace the id `1000` with `-5` and check the output in the console. You will only see `finished` printed because you caught the error and returned `Empty()`.

Nice work! The first method of the `API` type is complete and you exercised some of the concepts you covered in previous chapters like calling the network and decoding JSON. Additionally you got a gentle introduction to basic dispatch queue switching and some easy error handling. You will cover these in more detail in future chapters.

Despite what an incredibly nice exercise this task was, you're probably hungry for more. So, in the next section, you will dig deeper and lay some serious code down.

Multiple stories via merging publishers

Getting a single story out of the API server was a relatively straight forward task. Next, you'll touch on a few more of the concepts you've been learning by creating a custom publisher to fetch multiple stories at the same time.

The new method `mergedStories(ids:)` will get a story publisher for each of the given story `ids` and merge them all together. Add this new method declaration to the `API` type after the `story(id:)` method you implemented earlier:

```
func mergedStories(ids storyIDs: [Int]) -> AnyPublisher<Story, Error> {

}
```

What this method will essentially do is call `story(id:)` for each of the given `ids` and then flatten the result into a single stream of output values.

First of all, to reduce the number of network calls during development, you will fetch only the first `maxStories` ids from the provided list. Start the new method by inserting the following code:

```
let storyIDs = Array(storyIDs.prefix(maxStories))
```

To get started, create the first publisher:

```
precondition(!storyIDs.isEmpty)

let initialPublisher = story(id: storyIDs[0])
let remainder = Array(storyIDs.dropFirst())
```

By using `story(id:)`, you create the `initialPublisher` publisher that fetches the story with the first `id` in the list.

Next, you will use `reduce(_:_:)` from the Swift standard library on the remaining story ids to merge each next story publisher into the initial publisher like so:

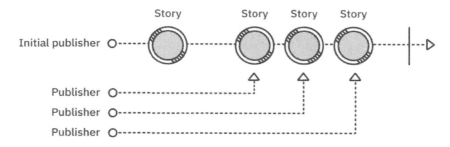

To reduce the rest of the stories into the initial publisher add:

```
return remainder.reduce(initialPublisher) { combined, id in

}
```

`reduce(_:_:)` will start with the initial publisher and provide each of the `ids` in the `remainder` array to the closure to process. Insert this code to create a new publisher for the given story `id` in the empty closure, and merge it to the current combined result:

```
return combined
  .merge(with: story(id: id))
  .eraseToAnyPublisher()
```

The final result is a publisher which emits each successfully fetched story and ignores any errors that each of the single-story publishers might encounter.

> **Note**: Congratulations, you just created a custom implementation of the `MergeMany` publisher. Working through the code yourself was not in vain though. You learned about operator composition and how to apply operators like `merge` and `reduce` in a real-world use case.

With the new API method completed, scroll down to this code and comment or delete it to speed up the execution of the playground while testing your newer code:

```
api.story(id: -5)
    .sink(receiveCompletion: { print($0) },
          receiveValue: { print($0) })
    .store(in: &subscriptions)
```

In place of the just deleted code, insert:

```
api.mergedStories(ids: [1000, 1001, 1002])
    .sink(receiveCompletion: { print($0) },
          receiveValue: { print($0) })
    .store(in: &subscriptions)
```

Let the playground run one more time with your latest code. This time, you should see in the console these three story summaries:

```
How Important is the .com TLD?
by python_kiss
http://www.netbusinessblog.com/2007/02/19/how-important-is-the-
dot-com/
-----

Wireless: India's Hot, China's Not
by python_kiss
http://www.redherring.com/Article.aspx?a=21355
-----

The Battle for Mobile Search
by python_kiss
http://www.businessweek.com/technology/content/feb2007/
tc20070220_828216.htm?campaign_id=rss_daily
-----
finished
```

Another glorious success along your path of learning Combine! In this section, you wrote a method that combines any number of publishers and reduces them to a single one. That's very helpful code to have around, as the built-in `merge` operator can merge only up to 8 publishers. Sometimes, however, you just don't know how many publishers you'll need in advance!

Getting the latest stories

In this final chapter section, you will work on creating an API method that fetches the list of latest Hacker News stories.

This chapter is following a bit of a pattern. First, you reused your single story method to fetch multiple stories. Now, you are going to reuse the multiple stories method to fetch the list of latest stories.

Add the new empty method declaration to the `API` type as follows:

```
func stories() -> AnyPublisher<[Story], Error> {
  return Empty().eraseToAnyPublisher()
}
```

Like before, you return an `Empty` object to prevent any compilation errors while you construct your method body and publisher.

Unlike before, though, this time your returned publisher's output is a list of stories. You will design the publisher to fetch multiple stories and accumulate them in an array, emitting each intermediary state as the responses come in from the server.

This behavior will allow you to, in the next chapter, bind this new publisher directly to a `List` UI control that will automatically animate the stories live on-screen as they come in from the server.

Begin, as you did previously, by firing off a network request to the Hacker News API. Insert the following in your new method, above the `return` statement:

```
URLSession.shared
  .dataTaskPublisher(for: EndPoint.stories.url)
```

The `stories` endpoint lets you hit the following URL to get the latest story ids: https://hacker-news.firebaseio.com/v0/newstories.json.

Again, you need to grab the data component of the emitted result. So, map the output by adding:

```
.map(\.data)
```

The JSON response you will get from the server is a plain list like this:

```
[1000, 1001, 1002, 1003]
```

You need to parse the list as an array of integer numbers and, if that succeeds, you can use the ids to fetch the matching stories.

Append to the subscription:

```
.decode(type: [Int].self, decoder: decoder)
```

This will map the current subscription output to an [Int] and you will use it to fetch the corresponding stories one-by-one from the server.

Now is the moment, however, to go back to the topic of error handling for a moment. When fetching a single story, you just ignore any errors. But, in stories(), let's see how you can do a little more than that.

API.Error is the error type to which you will constrain the errors thrown from stories(). You have two errors defined as enumeration cases:

- invalidResponse: for when you cannot decode the server response into the expected type.
- addressUnreachable(URL): for when you cannot reach the endpoint URL.

Currently, your subscription code in stories() can throw two types of errors:

- dataTaskPublisher(for:) could throw different variations of a URLError when a network problem occurs.
- decode(type:decoder:) could throw a decoding error when the JSON doesn't match the expected type.

Your next task is to handle those various errors in a way that would map them to the single API.Error type to match the expected failure of the returned publisher.

You will jump the gun yet another time and get a "soft" introduction to another error handling operator. Append this code to your current subscription, after decode:

```
.mapError { error -> API.Error in
  switch error {
  case is URLError:
    return Error.addressUnreachable(EndPoint.stories.url)
  default:
    return Error.invalidResponse
  }
}
```

`mapError` handles any errors occurring upstream and allows you to map them into a single error type — similar to how you use `map` to change the type of the output.

In the code above, you switch over any errors and:

- In case `error` is of type `URLError` and therefore occurred while trying to reach the `stories` server endpoint, you return `.addressUnreachable(_)`.

- Otherwise, you return `.invalidResponse` as the only other place where an error could occur. Once successfully fetched, the network response is decoding the JSON data.

With that, you matched the expected failure type in `stories()` and can leave it to the API consumers to handle errors downstream. You will use `stories()` in the next chapter. So, you will do a little more with error handling before you get to Chapter 16, "Error Handling," and dive into the details.

So far, the current subscription fetches a list of `ids` from the JSON API but doesn't do much on top of that. Next, you will use a few operators to filter unwanted content and map the `id` list to the actual stories.

First, filter empty results — in case the API goes bonkers and returns an empty list for its latest stories. Append:

```
.filter { !$0.isEmpty }
```

This will guarantee that downstream operators receive a list of story `ids` with at least one element. This is very handy because, as you remember, `mergedStories(ids:)` has a precondition ensuring that its input parameter is not empty.

To use `mergedStories(ids:)` and fetch the story details, you will flatten all the story publishers by appending a `flatMap` operator:

```
.flatMap { storyIDs in
  return self.mergedStories(ids: storyIDs)
}
```

Merging all the publishers into a single downstream will produce a continuous stream of Story values. The publisher emits these downstream as soon as they are fetched from the network:

You could leave the current subscription as is right now but you'd like to design the API to be easily bindable to a list UI control. This will allow the consumers to simply subscribe stories() and assign the result to an [Story] property in their view controller or SwiftUI view.

To achieve that, you will need to aggregate the emitted stories and map the subscription to return an ever-growing array — instead of single Story values.

It's time for some serious magic! Remember the scan operator from Chapter 3, "Transforming Operators" I know that was some time ago, but, this is the operator that will help you achieve your current task. So, if needed, jump back to that chapter and come back here when refreshed on scan.

Append to your current subscription:

```
.scan([]) { stories, story -> [Story] in
  return stories + [story]
}
```

You let scan(...) start emitting with an empty array. Each time a new story is being emitted, you append it to the current aggregated result via stories + [story].

This addition to the subscription code changes its behavior so that you get the — sort of — buffered contents each time you receive a new story from the batch you are working on:

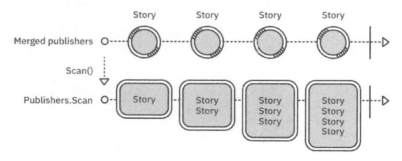

Finally, it can't hurt to sort the stories before emitting output. `Story` conforms to `Comparable` so you don't need to implement any custom sorting. You just need to call `sorted()` on the result. Append:

```
.map { $0.sorted() }
```

Wrap up the current, rather long, subscription by type erasing the returned publisher. Append one last operator:

```
.eraseToAnyPublisher()
```

At this point, you can find the following temporary return statement, and remove it:

```
return Empty().eraseToAnyPublisher()
```

Your playground should now finally compile with no errors. However, it still shows the test data from the previous chapter section. Find and comment out:

```
api.mergedStories(ids: [1000, 1001, 1002])
    .sink(receiveCompletion: { print($0) },
          receiveValue: { print($0) })
    .store(in: &subscriptions)
```

In its place, insert:

```
api.stories()
    .sink(receiveCompletion: { print($0) },
          receiveValue: { print($0) })
    .store(in: &subscriptions)
```

This code subscribes to `api.stories()` and prints any returned output and completion events.

Once you let the playground run one more time, you should see a dump of the latest Hacker News stories in the console. You print the list **iteratively**. Initially, you will see the story fetched first on its own:

```
[
More than 70% of America's packaged food supply is ultra-
processed
by xbeta
https://news.northwestern.edu/stories/2019/07/us-packaged-food-
supply-is-ultra-processed/
-----]
```

Then, the same one accompanied by a second story:

```
[
More than 70% of America's packaged food supply is ultra-
processed
by xbeta
https://news.northwestern.edu/stories/2019/07/us-packaged-food-
supply-is-ultra-processed/
-----,
New AI project expects to map all the word's reefs by end of
next year
by Biba89
https://www.independent.co.uk/news/science/coral-bleaching-ai-
reef-paul-allen-climate-a9022876.html
-----]
```

Then, a list of the same stories plus a third one and so on:

```
[
More than 70% of America's packaged food supply is ultra-
processed
by xbeta
https://news.northwestern.edu/stories/2019/07/us-packaged-food-
supply-is-ultra-processed/
-----,
New AI project expects to map all the word's reefs by end of
next year
by Biba89
https://www.independent.co.uk/news/science/coral-bleaching-ai-
reef-paul-allen-climate-a9022876.html
-----,
People forged judges' signatures to trick Google into changing
results
by lnguyen
https://arstechnica.com/tech-policy/2019/07/people-forged-
judges-signatures-to-trick-google-into-changing-results/
-----]
```

Please note, since you're fetching live data from the Hacker News website the stories, what you see in your console **will be different** as more and more stories are added every few minutes. To see that you are indeed fetching live data, wait a few minutes and re-run the playground. You should see some new stories show up alongside the ones you already saw.

Nice effort working through this somewhat longer section of the chapter! You've completed the development of the Hacker News API client and are ready to move on to the next chapter. There, you will use SwiftUI to build a proper Hacker News reader app.

Challenges

There is nothing to add per se to the API client but you can still play around a little if you'd like to put some more work into this chapter's project.

Challenge: Integrating the API client with UIKit

As already mentioned, in the next chapter, you will learn about SwiftUI and how to integrate it with your Combine code.

In this challenge, try to build an iOS app that uses your completed API client to display the latest stories in a table view. You can develop as many details as you want and add some styling or fun features but the main point to exercise in this challenge is subscribing the `API.stories()` and binding the result to a table view — much like the bindings you worked on in Chapter 8, "In Practice: Project 'Collage'."

In case you're not interested in working with UIKit - no worries, this challenge is just an excercise you can also skip and dive head first into Chapter 15, "In Practice: Combine & SwiftUI".

If you successfully work through the challenge as described, you should see the latest stories "pour in" when you launch the app in the simulator, or on your device:

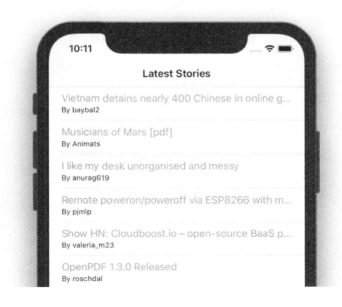

Key points

- Foundation includes several publishers that mirror counterpart methods in the Swift standard library and you can even use them interchangeably as you did with `reduce` in this chapter.

- Many of the pre-existing APIs, such as `Decodable`, have also integrated Combine support. This lets you use one standard approach across all of your code.

- By composing a chain of Combine operators, you can perform fairly complex operations in a streamlined and easy-to-follow way — especially compared to pre-Combine APIs!

Where to go from here?

Congratulations on completing the "Combine in Action" section! What a ride this was, wasn't it?

You've learned most of what Combine's foundations has to offer, so it's now times to pull out the big guns in an entire section dedicated to advanced topics in the Combine framework, starting with building an app that uses both SwiftUI *and* Combine.

Section IV: Advanced Combine

With a huge portion of Combine foundations already in your tool belt, it's time to learn some of the more advanced concepts and topics Combine has to offer on your way to true mastery.

You'll start by learning how to use SwiftUI with Combine to build truly reactive and fluent UI experiences and switch to learn how to properly handle errors in your Combine apps. You'll then learn about schedulers, the core concept behind scheduling work in different execution contexts and follow up with how you can create your own custom publishers and handling the demand of subscribers by understanding backpressure.

Finally, having a slick code base is great, but it doesn't help much if it's not well tested, so you'll wrap up this section by learning how to properly test your new Combine code.

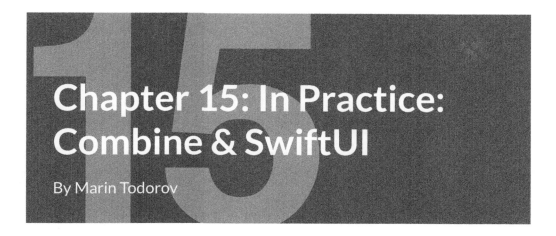

Chapter 15: In Practice: Combine & SwiftUI

By Marin Todorov

SwiftUI is Apple's latest technology for building app UIs declaratively. It's a big departure from the older UIKit and AppKit frameworks. It offers a very lean and easy to read and write syntax for building user interfaces.

> **Note**: In case you're already well versed with SwiftUI, you can skip ahead directly to _Getting started with "News"_.

The SwiftUI syntax clearly represents the view hierarchy you'd like to build:

```
HStack(spacing: 10) {
  Text("My photo")
  Image("myphoto.png")
    .padding(20)
    .resizable()
}
```

You can easily visually parse the hierarchy. The `HStack` view — a horizontal stack — contains two child views: A `Text` view and an `Image` view.

Each view can have a list of modifiers — which are methods you call on the view. In the example above, you use the view modifier `padding(20)` to add 20 points of padding around the image. Additionally, you also use `resizable()` to enable resizing of the image content.

SwiftUI also unifies the approach to building cross-platform UIs. For example, a `Picker` control displays a new modal view in your iOS app allowing the user to pick an item from a list, but on macOS the same `Picker` control displays a dropbox.

A quick code example of a data form could be something like this:

```
VStack {
  TextField("Name", text: $name)
  TextField("Proffesion", text: $profession)
  Picker("Type", selection: $type) {
    Text("Freelance")
    Text("Hourly")
    Text("Employee")
  }
}
```

This code will create two separate views on iOS. The **Type** picker control will be a button taking the user to a separate screen with a list of options like so:

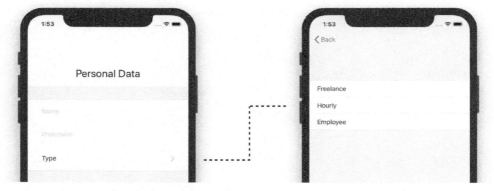

On macOS, however, SwiftUI will consider the abundant UI screen space on the mac and create a single form with a drop-down menu instead:

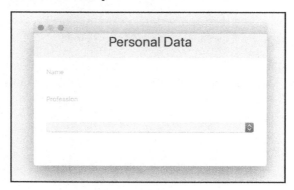

Finally, in SwiftUI, the user interface rendered on screen is a function of your state. You maintain a single copy of this state referred to as the "source of truth", and the UI is being derived dynamically from that state. Lucky for you, a Combine publisher can easily be plugged as a data source to SwiftUI views.

Hello, SwiftUI!

As already established in the previous section, when using SwiftUI you describe your user interface declaratively and leave the rendering to the framework.

Each of the views you declare for your UI — text labels, images, shapes, etc. — conform to the View protocol. The only requirement of View is a property called body.

Any time you change your data model, SwiftUI asks each of your views for their current body representation. This might be changing according to your latest data model changes. Then, the framework builds the view hierarchy to render on-screen by calculating only the views affected by changes in your model, resulting in a highly optimized and effective drawing mechanism.

In effect, SwiftUI makes UI "snapshots" triggered by any changes of your data model like so:

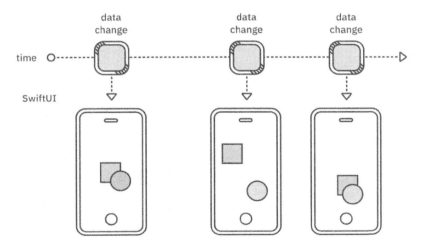

In this chapter, you will work through a number of tasks that cover both interoperations between Combine and SwiftUI along with some of the SwiftUI basics.

Memory management

Believe it or not, a big part of what makes all of the above roll is a shift in how memory management works for your UI.

No data duplication

Let's look at an example of what that means. When working with UIKit/AppKit you'd, in broad strokes, have your code separated between a data model, some kind of controller and a view:

Those three types can have several similar features. They include data storage, support mutability, can be reference types and more.

Let's say you want to display the current weather on-screen. For this example, let's say the model type is a struct called `Weather` and stores the current conditions in a text property called `conditions`. To display that information to the user, you need to create an instance of another type, namely `UILabel`, and copy the value of `conditions` into the `text` property of the label.

Now, you have two copies of the value you work with. One in your model type and the other stored in the `UILabel`, just for the purpose of displaying it on-screen:

There is no connection or binding between `text` and `conditions`. You simply need to copy the `String` value everywhere you need it.

Now you've added a **dependency** to your UI. The freshness of the information on-screen **depends** on `Weather.conditions`. It's your responsibility to update the label's `text` property manually with a new copy of `Weather.conditions` whenever the `conditions` property changes.

SwiftUI removes the need for duplicating your data for the purpose of showing it on-screen. Being able to offload data storage out of your UI allows you to effectively manage the data in a single place in your model and never have your app's users see stale information on-screen.

Less need to "control" your views

As an additional bonus, removing the need for having "glue" code between your model and your view allows you to get rid of most of your view controller code as well!

In this chapter, you will learn:

- Briefly about the basics of SwiftUI syntax for building declarative UIs.
- How to declare various types of UI inputs and connect them to their "sources of truth."
- How to use Combine to build data models and pipe the data into SwiftUI.

> **Note**: If you'd like to learn more about SwiftUI, consider checking out SwiftUI by Tutorials (https://bit.ly/2L5wLLi) for an in-depth learning experience.

And now, for our feature presentation: **Combine with SwiftUI**!

Getting started with "News"

The starter project for this chapter already includes some code so that you can focus on writing code connecting Combine and SwiftUI.

The project also includes some folders where you will find the following:

- **App** contains the main app type.
- **Network** includes the completed Hacker News API from last chapter.
- **Model** is where you will find simple model types like `Story`, `FilterKeyword` and `Settings`. Additionally, this is where `ReaderViewModel` resides, which is the model type that the main newsreader view uses.
- **View** contains the app views and, inside **View/Helpers**, you will find some simple reusable components like buttons, badges, etc.
- Finally, in **Util** there is a helper type that allows you to easily read and write JSON files to/from disk.

The completed project will display a list of Hacker News stories and allow the user to manage a keyword filter:

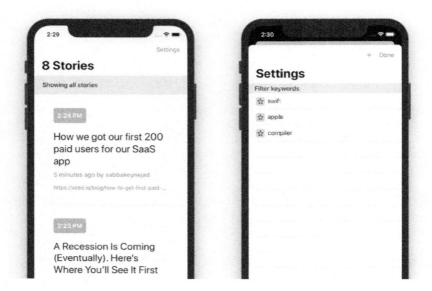

A first taste of managing view state

Build and run the starter project and you will see an empty table on screen and a single bar button titled "**Settings**":

This is where you start. To get a taste of how interacting with the UI via changes to your data works, you'll make the **Settings** button present `SettingsView` when tapped.

Open **View/ReaderView.swift** which contains the `ReaderView` view displaying the main app interface.

The type already includes a property called `presentingSettingsSheet` which is a simple Boolean value. Changing this value will either present or dismiss the settings view. Scroll down through the source code and find the comment `// Set presentingSettingsSheet to true here`.

This comment is in the Settings button callback so that's the perfect place to present the Settings view. Replace the comment with:

```
self.presentingSettingsSheet = true
```

As soon as you add this line, you will see the following error:

```
// Present the Settings sheet here.
self.presentingSettingsSheet = true          ● Cannot assign to property: 'self' is immutable
```

And indeed `self` **is** immutable because the view's body is a dynamic property and, therefore, cannot mutate `ReaderView`.

SwiftUI offers a number of built-in property wrappers to help you indicate that given properties are part of your state and any changes to those properties should trigger a new UI "snapshot."

Let's see what that means in practice. Adjust the plain old `presentingSettingsSheet` property so it looks as follows:

```
@State var presentingSettingsSheet = false
```

The `@State` property wrapper:

1. Moves the property storage out of the view, so modifying `presentingSettingsSheet` does not mutate `self`.

2. Marks the property as **local storage**. In other words, it denotes the piece of data is owned by the view.

3. Adds a publisher, somewhat like `@Published` does, to `ReaderView` called `$presentingSettingsSheet` which you can use to subscribe to the property or to bind it to UI controls or other views.

Once you add `@State` to `presentingSettingsSheet`, the error will clear as the compiler knows that you can modify this particular property from a non-mutating context.

Finally, to make use of presentingSettingsSheet, you need to declare how the new state affects the UI. In this case, you will add a sheet(...) view modifier to the view hierarchy and bind $presentingSettingsSheet to the sheet. Whenever you change presentingSettingsSheet, SwiftUI will take the current value and either present or dismiss your view, based on the boolean value.

Find the comment `// Present the Settings sheet here` and replace it with:

```
.sheet(isPresented: self.$presentingSettingsSheet, content: {
  SettingsView()
})
```

The `sheet(isPresented:content:)` modifier takes a `Bool` publisher and a view to render whenever the presentation publisher emits `true`.

Build and run the project. Tap **Settings** and your new presentation will display the target view:

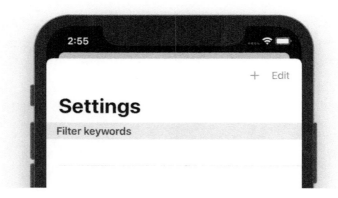

Fetching the latest stories

Next, time for you to go back to some Combine code. In this section, you will Combine-ify the existing `ReaderViewModel` and connect it to the `API` networking type.

Open **Model/ReaderViewModel.swift**. At the top, insert:

```
import Combine
```

This code, naturally, will allow you to use Combine types in **ReaderViewModel.swift**. Now, add a new `subscriptions` property to `ReaderViewModel` to store all of your subscriptions:

```
private var subscriptions = Set<AnyCancellable>()
```

With all that solid prep work, now it's time to create a new method and engage the network API. Add the following empty method to `ReaderViewModel`:

```
func fetchStories() {

}
```

In this method, you will subscribe to `API.stories()` and store the server response in the model type. You should be familiar with this method from the previous chapter.

Add the following inside `fetchStories()`:

```
api
  .stories()
  .receive(on: DispatchQueue.main)
```

You use the `receive(on:)` operator to receive any output on the main queue. Arguably, you could leave the thread management to the consumer of the API. However, since in `ReaderViewModel`'s case that's certainly `ReaderView`, you optimize right here and switch to the main queue to prepare for committing changes to the UI.

Next, you will use a `sink(...)` subscriber to store the stories and any emitted errors in the model. Append:

```
.sink(receiveCompletion: { completion in
  if case .failure(let error) = completion {
    self.error = error
  }
}, receiveValue: { stories in
  self.allStories = stories
  self.error = nil
})
.store(in: &subscriptions)
```

First, you check if the `completion` was a failure. If so, you store the associated error in `self.error`. In case you receive values from the stories publisher, you store them in `self.allStories`.

This is all the logic you're going to add to the model in this section. The fetchStories() method is now complete and you can "start-up" your model as soon as you display ReaderView on screen.

To do that, open **App/App.swift** and add a new onAppear(...) view modifier to ReaderView, like so:

```
ReaderView(model: viewModel)
  .onAppear {
    viewModel.fetchStories()
  }
```

Right now, ReaderViewModel is not really hooked up to ReaderView so you will not see any change on-screen. However, to quickly verify that everything works as expected, do the following: Go back to **Model/ReaderViewModel.swift** and add a didSet handler to the allStories property:

```
private var allStories = [Story]() {
  didSet {
    print(allStories.count)
  }
}
```

Run the app and observe the Console. You should see a reassuring output like so:

```
1
2
3
4
...
```

You can remove the didSet handler you just added in case you don't want to see that output every time you run the app.

Using ObservableObject for model types

ObservableObject is a protocol that makes plain old data models observable and lets an observing SwiftUI View know the data has changed, so its able to rebuild any user interface that dependa on this data.

The protocol requires types to implement a publisher called objectWillChange which emits any time the type's state is about to change.

There is already a default implementation of that publisher in the protoocol so in most cases you won't have to add anything to your data model. When you add `ObservableObject` conformance to your type, the default protocol implementation will automatically emit any time any of your `@Published` properties emit!

Open **ReaderViewModel.swift** and add `ObservableObject` conformance to `ReaderViewModel`, so it looks like this:

```
class ReaderViewModel: ObservableObject {
```

Next, you need to consider which properties of the data model constitute its state. The two properties you currently update in your `sink(...)` subscriber are `allStories` and `error`. You will consider those state-change worthy.

> **Note**: There is also a third property called `filter`. Ignore it for the moment and you'll come back to it later on.

Adjust `allStories` to include the `@Published` property wrapper like so:

```
@Published private var allStories = [Story]()
```

Then, do the same for `error`:

```
@Published var error: API.Error? = nil
```

The final step in this section is, since `ReaderViewModel` now conforms to `ObservableObject`, to actually bind the data model to `ReaderView`.

Open **View/ReaderView.swift** and add the `@ObservedObject` property wrapper to the line `var model: ReaderViewModel` like so:

```
@ObservedObject var model: ReaderViewModel
```

You bind the model so that, any time its state changes, your view will receive the latest data and generate its new UI "snapshot".

The `@ObservedObject` wrapper does the following:

1. Removes the property storage from the view and uses a binding to the original model instead. In other words, it doesn't duplicate the data.

2. Marks the property as **external storage**. In other words, it denotes that the piece of data is *not* owned by the view.

3. Like `@Published` and `@State`, it adds a publisher to the property so you could subscribe to it and/or bind to it further down the view hierarchy.

By adding `@ObservedObject`, you've made `model` dynamic. This means it'll get all updates while your view model fetches stories from the Hacker News server. In fact, run the app right now and you will see the view refreshes itself as the model fetches stories:

Displaying errors

You will also display errors in the same way you display the fetched stories. At present, the view model stores any errors in its `error` property which you could bind to a UI alert on-screen.

Open **View/ReaderView.swift** and find the comment `// Display errors here`. Replace this comment with the following code to bind the model to an alert view:

```
.alert(item: self.$model.error) { error in
  Alert(
    title: Text("Network error"),
    message: Text(error.localizedDescription),
    dismissButton: .cancel()
  )
}
```

The `alert(item:)` modifier controls an alert presentation on-screen. It takes a binding with an optional output called the `item`. Whenever that binding source emits a non-`nil` value, the UI presents the alert view.

The model's `error` property is `nil` by default and will only be set to a non-`nil` error value whenever the model experiences an error fetching stories from the server. This is an ideal scenario for presenting an alert as it allows you to bind `error` directly as `alert(item:)` input.

To test this, open **Network/API.swift** and modify the `baseURL` property to an invalid URL, for example, `https://123hacker-news.firebaseio.com/v0/`.

Run the app again and you will see the error alert show up as soon as the request to the stories endpoint fails:

Before moving on and working through the next section, take a moment to revert your changes to `baseURL` so your app once again connects to the server successfully.

Subscribing to an external publisher

Sometimes you don't want to go down the `ObservableObject`/`ObservedObject` route, because all you want to do is subscribe to a single publisher and receive its values in your SwiftUI view. For simpler situations like this, there is no need to create an extra type — you can simply use the `onReceive(_)` view modifier. It allows you to subscribe to a publisher directly from your view.

If you run the app right now, you will see that each of the stories has a relative time included alongside the name of the story author:

The relative time there is useful to instantly communicate the "freshness" of the story to the user. However, once rendered on-screen, the information becomes stale after a while. If the user has the app open for a long time, "1 minute ago" might be off by quite some time.

In this section, you will use a timer publisher to trigger UI updates at regular intervals so each row could recalculate and display correct times.

How the code works right now is as follows:

- `ReaderView` has a property called `currentDate` which is set once with the current date when the view is created.

- Each row in the stories list includes a `PostedBy(time:user:currentDate:)` view which compiles the author and time information by using `currentDate`'s value.

To make the information on-screen "refresh" periodically, you will add a new timer publisher. Every time it emits, you will update `currentDate`. Additionally, as you might've guessed already, you will add `currentDate` to the view's state so it will trigger a new UI "snapshot" as it changes.

To work with publishers, start by adding towards the top of **ReaderView.swift**:

```
import Combine
```

Then, add a new publisher property to `ReaderView` which creates a new timer publisher ready to go as soon as anyone subscribes to it:

```
private let timer = Timer.publish(every: 10, on: .main, in: .common)
  .autoconnect()
  .eraseToAnyPublisher()
```

As you already learned earlier in the book, `Timer.publish(every:on:in:)` returns a *connectable* publisher. This is a kind of "dormant" publisher that requires subscribers to connect to it to activate it. Above you use `autoconnect()` to instruct the publisher to automatically "awake" upon subscription.

What's left now is to update `currentDate` each time the timer emits. You will use a SwiftUI modifier called `onReceive(_)`, which behaves much like the `sink(receiveValue:)` subscriber. Scroll just a tad down and find the comment `// Add timer here` and replace it with:

```
.onReceive(timer) {
  self.currentDate = $0
}
```

The timer emits the current date and time so you just take that value and assign it to `currentDate`. Doing that will produce a somewhat familiar error:

```
.onReceive(timer) {
   self.currentDate = $0     ❶ Cannot assign to property: 'self' is immutable
}
```

Naturally, this happens because you cannot mutate the property from a non-mutating context. Just as before, you'll solve this predicament by adding `currentDate` to the view's local storage state.

Add a `@State` property wrapper to the property like so:

```
@State var currentDate = Date()
```

This way, any update to `currentDate` will trigger a new UI "snapshot" and will force each row to recalculate the relative time of the story and update the text if necessary.

Run the app one more time and leave it open. Make a mental note of how long ago the top story was posted, here's what I had when I tried that:

Wait for at least one minute and you will see the visible rows update their information with the current time. The orange time badge will still show the time when the story was posted but the text below the title will update with the correct "… minutes ago" text:

> **10:17 AM**
>
> **Scandinavia's reign as t…**
>
> 10 minutes ago by briantailor
>
> https://www.wired.co.uk/article/worlds-happiest-country-scandinavia

Besides having the publisher a property on your view, you can also inject any publisher from your Combine model into the view via the view's initializer or the environment. Then, it's only a matter of using `onReceive(...)` in the same way as above.

Initializing the app's settings

In this part of the chapter, you will move on to making the `Settings` view work. Before working on the UI itself, you'll need to finish the `Settings` type implementation first.

Open **Model/Settings.swift** and you'll see that, currently, the type is pretty much bare bones. It contains a single property holding a list of `FilterKeyword` values.

Now, open **Model/FilterKeyword.swift**. `FilterKeyword` is a helper model type that wraps a single keyword to use as a filter for the stories list in the main reader view. It conforms to `Identifiable`, which requires an `id` property that uniquely identifies each instance, such as when you use those types in your SwiftUI code. If you peruse the `API.Error` and `Story` definitions in **Network/API.swift** and **Model/Story.swift**, respectively, you'll see that these types also conform to `Identifiable`.

Let's go on the merry-go-round one more time. You need to turn the plain, old model `Settings` into a modern type to use with your Combine and SwiftUI code.

Get started by adding at the top of **Model/Settings.swift**:

```
import Combine
```

Then, add a publisher to keywords by adding the @Published property wrapper to it, so it looks as follow:

```
@Published var keywords = [FilterKeyword]()
```

Now, other types can subscribe to Settings's current keywords. You can also pipe in the keywords list to views that accept a binding.

Finally, to enable observation of Settings, make the type conform to ObservableObject like so:

```
final class Settings: ObservableObject {
```

There's no need to add anything else to make the ObservableObject conformance work. The default implementation will emit any time the $keywords publisher does.

This is how, in few easy steps, you turned Settings into a model type on steroids. Now, you can plug it into the rest of your reactive code in the app.

To bind the app's Settings, you'll instantiate it in your app. Open **App/App.swift** and add a new property to HNReader:

```
let userSettings = Settings()
```

As usual, you will also need a cancelable collection to store your subscriptions. Add one more property for that to HNReader:

```
private var subscriptions = Set<AnyCancellable>()
```

Now, you can bind Settings.keywords to ReaderViewModel.filter so that the main view will not only receive the initial list of keywords but also the update list each time the user edits the list of keywords.

You'll create that binding while intializing HNReader. Add a new initializer to that type:

```
init() {
  userSettings.$keywords
    .map { $0.map { $0.value } }
    .assign(to: \.filter, on: viewModel)
    .store(in: &subscriptions)
}
```

You subscribe to `userSettings.$keywords`, which outputs `[FilterKeyword]`, and map it to `[String]` by getting each keyword's `value` property. Then, you assign the resulting value to `viewModel.filter`.

Now, whenever you alter the contents of `Settings.keywords`, the binding to the view model will ultimately cause the generation of a new UI "snapshot" of `ReaderView` because the view model is part of its state.

The binding so far works. However, you still have to add the `filter` property to be part of `ReaderViewModel`'s state. You'll do this so that, each time you update the list of keywords, the new data is relayed onwards to the view.

To do that, open **Model/ReaderViewModel.swift** and add the `@Published` property wrapper to `filter` like so:

```
@Published var filter = [String]()
```

The complete binding from `Settings` to the view model and onwards to the view is now complete!

This is extremely handy because, in the next section, you will connect the `Settings` view to the `Settings` model and any change the user makes to the keyword list will trigger the whole chain of bindings and subscriptions to ultimately refresh the main app view story list like so:

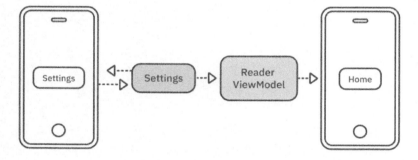

Editing the keywords list

In this last part of the chapter, you will look into the SwiftUI environment. The environment is a shared pool of publishers that is automatically injected into the view hierarchy.

System environment

The environment contains publishers injected by the system, like the current calendar, the layout direction, the locale, the current time zone and others. As you see, those are all values that could change over time. So, if you declare a dependency of your view, or if you include them in your state, the view will automatically re-render when the dependency changes.

To try out observing one of the system settings, open **View/ReaderView.swift** and add a new property to `ReaderView`:

```
@Environment(\.colorScheme) var colorScheme: ColorScheme
```

You use the `@Environment` property wrapper, which defines which key of the environment should be bound to the `colorScheme` property. Now, this property is part of your view's state. Each time the system appearance mode changes between light and dark, and vice-versa, SwiftUI will re-render your view.

Additionally, you will have access to the latest color scheme in the view's body. So, you can render it differently in light and dark modes.

Scroll down and find the line setting the color of the story link `.foregroundColor(Color.blue)`. Replace that line with:

```
.foregroundColor(self.colorScheme == .light ? .blue : .orange)
```

Now, depending on the current value of `colorScheme`, the link will be either blue or orange.

Try out this new miracle of code by changing the system appearance to dark. In Xcode, open **Debug ▶ View Debugging ▶ Configure Environment Overrides…** or tap the **Environment Overrides** button at Xcode's bottom toolbar. Then, toggle the switch next to **Interface Style** on.

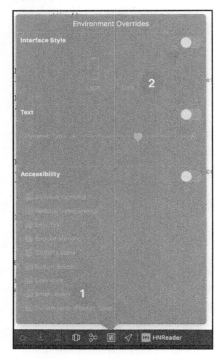

Feel free to stay in dark appearance mode. However, I'll switch back to light appearance for the remainder of the chapter because it will print screenshots better in the book.

Custom environment objects

As cool as observing the system settings via @Environment(_) is, that's not all that the SwiftUI environment has to offer. You can, in fact, environment-ify your objects as well!

This is very handy. Especially when you have deeply nested view hierarchies. Inserting a model or another shared resource into the environment removes the need to dependency-inject through a multitude of views until you reach the deeply nested view that actually needs the data.

Objects you insert in a view's environment are available automatically to any child views of that view and all their child views too.

This sounds like a great opportunity for sharing your user's `Settings` with all views of the app so they can make use of the user's story filter.

The place to inject dependencies into all your views is the main app file. This is where you previously created the `userSettings` instance of `Settings` and bound its `$keywords` to the `ReaderViewModel`. Now, you will inject `userSettings` into the environment as well.

Open **App/App.swift** and add the `environmentObject` view modifier to `ReaderView` by adding below `ReaderView(model: viewModel)`:

```
.environmentObject(userSettings)
```

The `environmentObject` modifier is a view modifier which inserts the given object in the view hierarchy. Since you already have an instance of `Settings`, you simply send that one off to the environment and you're done.

Next, you need to add the environment dependency to the views where you want to use your custom object. Open **View/SettingsView.swift** and add a new property with the `@EnvironmentObject` wrapper:

```
@EnvironmentObject var settings: Settings
```

The `settings` property will automatically be populated with the latest user settings from the environment.

For your own objects, you do not need to specify a key path like for the system environment. `@EnvironmentObject` will match the property type — in this case `Settings` — to the objects stored in the environment and find the right one.

Now, you can use `settings.keywords` like any of your other view states. You can either get the value directly, subscribe to it, or bind it to other views.

To complete the `SettingsView` functionality, you'll display the list of keywords and enable adding, editing and deleting keywords from the list.

Find the following line:

```
ForEach([FilterKeyword]()) { keyword in
```

And replace it with:

```
ForEach(settings.keywords) { keyword in
```

The updated code will use the filter keywords for the on-screen list. This will, however, still display an empty list as the user doesn't have a way to add new keywords.

The starter project includes a view for adding keywords. So, you simply need to present it when the user taps the + button. The + button action is set to addKeyword() in SettingsView.

Scroll to the private addKeyword() method and add inside it:

```
presentingAddKeywordSheet = true
```

presentingAddKeywordSheet is a published property, much like the one you already worked with earlier this chapter, to present an alert. You can see the presentation declaration slightly up in the source: .sheet(isPresented: $presentingAddKeywordSheet).

To try out how injecting objects manually to a given view works, switch to **View/ReaderView.swift** and find the spot where you present SettingsView — it's a single line where you just create a new instance like so: SettingsView().

The same way you injected the settings into ReaderView, you can inject them here as well. Add a new property to ReaderView:

```
@EnvironmentObject var settings: Settings
```

And then, add the .environmentObject modifier directly under SettingsView():

```
.environmentObject(self.settings)
```

Now, you declared a ReaderView dependency on Settings and you passed that dependency onwards to SettingsView via the environment. In this particular case, you could've just passed it as a parameter to the init of SettingsView as well.

Before moving on, run the app one more time. You should be able to tap **Settings** and see the SettingsView pop up.

Now, switch back to **View/SettingsView.swift** and complete the list editing actions as initially intended.

Inside `sheet(isPresented: $presentingAddKeywordSheet)`, a new `AddKeywordView` is already created for you. It's a custom view included with the starter project, which allows the user to enter a new keyword and tap a button to add it to the list.

`AddKeywordView` takes a callback, which it will call when the user taps the button to add the new keyword. In the empty completion callback of `AddKeywordView` add:

```
let new = FilterKeyword(value: newKeyword.lowercased())
self.settings.keywords.append(new)
self.presentingAddKeywordSheet = false
```

You create a new keyword, add it to user settings, and finally dismiss the presented sheet.

Remember, adding the keyword to the list here will update the settings model object and in turn, will update the reader view model and refresh `ReaderView` as well. All automatically as declared in your code.

To wrap up with `SettingsView`, let's add deleting and moving keywords. Find `// List editing actions` and replace it with:

```
.onMove(perform: moveKeyword)
.onDelete(perform: deleteKeyword)
```

This code sets `moveKeyword()` as the handler when the user moves one of the keywords up or down the list and `deleteKeyword()` as the handler when the user swipes right to delete a keyword.

In the currently empty `moveKeyword(from:to:)` method, add:

```
guard let source = source.first,
      destination != settings.keywords.endIndex else { return }

settings.keywords
  .swapAt(source,
          source > destination ? destination : destination - 1)
```

And inside `deleteKeyword(at:)`, add:

```
settings.keywords.remove(at: index.first!)
```

That's really all you need to enable editing in your list! Build and run the app one final time and you'll be able to fully manage the story filter including adding, moving and deleting keywords:

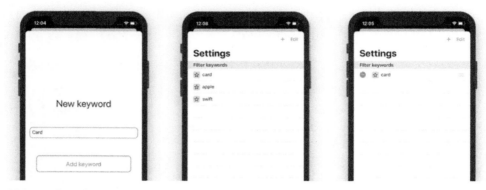

Additionally, when you navigate back to the story list, you will see that the settings are propagated along with your subscriptions and bindings across the application and the list displays only stories matching your filter. The title will display the number of matching stories as well:

Challenges

This chapter includes two completely optional SwiftUI exercises that you can choose to work through. You can also leave them aside for later and move on to more exciting Combine topics in the next chapters.

Challenge 1: Displaying the filter in the reader view

In the first challenge, you will insert a list of the filter's keywords in the story list header in `ReaderView`. Currently, the header always displays "Showing all stories". Change that text to display the list of keywords in case the user has added any, like so:

Challenge 2: Persisting the filter between app launches

The starter project includes a helper type called `JSONFile` which offers two methods: `loadValue(named:)` and `save(value:named:)`.

Use this type to:

- Save the list of keywords on disk any time the user modifies the filter by adding a `didSet` handler to `Settings.keywords`.
- Load the keywords from disk in `Settings.init()`.

This way, the user's filter will persist between app launches like in real apps.

If you're not sure about the solution to either of these challenges, or need some help, feel free to look into the finished project in the **projects/challenge** folder.

Key points

With SwiftUI, your UI is a **function of your state**. You cause your UI to render itself by committing changes to the data declared as the view's state, among other view dependencies. You learned various ways to manage state in SwiftUI:

- Use `@State` to add local state to a view and `@ObservedObject` to add a dependency on an external `ObservableObject` in your Combine code.

- Use `onReceive` view modifier to subscribe an external publisher directly.

- Use `@Environment` to add a dependency to one of the system-provided environment settings and `@EnvironmentObject` for your own custom environment objects.

Where to go from here?

Congratulations on getting down and dirty with SwiftUI and Combine! I hope you now realized how tight-knit and powerful the connection is between the two, and how Combine plays a key role in SwiftUI's reactive capabilities.

Even though you should always aim to write error-free apps, the world is rarely this perfect. Which is exactly why you'll spend the next chapter learning about how you can handle errors in Combine.

Chapter 16: Error Handling

By Shai Mishali

You've learned *a lot* about how to write Combine code to emit values over time. One thing you might have noticed, though: Throughout most of the code you've written so far, you didn't deal with errors at all, and mostly handled the "happy path."

Unless you write error-free apps, this chapter is for you! :]

As you learned in Chapter 1, "Hello, Combine!," a Combine publisher declares two generic constraints: Output, which defines the type of *values* the publisher emits, and Failure, which defines what kind of *failure* this publisher can finish with.

Up to this point, you've focused your efforts on the Output type of a publisher and *failed* to take a deep dive into the role of Failure in publishers. Well, don't worry, this chapter will change that!

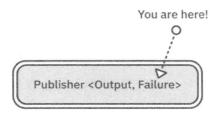

Getting started

Open the starter playground for this chapter in **projects/Starter.playground**. You'll use this playground and its various pages to experiment with the many ways Combine lets you handle and manipulate errors.

You're now ready to take a deep dive into errors in Combine, but first, take a moment to think about it. Errors are such a broad topic, where would you even start?

Well, how about starting with the *absence* of errors?

Never

A publisher whose `Failure` is of type `Never` indicates that the publisher can **never fail**.

While this might seem a tad strange at first, it provides some extremely powerful guarantees about these publishers. A publisher with `Never` failure type lets you focus on consuming the publisher's values while being absolutely sure the publisher will never fail. It can only complete successfully once it's done.

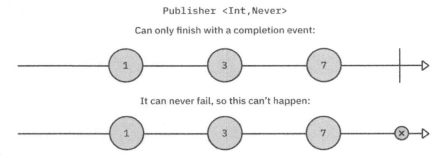

Open the **Project Navigator** in the starter playground by pressing **Command-1**, then select the **Never** playground page.

Add the following example to it:

```
example(of: "Never sink") {
  Just("Hello")
}
```

You create a `Just` with a string value of `Hello`. `Just` always declares a `Failure` of `Never`. To confirm this, **Command-click** the `Just` initializer and select **Jump to Definition**:

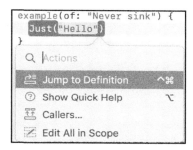

Looking at the definition, you can see a type alias for `Just`'s failure:

```
public typealias Failure = Never
```

Combine's no-failure guarantee for `Never` isn't just theoretical, but is deeply rooted in the framework and its various APIs.

Combine offers several operators that are only available when the publisher is guaranteed to never fail. The first one is a variation of `sink` to handle *only* values.

Go back to the **Never** playground page and update the above example so it looks like this:

```
example(of: "Never sink") {
  Just("Hello")
    .sink(receiveValue: { print($0) })
    .store(in: &subscriptions)
}
```

Run your playground and you'll see the `Just`'s value printed out:

```
——— Example of: Never sink ———
Hello
```

In the above example, you use `sink(receiveValue:)`. This specific overload of `sink` lets you ignore the publisher's completion event and only deal with its emitted values.

This overload is only available for infallible publishers. Combine is smart and safe when it comes to error handling, and forces you to deal with a completion event if an error may be thrown — i.e., for a non-failing publisher.

To see this in action, you'll want to turn your `Never`-failing publisher into one that may fail. There are a few ways to do this, and you'll start with the most popular one — the `setFailureType` operator.

setFailureType

The first way to turn an infallible publisher into a fallible one is to use `setFailureType`. This is another operator only available for publishers with a failure type of `Never`.

Add the following code and example to your playground page:

```
enum MyError: Error {
  case ohNo
}

example(of: "setFailureType") {
  Just("Hello")
}
```

You start by defining a `MyError` error type *outside* the scope of the example. You'll reuse this error type in a bit. You then start the example by creating a `Just` similar to the one you used before.

Now, you can use `setFailureType` to change the failure type of the publisher to `MyError`. Add the following line immediately after the `Just`:

```
.setFailureType(to: MyError.self)
```

To confirm this actually changed the publisher's failure type, start typing `.eraseToAnyPublisher()`, and the auto-completion will show you the erased publisher type:

```
17        Just("Hello")
18          .setFailureType(to: MyError.self)
19          .erase
AnyPublisher<String, MyError> eraseToAnyPublisher()
```

Delete the `.erase...` line you started typing before proceeding.

Now it's time to use `sink` to consume the publisher. Add the following code immediately after your last call to `setFailureType`:

```
// 1
.sink(
  receiveCompletion: { completion in
    switch completion {
    // 2
    case .failure(.ohNo):
      print("Finished with Oh No!")
    case .finished:
      print("Finished successfully!")
    }
  },
  receiveValue: { value in
    print("Got value: \(value)")
  }
)
.store(in: &subscriptions)
```

You might have noticed two interesting facts about the above code:

1. It's using `sink(receiveCompletion:receiveValue:)`. The `sink(receiveValue:)` overload is no longer available since this publisher may complete with a failure event. Combine forces you to deal with the completion event for such publishers.

2. The failure type is strictly typed as `MyError`, which lets you target the `.failure(.ohNo)` case without unnecessary casting to deal with that specific error.

Run your playground, and you'll see the following output:

```
——— Example of: setFailureType ———
Got value: Hello
Finished successfully!
```

Of course, `setFailureType`'s effect is only a type-system definition. Since the original publisher is a `Just`, no error is actually thrown.

You'll learn more about how to actually produce errors from your own publishers later in this chapter. But first, there are still a few more operators that are specific to never-failing publishers.

assign(to:on:)

The `assign` operator you learned about in Chapter 2, "Publishers & Subscribers," only works on publishers that cannot fail, same as `setFailureType`. If you think about it, it makes total sense. Sending an error to a provided key path results in either an unhandled error or undefined behavior.

Add the following example to test this:

```
example(of: "assign(to:on:)") {
  // 1
  class Person {
    let id = UUID()
    var name = "Unknown"
  }

  // 2
  let person = Person()
  print("1", person.name)

  Just("Shai")
    .handleEvents( // 3
      receiveCompletion: { _ in print("2", person.name) }
    )
    .assign(to: \.name, on: person) // 4
    .store(in: &subscriptions)
}
```

In the above piece of code, you:

1. Define a `Person` class with `id` and `name` properties.

2. Create an instance of `Person` and immediately print its name.

3. Use `handleEvents`, which you learned about previously, to print the person's name again once the publisher sends a completion event.

4. Finish up by using `assign` to set the person's name to whatever the publisher emits.

Run your playground and look at the debug console:

```
——— Example of: assign(to:on:) ———
1 Unknown
2 Shai
```

As expected, `assign` updates the person's name as soon as `Just` emits its value, which works because `Just` cannot fail. In contrast, what do you think would happen if the publisher had a non-`Never` failure type?

Add the following line immediately below `Just("Shai")`:

```
.setFailureType(to: Error.self)
```

In this code, you've set the failure type to a standard Swift error. This means that instead of being a `Publisher<String, Never>`, it's now a `Publisher<String, Error>`.

Try to run your playground. Combine is very verbose about the issue at hand:

```
referencing instance method 'assign(to:on:)' on 'Publisher'
requires the types 'Error' and 'Never' be equivalent
```

Remove the call to `setFailureType` you just added, and make sure your playground runs with no compilation errors.

assign(to:)

There is one tricky part about `assign(to:on:)` — It'll **strongly capture** the object provided to the on argument.

Let's explore why this is problematic.

Add the following code immediately after the previous example:

```
example(of: "assign(to:)") {
  class MyViewModel: ObservableObject {
    // 1
    @Published var currentDate = Date()

    init() {
      Timer.publish(every: 1, on: .main, in: .common) // 2
        .autoconnect()
        .prefix(3) // 3
        .assign(to: \.currentDate, on: self) // 4
        .store(in: &subscriptions)
    }
  }

  // 5
  let vm = MyViewModel()
  vm.$currentDate
    .sink(receiveValue: { print($0) })
    .store(in: &subscriptions)
}
```

This code is a tad long, so let's break it down. You:

1. Define a `@Published` property inside a view model object. Its initial value is the current date.

2. Create a timer publisher which emits the current date every second.

3. Use the `prefix` operator to only accept 3 date updates.

4. Apply the `assign(to:on:)` operator to assign every date update to your `@Published` property.

5. Instantiate your view model, `sink` over the published publisher, and print out every value.

If you run your playground, you'll see output similar to the following:

```
—— Example of: assign(to:on:) strong capture ——
2021-08-21 12:43:32 +0000
2021-08-21 12:43:33 +0000
2021-08-21 12:43:34 +0000
2021-08-21 12:43:35 +0000
```

As expected, the code above prints the initial date assigned to the published property, and then 3 consecutive updated (limited by the `prefix` operator).

Seemingly, everything is working just fine, so what's actually wrong here?

The call to `assign(to:on:)` creates a subscription that strongly retains `self`. Essentially — `self` hangs on to the subscription, and the subscription hangs on to `self`, creating a **retain cycle** resulting in a memory leak.

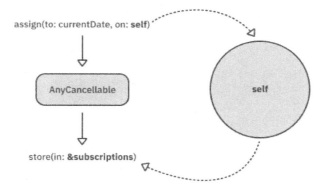

Fortunately, the good folks at Apple realized how problematic this is and introduced another overload of this operator - `assign(to:)`.

This operator specifically deals with reassigning published values to a `@Published` property by providing an `inout` reference to its projected publisher.

Go back to the example code, find the following two lines:

```
.assign(to: \.currentDate, on: self) // 3
.store(in: &subscriptions)
```

And replace them with the following line:

```
.assign(to: &$currentDate)
```

Using the `assign(to:)` operator and passing it an `inout` reference to the projected publisher breaks the retain cycle and lets you easily deal with the problem presented above.

Also, it automatically takes care of memory management for the subscription internally, which lets you omit the `store(in: &subscriptions)` line.

> **Note**: Before moving on, it's recommended to comment out the previous example so the printed out timer events won't add unnecessary noise to your console output.

You're almost done with infallible publishers at this point. But before you start dealing with errors, there's one final operator related to infallible publishers you should know: `assertNoFailure`.

assertNoFailure

The `assertNoFailure` operator is useful when you want to protect yourself during development and confirm a publisher can't finish with a failure event. It doesn't *prevent* a failure event from being emitted by the upstream. However, it will crash with a `fatalError` if it detects an error, which gives you a good incentive to fix it in development.

Add the following example to your playground:

```
example(of: "assertNoFailure") {
  // 1
  Just("Hello")
    .setFailureType(to: MyError.self)
    .assertNoFailure() // 2
    .sink(receiveValue: { print("Got value: \($0) ")}) // 3
    .store(in: &subscriptions)
}
```

In the previous code, you:

1. Use `Just` to create an infallible publisher and set its failure type to `MyError`.

2. Use `assertNoFailure` to crash with a `fatalError` if the publisher completes with a failure event. This turns the publisher's failure type back to `Never`.

3. Print out any received values using `sink`. Notice that since `assertNoFailure` sets the failure type back to `Never`, the `sink(receiveValue:)` overload is at your disposal again.

Run your playground, and as expected it should work with no issues:

```
——— Example of: assertNoFailure ———
Got value: Hello
```

Now, after `setFailureType`, add the following line:

```
.tryMap { _ in throw MyError.ohNo }
```

You just used `tryMap` to throw an error once `Hello` is pushed downstream. You'll learn more about `try`-prefixed operators later in this chapter.

Run your playground again and take a look at the console. You'll see output similar to the following:

```
Playground execution failed:

error: Execution was interrupted, reason: EXC_BAD_INSTRUCTION
(code=EXC_I386_INVOP, subcode=0x0).

...

frame #0: 0x00007fff232fbbf2
Combine`Combine.Publishers.AssertNoFailure...
```

The playground crashes because a failure occurred in the publisher. In a way, you can think of `assertFailure()` as a guarding mechanism for your code. While not something you should use in production, it is extremely useful during development to "crash early and crash hard."

Comment out the call to `tryMap` before moving on to the next section.

Dealing with failure

Wow, so far you've learned a lot about how to deal with publishers that *can't fail at all*... in an error-handling chapter! :] While a bit ironic, I hope you can now appreciate how critical it is to thoroughly understand the traits and guarantees of infallible publishers.

With that in mind, it's time for you to learn about some techniques and tools Combine provides to deal with publishers that actually fail. This includes both built-in publishers and *your own* publishers!

But first, how do you actually *produce* failure events? As mentioned in the previous section, there are several ways to do this. You just used `tryMap`, so why not learn more about how these `try` operators work?

try* operators

In Section II, "Operators," you learned about most of Combine's operators and how you can use them to manipulate the values and events your publishers emit. You also learned how to compose a logical chain of multiple operators to produce the output you want.

In these chapters, you learned that most operators have parallel operators prefixed with `try`, and that you'll "*learn about them later in this book.*" Well, later is now!

Combine provides an interesting distinction between operators that *may* throw errors and ones that may not.

> **Note:** All `try`-prefixed operators in Combine behave the same way when it comes to errors. In the essence of time, you'll only experiment with the `tryMap` operator throughout this chapter.

First, select the *try operators** playground page from the Project navigator. Add the following code to it:

```
example(of: "tryMap") {
  // 1
  enum NameError: Error {
    case tooShort(String)
    case unknown
  }
```

```
// 2
let names = ["Marin", "Shai", "Florent"].publisher

names
  // 3
  .map { value in
    return value.count
  }
  .sink(
    receiveCompletion: { print("Completed with \($0)") },
    receiveValue: { print("Got value: \($0)") }
  )
}
```

In the above example, you:

1. Define a `NameError` error enum, which you'll use momentarily.

2. Create a publisher emitting three different strings.

3. Map each string to its length.

Run the example and check out the console output:

```
——— Example of: tryMap ———
Got value: 5
Got value: 4
Got value: 7
Completed with finished
```

All names are mapped with no issues, as expected. But then you receive a new product requirement: Your code should throw an error if it accepts a name shorter than 5 characters.

Replace the map in the above example with the following:

```
.map { value -> Int in
  // 1
  let length = value.count

  // 2
  guard length >= 5 else {
    throw NameError.tooShort(value)
  }

  // 3
  return value.count
}
```

In the above map, you check that the length of the string is greater or equal to 5.

Otherwise, you *try* to throw an appropriate error.

However, as soon as you add the above code or attempt to run it, you'll see that the compiler produces an error:

```
Invalid conversion from throwing function of type '(_) throws ->
_' to non-throwing function type '(String) -> _'
```

Since `map` is a non-throwing operator, you can't throw errors from within it. Luckily, the `try*` operators are made just for that purpose.

Replace `map` with `tryMap` and run your playground again. It will now compile and produce the following output (truncated):

```
——— Example of: tryMap ———
Got value: 5
Got value: 5
Completed with failure(...NameError.tooShort("Shai"))
```

Mapping errors

The differences between `map` and `tryMap` go beyond the fact that the latter allows throwing errors. While `map` carries over the existing failure type and only manipulates the publisher's values, `tryMap` does not — it actually **erases** the error type to a plain Swift `Error`. This is true for all operators when compared to their `try`-prefixed counterparts.

Switch to the **Mapping errors** playground page and add the following code to it:

```
example(of: "map vs tryMap") {
  // 1
  enum NameError: Error {
    case tooShort(String)
    case unknown
  }

  // 2
  Just("Hello")
    .setFailureType(to: NameError.self) // 3
    .map { $0 + " World!" } // 4
    .sink(
      receiveCompletion: { completion in
        // 5
        switch completion {
        case .finished:
          print("Done!")
        case .failure(.tooShort(let name)):
```

```
        print("\(name) is too short!")
      case .failure(.unknown):
        print("An unknown name error occurred")
      }
    },
    receiveValue: { print("Got value \($0)") }
  )
  .store(in: &subscriptions)
}
```

In the above example, you:

1. Define a `NameError` to use for this example.

2. Create a `Just` which only emits the string `Hello`.

3. Use `setFailureType` to set the failure type to `NameError`.

4. Append another string to the published string using `map`.

5. Finally, use `sink`'s `receiveCompletion` to print out an appropriate message for every failure case of `NameError`.

Run the playground and you'll see the following output:

```
——— Example of: map vs tryMap ———
Got value Hello World!
Done!
```

Next, find the `switch completion {` line and **Option-click** on `completion`:

```
19          receiveCompletion: { completion in
20            // 5
21            switch completion {
22            case .finished:
```

Declaration
let completion: Subscribers.Completion<NameError>

Declared In
Mapping errors.xcplaygroundpage

Notice that the `Completion`'s failure type is `NameError`, which is exactly what you want. The `setFailureType` operator lets you specifically target `NameError` failures such as `failure(.tooShort(let name))`.

Next, change `map` to `tryMap`. You'll immediately notice the playground no longer compiles. **Option-click** on `completion` again:

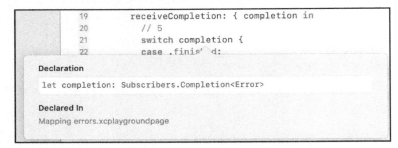

Very interesting! `tryMap` erased your strictly-typed error and replaced it with a general `Swift.Error` type. This happens even though you didn't actually throw an error from within `tryMap` — you simply used it! Why is that?

The reasoning is quite simple when you think about it: Swift doesn't support typed throws *yet*, even though discussions around this topic have been taking place in Swift Evolution since 2015. This means when you use `try`-prefixed operators, your error type will always be erased to the most common ancestor: `Swift.Error`.

So, what can you do about it? The entire point of a strictly-typed `Failure` for publishers is to let you deal with — in this example — `NameError` specifically, and not any other kind of error.

A naive approach would be to cast the generic error manually to a specific error type, but that's quite suboptimal. It breaks the entire purpose of having strictly-typed errors. Luckily, Combine provides a great solution to this problem, called `mapError`.

Immediately after the call to `tryMap`, add the following line:

```
.mapError { $0 as? NameError ?? .unknown }
```

`mapError` receives any error thrown from the upstream publisher and lets you map it to *any* error you want. In this case, you can utilize it to cast the error back to a `NameError` or fall back to a `NameError.unknown` error. You must provide a fallback error in this case, because the cast could theoretically fail — even though it won't here — and you have to return a `NameError` from this operator.

This restores `Failure` to its original type and turns your publisher back to a `Publisher<String, NameError>`.

Build and run the playground. It should finally compile and work as expected:

```
——— Example of: map vs tryMap ———
Got value Hello World!
Done!
```

Finally, replace the entire call to `tryMap` with:

```
.tryMap { throw NameError.tooShort($0) }
```

This call will immediately throw an error from within the `tryMap`. Check out the console output once again, and make sure you get the properly-typed `NameError`:

```
——— Example of: map vs tryMap ———
Hello is too short!
```

Designing your fallible APIs

When constructing your own Combine-based code and APIs, you'll often use APIs from other sources that return publishers that fail with various types. When creating your own APIs, you would usually want to provide your own errors around that API as well. It's easier to experiment with this instead of just theorizing, so you'll go ahead and dive into an example!

In this section, you'll build a quick API that lets you fetch somewhat-funny dad jokes from the icanhazdadjoke API, available at https://icanhazdadjoke.com/api.

Start by switching to the **Designing your fallible APIs** playground page and add the following code to it, which makes up the first portion of the next example:

```swift
example(of: "Joke API") {
  class DadJokes {
    // 1
    struct Joke: Codable {
      let id: String
      let joke: String
    }

    // 2
    func getJoke(id: String) -> AnyPublisher<Joke, Error> {
      let url = URL(string: "https://icanhazdadjoke.com/j/\(id)")!
      var request = URLRequest(url: url)
      request.allHTTPHeaderFields = ["Accept": "application/json"]

      // 3
```

```
    return URLSession.shared
      .dataTaskPublisher(for: request)
      .map(\.data)
      .decode(type: Joke.self, decoder: JSONDecoder())
      .eraseToAnyPublisher()
  }
 }
}
```

In the above code, you created the shell of your new `DadJokes` class by:

1. Defining a `Joke` struct. The API response will be decoded into an instance of `Joke`.

2. Providing a `getJoke(id:)` method, which currently returns a publisher that emits a `Joke` and can fail with a standard `Swift.Error`.

3. Using `URLSession.dataTaskPublisher(for:)` to call the icanhazdadjoke API and decode the resulting data into a `Joke` using a `JSONDecoder` and the decode operator. You might remember this technique from Chapter 9, "Networking."

Finally, you'll want to actually use your new API. Add the following directly below the `DadJokes` class, while still in the scope of the example:

```
// 4
let api = DadJokes()
let jokeID = "9prWnjyImyd"
let badJokeID = "123456"

// 5
api
  .getJoke(id: jokeID)
  .sink(receiveCompletion: { print($0) },
        receiveValue: { print("Got joke: \($0)") })
  .store(in: &subscriptions)
```

In this code, you:

4. Create an instance of `DadJokes` and define two constants with valid and invalid joke IDs.

5. Call `DadJokes.getJoke(id:)` with the valid joke ID and print any completion event or the decoded joke itself.

Run your playground and look at the console:

```
─── Example of: Joke API ───
Got joke: Joke(id: "9prWnjyImyd", joke: "Why do bears have hairy
coats? Fur protection.")
finished
```

A polar bear on this book's cover and a bear joke inside? Ah, classic.

So your API currently deals with the happy path perfectly, but this is an error-handling chapter. When wrapping other publishers, you need to ask yourself: "*What kinds of errors can result from this specific publisher?*"

In this case:

- Calling `dataTaskPublisher` can fail with a `URLError` for various reasons, such as a bad connection or an invalid request.

- The provided joke ID might not exist.

- Decoding the JSON response might fail if the API response changes or its structure is incorrect.

- Any other unknown error! Errors are plenty and random, so it's impossible to think of every edge case. For this reason, you always want to have a case to cover an unknown or unhandled error.

With this list in mind, add the following piece of code inside the `DadJokes` class, immediately below the `Joke` struct:

```
enum Error: Swift.Error, CustomStringConvertible {
  // 1
  case network
  case jokeDoesntExist(id: String)
  case parsing
  case unknown

  // 2
  var description: String {
    switch self {
    case .network:
      return "Request to API Server failed"
    case .parsing:
      return "Failed parsing response from server"
    case .jokeDoesntExist(let id):
      return "Joke with ID \(id) doesn't exist"
    case .unknown:
      return "An unknown error occurred"
    }
  }
```

```
    }
}
```

This error definition:

1. Outlines all the possible errors that can occur in the `DadJokes` API.

2. Conforms to `CustomStringConvertible`, which lets you provide a friendly `description` for each error case.

After adding the above `Error` type, your playground won't compile anymore. This is because `getJoke(id:)` returns a `AnyPublisher<Joke, Error>`. Before, `Error` referred to `Swift.Error`, but now it refers to `DadJokes.Error` — which is actually what you want, in this case.

So, how can you take the various possible and differently-typed errors and *map* them all into your `DadJoke.Error`? If you've been following this chapter, you've probably guessed the answer: `mapError` is your friend here.

Add the following to `getJoke(id:)`, between the calls to decode and `eraseToAnyPublisher()`:

```
.mapError { error -> DadJokes.Error in
  switch error {
  case is URLError:
    return .network
  case is DecodingError:
    return .parsing
  default:
    return .unknown
  }
}
```

That's it! This simple `mapError` uses a `switch` statement to replace any kind of error the publisher may throw with a `DadJokes.Error`. You might ask yourself: "*Why should I wrap these errors?*" The answer to this is two-fold:

1. Your publisher is now guaranteed to only fail with a `DadJokes.Error`, which is useful when consuming the API and dealing with its possible errors. You know exactly what you'll get from the type system.

2. You don't leak the implementation details of your API. Think about it, does the consumer of your API care if you use `URLSession` to perform a network request and a `JSONDecoder` to decode the response? Obviously not! The consumer only cares about what your API itself defines as errors — not about its internal dependencies.

There's still one more error you haven't dealt with: a non-existent joke ID. Try replacing the following line:

```
.getJoke(id: jokeID)
```

With:

```
.getJoke(id: badJokeID)
```

Run the playground again. This time, you'll get the following error:

```
failure(Failed parsing response from server)
```

Interestingly enough, icanhazdadjoke's API doesn't fail with an HTTP code of 404 (Not Found) when you send a non-existent ID — as would be expected of most APIs. Instead, it sends back a different but *valid* JSON response:

```
{
    message = "Joke with id \"123456\" not found";
    status = 404;
}
```

Dealing with this case requires a bit of hackery, but it's definitely nothing you can't handle!

Back in getJoke(id:), replace the call to map(\.data) with the following code:

```
.tryMap { data, _ -> Data in
  // 6
  guard let obj = try? JSONSerialization.jsonObject(with: data),
        let dict = obj as? [String: Any],
        dict["status"] as? Int == 404 else {
    return data
  }

  // 7
  throw DadJokes.Error.jokeDoesntExist(id: id)
}
```

In the above code, you use tryMap to perform additional validation before passing the raw data to the decode operator:

6. You use JSONSerialization to try and check if a status field exists and has a value of 404 — i.e., the joke doesn't exist. If that's *not* the case, you simply return the data so it's pushed downstream to the decode operator.

7. If you *do* find a 404 status code, you throw a .jokeDoesntExist(id:) error.

Run your playground again and you'll notice another tiny nitpick you need to solve:

```
—— Example of: Joke API ——
failure(An unknown error occurred)
```

The failure is actually treated as an unknown error, and not as a `DadJokes.Error`, because you didn't deal with that type inside `mapError`.

Inside your `mapError`, find the following line:

```
return .unknown
```

And replace it with:

```
return error as? DadJokes.Error ?? .unknown
```

If none of the other error types match, you attempt to cast it to a `DadJokes.Error` before giving up and falling back to an unknown error.

Run your playground again and take a look at the console:

```
—— Example of: Joke API ——
failure(Joke with ID 123456 doesn't exist)
```

This time around, you receive the correct error, with the correct type! Awesome. :]

Before you wrap up this example, there's one final optimization you can make in `getJoke(id:)`.

As you might have noticed, joke IDs consist of letters *and* numbers. In the case of our "Bad ID", you've sent only numbers. Instead of performing a network request, you can preemptively validate your ID and fail without wasting resources.

Add the following final piece of code at the beginning of `getJoke(id:)`:

```
guard id.rangeOfCharacter(from: .letters) != nil else {
  return Fail<Joke, Error>(
    error: .jokeDoesntExist(id: id)
  )
  .eraseToAnyPublisher()
}
```

In this code, you start by making sure `id` contains at least one letter. If that's not the case, you immediately return a `Fail`.

`Fail` is a special kind of publisher that lets you immediately and imperatively fail with a provided error. It's perfect for these cases where you want to fail early based on some condition. You finish up by using `eraseToAnyPublisher` to get the expected `AnyPublisher<Joke, DadJokes.Error>` type.

That's it! Run your example again with the invalid ID and you'll get the same error message. However, it will post immediately and won't perform a network request. Great success!

Before moving on, revert your call to `getJoke(id:)` to use `jokeID` instead of `badJokeId`.

At this point, you can validate your error logic by manually "breaking" your code. After performing each of the following actions, undo your changes so you can try the next one:

1. When you create the URL above, add a random letter inside it to break the URL. Run the playground and you'll see: `failure(Request to API Server failed)`.

2. Comment out the line that starts with `request.allHttpHeaderFields` and run the playground. Since the server response will no longer be JSON, but instead just be plain text, you'll see the output: `failure(Failed parsing response from server)`.

3. Send a random ID to `getJoke(id:)`, as you did before. Run the playground and you'll get: `failure(Joke with ID {your ID} doesn't exist)`.

And that's it! You've just built your very own Combine-based, production-class API layer with its own errors. What more could a person want? :]

Catching and retrying

You learned a ton about error handling for your Combine code, but we've saved the best for last with two final topics: catching errors and retrying failed publishers.

The great thing about `Publisher` being a unified way to represent work is that you have many operators that let you do an incredible amount of work with very few lines of code.

Go ahead and dive right into the example.

Start by switching to the **Catching and retrying** page in the Project navigator. Expand the playground's **Sources** folder and open **PhotoService.swift**.

It includes a `PhotoService` with a `fetchPhoto(quality:failingTimes:)` method that you'll use in this section. `PhotoService` fetches a photo in either high or low quality using a custom publisher. For this example, asking for a high-quality image will always fail — so you can experiment with the various techniques to retry and catch failures as they occur.

Head back to the **Catching and retrying** playground page and add this bare-bones example to your playground:

```
let photoService = PhotoService()

example(of: "Catching and retrying") {
  photoService
    .fetchPhoto(quality: .low)
    .sink(
      receiveCompletion: { print("\($0)") },
      receiveValue: { image in
        image
        print("Got image: \(image)")
      }
    )
    .store(in: &subscriptions)
}
```

The above code should be familiar by now. You instantiate a `PhotoService` and call `fetchPhoto` with a `.low` quality. Then you use `sink` to print out any completion event or the fetched image.

Notice that the instantiation of `photoService` is outside the scope of the example so that it doesn't get deallocated immediately.

Run your playground and wait for it to finish. You should see the following output:

```
——— Example of: Catching and retrying ———
Got image: <UIImage:0x600000790750 named(lq.jpg) {300, 300}>
finished
```

Tap the **Show Result** button next to the first line in receiveValue and you'll see a beautiful low-quality picture of... well, a combine.

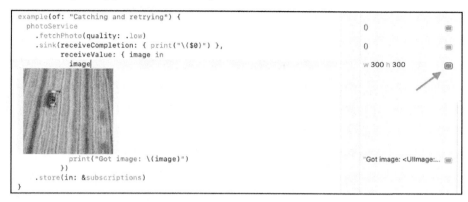

Next, change the quality from .low to .high and run the playground again. You'll see the following output:

```
——— Example of: Catching and retrying ———
 failure(Failed fetching image with high quality)
```

As mentioned earlier, asking for a high-quality image will fail. This is your starting point! There are a few things that you could improve here. You'll start by retrying upon a failure.

Many times, when you request a resource or perform some computation, a failure might be a one-off occurrence resulting from a bad network connection or another unavailable resource.

In these cases, you'd usually write a big ol' mechanism to retry different pieces of work while tracking the number of attempts and deciding what to do if all attempts fail. Fortunately, Combine makes this much, *much* simpler.

Like all good things in Combine, there's an operator for that!

The retry operator accepts a number. If the publisher fails, it will resubscribe to the upstream and *retry* up to the number of times you specify. If all retries fail, it simply pushes the error downstream as it would without the retry operator.

It's time for you to try this. Below the line fetchPhoto(quality: .high), add the following line:

```
.retry(3)
```

Wait, is that it?! Yup. That's it.

You get a free retry mechanism for **every piece of work wrapped in a publisher**, and it's as easy as calling this simple retry operator.

Before running your playground, add this code *between* the calls to `fetchPhoto` and `retry`:

```
.handleEvents(
  receiveSubscription: { _ in print("Trying ...") },
  receiveCompletion: {
    guard case .failure(let error) = $0 else { return }
    print("Got error: \(error)")
  }
)
```

This code will help you see when retries occur — it prints out the subscriptions and failures that occur in `fetchPhoto`.

Now you're ready! Run your playground and wait for it to complete. You'll see the following output:

```
——— Example of: Catching and retrying ———
Trying ...
Got error: Failed fetching image with high quality
Trying ...
Got error: Failed fetching image with high quality
Trying ...
Got error: Failed fetching image with high quality
Trying ...
Got error: Failed fetching image with high quality
failure(Failed fetching image with high quality)
```

As you can see, there are four attempts. The initial attempt, plus three retries triggered by the `retry` operator. Because fetching a high-quality photo constantly fails, the operator exhausts all its retry attempts and pushes the error down to `sink`.

Replace the following call to `fetchPhoto`:

```
.fetchPhoto(quality: .high)
```

With:

```
.fetchPhoto(quality: .high, failingTimes: 2)
```

The `faliingTimes` parameter will limit the number of times that fetching a high-quality image will fail. In this case, it will fail the first two times you call it, then succeed.

Run your playground again, and take a look at the output:

```
——— Example of: Catching and retrying ———
Trying ...
Got error: Failed fetching image with high quality
Trying ...
Got error: Failed fetching image with high quality
Trying ...
Got image: <UIImage:0x600001268360 named(hq.jpg) {1835, 2446}>
finished
```

As you can see, this time there are three attempts, the initial one plus two more retries. The method fails for the first two attempts, and then succeeds and returns this gorgeous, high-quality photo of a combine in a field:

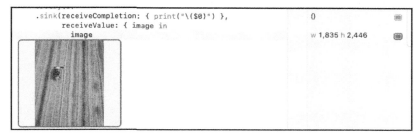

Awesome! But there's still one final feature you'll improve in this service call. Your product folks asked that you fall back to a low-quality image if fetching a high-quality image fails. If fetching a low-quality image fails *as well*, you should fall back to a hard-coded image.

You'll start with the latter of the two tasks. Combine includes a handy operator called replaceError(with:) that lets you fall back to a default value of the publisher's type if an error occurs. This also changes your publisher's Failure type to Never, since you replace every possible failure with a fallback value.

First, remove the failingTimes argument from fetchPhoto, so it constantly fails as it did before.

Then add the following line, immediately after the call to retry:

```
.replaceError(with: UIImage(named: "na.jpg")!)
```

Run your playground again and take a look at the image result this time around. After four attempts — i.e., the initial plus three retries — you fall back to a hard-coded image on disk:

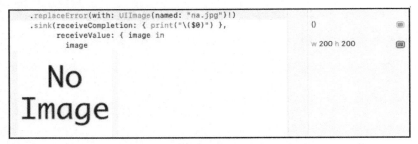

Also, looking at the console output reveals what you'd expect: There are four failed attempts, followed by the hard-coded fallback image:

```
—— Example of: Catching and retrying ——
Trying ...
Got error: Failed fetching image with high quality
Trying ...
Got error: Failed fetching image with high quality
Trying ...
Got error: Failed fetching image with high quality
Trying ...
Got error: Failed fetching image with high quality
Got image: <UIImage:0x6000020e9200 named(na.jpg) {200, 200}>
finished
```

Now, for the second task and final part of this chapter: Fall back to a low-quality image if the high-quality image fails. Combine provides the perfect operator for this task, called `catch`. It lets you *catch* a failure from a publisher and recover from it with a different publisher.

To see this in action, add the following code after `retry`, but before `replaceError(with:)`:

```
.catch { error -> PhotoService.Publisher in
  print("Failed fetching high quality, falling back to low quality")
  return photoService.fetchPhoto(quality: .low)
}
```

Run your playground one final time and take a look at the console:

```
—— Example of: Catching and retrying ——
Trying ...
Got error: Failed fetching image with high quality
Trying ...
Got error: Failed fetching image with high quality
Trying ...
Got error: Failed fetching image with high quality
Trying ...
Got error: Failed fetching image with high quality
Failed fetching high quality, falling back to low quality
Got image: <UIImage:0x60000205c480 named(lq.jpg) {300, 300}>
finished
```

Like before, the initial attempt plus three retries to fetch the high-quality image fail. Once the operator has exhausted all retries, `catch` plays its role and subscribes to `photoService.fetchPhoto`, requesting a low-quality image. This results in a fallback from the failed high-quality request to the successful low-quality request.

Key points

- Publishers with a `Failure` type of `Never` are guaranteed to not emit a failure completion event.
- Many operators only work with infallible publishers. For example: `sink(receiveValue:)`, `setFailureType`, `assertNoFailure` and `assign(to:on:)`.
- The `try`-prefixed operators let you throw errors from within them, while non-`try` operators do not.
- Since Swift doesn't support typed throws, calling `try`-prefixed operators erases the publisher's `Failure` to a plain Swift `Error`.
- Use `mapError` to map a publisher's `Failure` type, and unify all failure types in your publisher to a single type.
- When creating your own API based on other publishers with their own `Failure` types, wrap all possible errors into your own `Error` type to unify them and hide your API's implementation details.
- You can use the `retry` operator to resubscribe to a failed publisher for an additional number of times.
- `replaceError(with:)` is useful when you want to provide a default fallback value for your publisher, in case of failure.
- Finally, you may use `catch` to replace a failed publisher with a different fallback publisher.

Where to go from here?

Congratulations on getting to the end of this chapter. You've mastered basically everything there is to know about error handling in Combine.

You only experimented with the `tryMap` operator in the **try* operators** section of this chapter. You can find a full list of `try`-prefixed operators in Apple's official documentation at https://apple.co/3233VRB.

With your mastery of error handling, it's time to learn about one of the lower-level, but most crucial topics in Combine: Schedulers. Continue to the next chapter to find out what schedulers are and how to use them.

Chapter 17: Schedulers

By Florent Pillet

As you've been progressing through this book, you've read about this or that operator taking a scheduler as a parameter. Most often you'd simply use DispatchQueue.main because it's convenient, well understood and brings a reassuring feeling of safety. This is the comfort zone!

As a developer, you have at least a general idea of what a DispatchQueue is. Besides DispatchQueue.main, you most certainly already used either one of the global, concurrent queues, or created a serial dispatch queue to run actions serially on. Don't worry if you haven't or don't remember the details. You'll re-assess some important information about dispatch queues throughout this chapter.

But then, why does Combine need a new similar concept? It is now time for you to dive into the real nature, meaning and purpose of Combine schedulers!

In this chapter, you'll learn why the concept of schedulers came about. You'll explore how Combine makes asynchronous events and actions easy to work with and, of course, you'll get to experiment with all the schedulers that Combine provides.

An introduction to schedulers

Per Apple's documentation, a **scheduler** is *a protocol that defines when and how to execute a closure*. Although the definition is correct, it's only part of the story.

A scheduler provides the context to execute a future action, either as soon as possible or at a future date. The action is a closure as defined in the protocol itself. But the term *closure* can also hide the delivery of some value by a `Publisher`, performed on a particular scheduler.

Did you notice that this definition purposely avoids any reference to threading? This is because the concrete implementation is the one that defines where the "context" provided by the scheduler protocol executes!

The exact details of *which thread* your code will execute on therefore depends on the scheduler you pick.

Remember this important concept: **A scheduler is not equal to a thread**. You'll get into the details of what this means for each scheduler later in this chapter.

Let's look at the concept of schedulers from an event flow standpoint:

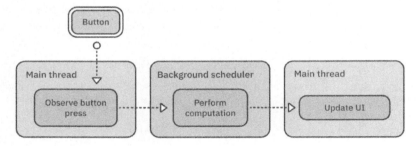

What you see in the figure above:

- A user action (button press) occurs on the main (UI) thread.
- It triggers some work to process on a background scheduler.
- Final data to display is delivered to subscribers on the main thread, so subscribers can update the app's UI.

You can see how the notion of scheduler is deeply rooted in the notions of foreground/background execution. Moreover, depending on the implementation you pick, work can be **serialized** or **parallelized**.

Therefore, to fully understand schedulers, you need to look at which classes conform to the `Scheduler` protocol.

But first, you need to learn about two important operators related to schedulers!

> **Note**: In the next section, you'll primarily use `DispatchQueue` which conforms to Combine's `Scheduler` protocol.

Operators for scheduling

The Combine framework provides two fundamental operators to work with schedulers:

- `subscribe(on:)` and `subscribe(on:options:)` **creates** the subscription (start the work) on the specified scheduler.
- `receive(on:)` and `receive(on:options:)` **delivers** values on the specified scheduler.

In addition, the following operators take a scheduler and scheduler options as parameters. You learned about them in Chapter 6, "Time Manipulation Operators:"

- `debounce(for:scheduler:options:)`
- `delay(for:tolerance:scheduler:options:)`
- `measureInterval(using:options:)`
- `throttle(for:scheduler:latest:)`
- `timeout(_:scheduler:options:customError:)`

Don't hesitate to take a look back at Chapter 6 if you need to refresh your memory on these operators. Then you can look into the two new ones.

Introducing subscribe(on:)

Remember — a publisher is an inanimate entity until you subscribe to it. But what happens when you subscribe to a publisher? Several steps take place:

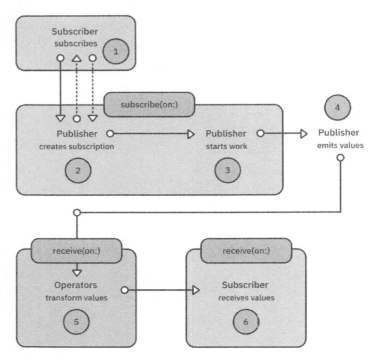

1. `Publisher` receives the subscriber and creates a `Subscription`.
2. `Subscriber` receives the subscription and requests values from the publisher (dotted lines).
3. `Publisher` starts work (via the `Subscription`).
4. `Publisher` emits values (via the `Subscription`).
5. Operators transform values.
6. `Subscriber` receives the final values.

Steps one, two and three usually happen on the thread that is current when your code subscribes to the publisher. But when you use the `subscribe(on:)` operator, all these operations run *on the scheduler you specified*.

> **Note**: You'll come back to this diagram when looking at the `receive(on:)` operator. You'll then understand the two boxes at the bottom with steps labeled five and six.

You may want a publisher to perform some expensive computation in the background to avoid blocking the main thread. The simple way to do this is to use `subscribe(on:)`.

It's time to look at an example!

Open **Starter.playground** in the **projects** folder and select the **subscribeOn-receiveOn** page. Make sure the Debug area is displayed, then start by adding the following code:

```
// 1
let computationPublisher =
Publishers.ExpensiveComputation(duration: 3)

// 2
let queue = DispatchQueue(label: "serial queue")

// 3
let currentThread = Thread.current.number
print("Start computation publisher on thread \(currentThread)")
```

Here's a breakdown of the above code:

1. This playground defines a special publisher in **Sources/Computation.swift** called `ExpensiveComputation`, which *simulates* a long-running computation that emits a string after the specified duration.

2. A serial queue you'll use to trigger the computation on a specific scheduler. As you learned above, `DispatchQueue` conforms to the `Scheduler` protocol.

3. You obtain the current execution thread number. In a playground, the main thread (thread number 1) is the default thread your code runs in. The `number` extension to the `Thread` class is defined in **Sources/Thread.swift**.

> **Note**: The details of how the `ExpensiveComputation` publisher is implemented do not matter for now. You will learn more about creating your own publishers in the next chapter, "Custom Publishers & Handling Backpressure."

Back to the **subscribeOn-receiveOn** playground page, you'll need to subscribe to `computationPublisher` and display the value it emits:

```
let subscription = computationPublisher
  .sink { value in
    let thread = Thread.current.number
    print("Received computation result on thread \(thread): '\(value)'")
  }
```

Execute the playground and look at the output:

```
Start computation publisher on thread 1
ExpensiveComputation subscriber received on thread 1
Beginning expensive computation on thread 1
Completed expensive computation on thread 1
Received computation result on thread 1 'Computation complete'
```

Let's dig into the various steps to understand what happens:

- Your code is running on the main thread. From there, it subscribes to the computation publisher.
- The `ExpensiveComputation` publisher receives a subscriber.
- It creates a subscription, then starts the work.
- When work completes, publisher delivers the result through the subscription and completes.

You can see that all of this happen on thread 1 which is the main thread.

Now, change the publisher subscription to insert a `subscribe(on:)` call:

```
let subscription = computationPublisher
  .subscribe(on: queue)
  .sink { value in...
```

Execute the playground again to see output similar to the following:

```
Start computation publisher on thread 1
ExpensiveComputation subscriber received on thread 5
Beginning expensive computation from thread 5
Completed expensive computation on thread 5
Received computation result on thread 5 'Computation complete'
```

Ah! This is different! Now you can see that you're still subscribing from the main thread, but Combine delegates to the queue you provided to perform the subscription effectively. The queue runs the code on one of its threads. Since the computation starts and completes on thread 5 and then emits the resulting value from this thread, your sink receives the value on this thread as well.

> **Note**: Due to the dynamic thread management nature of `DispatchQueue`, you may see different thread numbers in this log and further logs in this chapter. What matters is consistency: The same thread number should be shown at the same steps.

But what if you wanted to update some on-screen info? You would need to do something like `DispatchQueue.main.async { ... }` in your sink closure, just to make sure you're performing UI updates from the main thread.

There is a more effective way to do this with Combine!

Introducing receive(on:)

The second important operator you want to know about is `receive(on:)`. It lets you specify which scheduler should be used to deliver values to subscribers. But what does this mean?

Insert a call to `receive(on:)` just before your sink in the subscription:

```
let subscription = computationPublisher
  .subscribe(on: queue)
  .receive(on: DispatchQueue.main)
  .sink { value in
```

Then, execute the playground again. Now you see this output:

```
Start computation publisher on thread 1
ExpensiveComputation subscriber received on thread 4
Beginning expensive computation from thread 4
Completed expensive computation on thread 4
Received computation result on thread 1 'Computation complete'
```

> **Note**: You may see the second message ("ExpensiveComputation subscriber received...") on a different thread than the two next steps. Due to internal plumbing in Combine, this step and the next may execute asynchronously on the same queue. Since `Dispatch` dynamically manages its own thread pool, you may see a different thread number for this line and the next, but you won't see `thread 1`.

Success! Even though the computation works and emits results from a background thread, you are now guaranteed to always receive values on the main queue. This is what you need to perform your UI updates safely.

In this introduction to scheduling operators, you used `DispatchQueue`. Combine extends it to implement the `Scheduler` protocol, but it's not the only one! It's time to dive into schedulers!

Scheduler implementations

Apple provides several concrete implementations of the `Scheduler` protocol:

- `ImmediateScheduler`: A simple scheduler that executes code immediately on the current thread, which is the default execution context unless modified using `subscribe(on:)`, `receive(on:)` or any of the other operators which take a scheduler as parameter.

- `RunLoop`: Tied to Foundation's `Thread` object.

- `DispatchQueue`: Can either be serial or concurrent.

- `OperationQueue`: A queue that regulates the execution of work items.

In the rest of this chapter, you'll go over all of these and their specific details.

> **Note**: One glaring omission here is the lack of a `TestScheduler`, an indispensable part of the testing portion of any reactive programming framework. Without such a virtual, simulated scheduler, it's challenging to test your Combine code thoroughly. You'll explore more details about this particular kind of scheduler in Chapter 19, "Testing."

ImmediateScheduler

The easiest entry in the scheduler category is also the simplest one the Combine framework provides: `ImmediateScheduler`. The name already spoils the details, so have a look at what it does!

Open the **ImmediateScheduler** page of the playground. You won't need the debug area for this one, but make sure you make the Live View visible. If you're not sure how to do that, see the beginning of Chapter 6, "Time Manipulation Operators."

You're going to use some fancy new tools built into this playground to follow your publisher values across schedulers!

Start by creating a simple timer as you did in previous chapters:

```
let source = Timer
  .publish(every: 1.0, on: .main, in: .common)
  .autoconnect()
  .scan(0) { counter, _ in counter + 1 }
```

Next, prepare a closure that creates a publisher. You'll make use of a custom operator defined in the **Sources/Record.swift**: `recordThread(using:)`. This operator records the thread that is current at the time the operator sees a value passing through, and can record multiple times from the publisher source to the final sink.

> **Note**: This `recordThread(using:)` operator is for testing purposes only, as the operator changes the type of data to an internal value type. The details of its implementation are beyond the scope of this chapter, but the adventurous reader may find it interesting to look into.

Add this code:

```
// 1
let setupPublisher = { recorder in
  source
    // 2
    .recordThread(using: recorder)
    // 3
    .receive(on: ImmediateScheduler.shared)
    // 4
    .recordThread(using: recorder)
    // 5
    .eraseToAnyPublisher()
}
```

```
// 6
let view = ThreadRecorderView(title: "Using ImmediateScheduler",
setup: setupPublisher)
PlaygroundPage.current.liveView = UIHostingController(rootView:
view)
```

In the above code, you:

1. Prepare a closure that returns a publisher, using the given recorder object to setup current thread recording via recordThread(using:).

2. At this stage, the timer emitted a value, so you record the current thread. Can you already guess which one it is?

3. Make sure the publisher delivers values on the shared ImmediateScheduler.

4. Record which thread you're now on.

5. The closure **must** return an AnyPublisher type. This is mainly for convenience in the internal implementation.

6. Prepare and instantiate a ThreadRecorderView which displays the migration of a published value across threads at various record points.

Execute the playground page and look at the output after a few seconds:

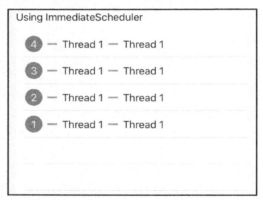

This representation shows each value the source publisher (the timer) emits. On each line, you see the threads the value is going through. Every time you add a recordThread(using:) operator, you see an additional thread number logged on the line.

Here you see that at the two recording points you added, the current thread was the main thread. This is because the ImmediateScheduler "schedules" immediately on the current thread.

To verify this, you can do a little experiment! Go back to your `setupPublisher` closure definition, and just before the first `recordThread` line, insert the following:

```
.receive(on: DispatchQueue.global())
```

This requests that values the source emits be further made available on the global concurrent queue. Is this going to yield interesting results? Execute the playground to find out:

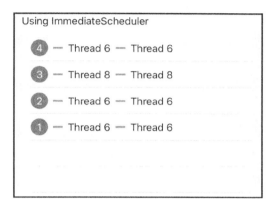

This is completely different! Can you guess why the thread changes all the time? You'll learn more about this in the coverage of `DispatchQueue` in this chapter!

ImmediateScheduler options

With most of the operators accepting a `Scheduler` in their arguments, you can also find an `options` argument which accepts a `SchedulerOptions` value. In the case of `ImmediateScheduler`, this type is defined as `Never` so when using `ImmediateScheduler`, you should never pass a value for the `options` parameter of the operator.

ImmediateScheduler pitfalls

One specific thing about `ImmediateScheduler` is that it is *immediate*. You won't be able to use any of the `schedule(after:)` variants of the `Scheduler` protocol, because the `SchedulerTimeType` you need to specify a delay has no public initializer and is meaningless for immediate scheduling.

Similar but different pitfalls exist for the second type of `Scheduler` you'll learn about in this chapter: `RunLoop`.

RunLoop scheduler

Long-time iOS and macOS developers are familiar with `RunLoop`. Predating `DispatchQueue`, it is a way to manage input sources at the thread level, including in the Main (UI) thread. Your application's main thread still has an associated `RunLoop`. You can also obtain one for any Foundation `Thread` by calling `RunLoop.current` from the current thread.

> **Note**: Nowadays `RunLoop` is a less useful class, as `DispatchQueue` is a sensible choice in most situations. This said, there are still some specific cases where run loops are useful. For example, `Timer` schedules itself on a `RunLoop`. UIKit and AppKit rely on `RunLoop` and its execution modes for handling various user input situations. Describing everything about `RunLoop` is outside the scope of this book.

To have a look at `RunLoop`, open the **RunLoop** page in the playground. The `Timer` source you used earlier is the same, so it's already written for you. Add this code after it:

```
let setupPublisher = { recorder in
  source
    // 1
    .receive(on: DispatchQueue.global())
    .recordThread(using: recorder)
    // 2
    .receive(on: RunLoop.current)
    .recordThread(using: recorder)
    .eraseToAnyPublisher()
}

let view = ThreadRecorderView(title: "Using RunLoop", setup: setupPublisher)
PlaygroundPage.current.liveView = UIHostingController(rootView: view)
```

1. As you previously did, you first make values go through the global concurrent queue. Why? Because it's fun!

2. Then, you ask values to be received on `RunLoop.current`.

But what is `RunLoop.current`? It is the *RunLoop associated with the thread that was current when the call was made*. The closure is being called by `ThreadRecorderView`, from the main thread to set up the publisher and the recorder. Therefore, `RunLoop.current` is the main thread's `RunLoop`.

Execute the playground to see what happens:

```
Using RunLoop
    4  — Thread 5  — Thread 1
    3  — Thread 5  — Thread 1
    2  — Thread 5  — Thread 1
    1  — Thread 4  — Thread 1
```

As you requested it, the first `recordThread` shows that each value goes through one of the global concurrent queue's threads, then continues on the main thread.

A little comprehension challenge

What would happen if you had used `subscribe(on: DispatchQueue.global())` instead of `receive(on:)` the first time? Try it!

You see that everything is recorded on thread one. It may not be obvious at first, but it is entirely logical. Yes, the publisher was subscribed to on the concurrent queue. But remember that you are using a `Timer` which is emitting its values… on the main RunLoop! Therefore, regardless of the scheduler you pick to subscribe to this publisher on, values will always begin their journey on the main thread.

Scheduling code execution with RunLoop

The `Scheduler` lets you schedule code that executes *as soon as possible, or after a future date*. While it was not possible to use the latter form with `ImmediateScheduler`, `RunLoop` is perfectly capable of deferred execution.

Each scheduler implementation defines its own `SchedulerTimeType`. It makes things a little complicated to grasp until you figure out what type of data to use. In the case of `RunLoop`, the `SchedulerTimeType` value is a `Date`.

You'll schedule an action that will cancel the `ThreadRecorderView`'s subscription after a few seconds. It turns out the `ThreadRecorder` class has an optional `Cancellable` that can be used to stop its subscription to the publisher.

First, you need a variable to hold a reference to the `ThreadRecorder`. At the beginning of the page, add this line:

```
var threadRecorder: ThreadRecorder? = nil
```

Now you need to capture the thread recorder instance. The best place to do this is on the `setupPublisher` closure. But how? You could:

- Add explicit types to the closure, assign the `threadRecorder` variable and return the publisher. You'll need to add explicit types because the poor Swift compiler will complain "may be unable to infer complex closure return type."
- Use some operator to capture the recorder at subscription time.

Go wild and do the latter!

Add this line in your `setupPublisher` closure before `eraseToAnyPublisher()`:

```
.handleEvents(receiveSubscription: { _ in threadRecorder = recorder })
```

Interesting choice to capture the recorder!

> **Note**: You already learned about `handleEvents` in Chapter 10, "Debugging." It has a long signature and lets you execute code at various points in the lifecycle of a publisher (in the reactive programming terminology this is called *injecting side effects*) without actually interacting with the values it emits. In this case, you're intercepting the moment when the recorder subscribes to the publisher, so as to capture the recorder in your global variable. Not pretty, but it does the job in a fun way!

Now you're all set and can schedule some action after a few seconds. Add this code at the end of the page:

```
RunLoop.current.schedule(
  after: .init(Date(timeIntervalSinceNow: 4.5)),
  tolerance: .milliseconds(500)) {
    threadRecorder?.subscription?.cancel()
  }
```

This `schedule(after:tolerance:)` lets you schedule when the provided closure should execute along with the tolerable drift in case the system can't precisely execute the code at the selected time. You add `4.5` seconds to the current date to allow four values to be sent before the execution.

Run the playground. You can see that the list stops updating after the fourth item. This is your cancellation mechanism working!

> **Note:** If you only get three values, it might mean your Mac is running a little slow and cannot accommodate a half-second tolerance, so you can try bumping the dates out more, e.g., set `timeIntervalSinceNow` to `5.0` and `tolerance` to `1.0`.

RunLoop options

Like `ImmediateScheduler`, `RunLoop` does not offer any suitable options for the calls which take a `SchedulerOptions` parameter.

RunLoop pitfalls

Usages of `RunLoop` should be restricted to the main thread's run loop, and to the `RunLoop` available in Foundation threads that you control if needed. That is, anything you started yourself using a `Thread` object.

One particular pitfall to avoid is using `RunLoop.current` in code executing on a `DispatchQueue`. This is because `DispatchQueue` threads can be ephemeral, which makes them nearly impossible to rely on with `RunLoop`.

You are now ready to learn about the most versatile and useful scheduler: `DispatchQueue`!

DispatchQueue scheduler

Throughout this chapter and previous chapters, you've been using `DispatchQueue` in various situations. It comes as no surprise that `DispatchQueue` conforms to the `Scheduler` protocol and is fully usable with all operators that take a `Scheduler` as a parameter.

But first, a quick refresher on dispatch queues. The Dispatch framework is a powerful component of Foundation that allows you to *execute code concurrently on multicore hardware by submitting work to dispatch queues managed by the system.*

A `DispatchQueue` can be either **serial** (the default) or **concurrent**. A serial queue executes all the work items you feed it, in sequence. A concurrent queue will start multiple work items in parallel, to maximize CPU usage. Both queue types have different usages:

- **A serial queue** is typically used to guarantee that some operations do not overlap. So, they can use shared resources without locking if all operations occur in the same queue.
- **A concurrent queue** will execute as many operations concurrently as possible. So, it is better suited for pure computation.

Queues and threads

The most familiar queue you work with all the time is `DispatchQueue.main`. It directly maps to the main (UI) thread, and all operations executing on this queue can freely update the user interface. UI updates are only permitted from the main thread.

All other queues, serial or concurrent, execute their code in a pool of threads managed by the system. Meaning you should never make any assumption about the current thread in code that runs in a queue. In particular, you should not schedule work using `RunLoop.current` because of the way `DispatchQueue` manages its threads.

All dispatch queues share the same pool of threads. A serial queue you give work to perform will use any available thread in that pool. A direct consequence is that two successive work items from the same queue may use different threads while still executing sequentially.

This is an important distinction: When using `subscribe(on:)`, `receive(on:)` or any of the other operators taking a `Scheduler` parameter, you should never assume that the thread backing the scheduler is the same every time.

Using DispatchQueue as a scheduler

It's time for you to experiment! As usual, you're going to use a timer to emit values and watch them migrate across schedulers. But this time around, you're going to create the timer using a Dispatch Queue timer.

Open the playground page named **DispatchQueue**. First, you'll create a couple queues to work with. Add this code to your playground:

```
let serialQueue = DispatchQueue(label: "Serial queue")
let sourceQueue = DispatchQueue.main
```

You'll use `sourceQueue` to publish values from a timer, and later use `serialQueue` to experiment with switching schedulers.

Now add this code:

```
// 1
let source = PassthroughSubject<Void, Never>()

// 2
let subscription = sourceQueue.schedule(after: sourceQueue.now,
                                        interval: .seconds(1)) {
  source.send()
}
```

1. You'll use a `Subject` to emit a value when the timer fires. You don't care about the actual output type, so you just use `Void`.

2. As you learned in Chapter 11, "Timers," queues are perfectly capable of generating timers, but there is no `Publisher` API for queue timers. It is a surprising omission from the API! You have to use the repeating variant of the `schedule()` method from the `Schedulers` protocol. It starts immediately and returns a `Cancellable`. Every time the timer fires, you'll send a `Void` value through the source subject.

> **Note**: Did you notice how you're using the now property to specify the starting time of the timer? This is part of the `Scheduler` protocol and returns the current time expressed using the scheduler's `SchedulerTimeType`. Each class implementing the `Scheduler` protocol defines its own type for this.

Now, you can start exercising scheduler hopping. Setup your Publisher by adding the following code:

```
let setupPublisher = { recorder in
  source
    .recordThread(using: recorder)
    .receive(on: serialQueue)
    .recordThread(using: recorder)
    .eraseToAnyPublisher()
}
```

Nothing new here, you've coded similar patterns several times in this chapter.

Then, as in your the previous examples, set up the display:

```
let view = ThreadRecorderView(title: "Using DispatchQueue",
                              setup: setupPublisher)
PlaygroundPage.current.liveView = UIHostingController(rootView:
view)
```

Execute the playground. Easy enough, you see what was intended:

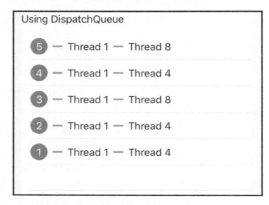

1. The timer fires on the main queue and sends `Void` values through the subject.

2. The publisher receive values on your serial queue.

Did you notice how the second `recordThread(using:)` records changes in the current thread after the `receive(on:)` operator? This is a perfect example of how `DispatchQueue` makes no guarantee over which thread each work item executes on. In the case of `receive(on:)`, a **work item** is a value that hops from the current scheduler to another.

Now, what would happen if you emitted values from the serial queue and kept the same `receive(on:)` operator? Would values still change threads on the go?

Try it! Go back to the beginning of the code and change the `sourceQueue` definition to:

```
let sourceQueue = serialQueue
```

Now, execute the playground again:

```
Using DispatchQueue
  5  — Thread 7 — Thread 7
  4  — Thread 5 — Thread 5
  3  — Thread 4 — Thread 4
  2  — Thread 5 — Thread 5
  1  — Thread 7 — Thread 7
```

Interesting! Again you see the no-thread-guarantee effect of DispatchQueue, but you also see that the `receive(on:)` operator never switches threads! It looks like some optimization is internally happening to avoid extra switching. You'll explore this in this chapter's challenge!

DispatchQueue options

`DispatchQueue` is the only scheduler providing a set of options you can pass when operators take a `SchedulerOptions` argument. These options mainly revolve around specifying QoS (Quality of Service) values independently of those already set on the `DispatchQueue`. There are some additional flags for work items, but you won't need them in the vast majority of situations.

To see how you would specify the QoS though, modify the `receive(on:options:)` in your `setupPublisher` to the following:

```
.receive(
  on: serialQueue,
  options: DispatchQueue.SchedulerOptions(qos: .userInteractive)
)
```

You pass an instance of `DispatchQueue.SchedulerOptions` to `options` that specifies the highest quality of service: `.userInteractive`. It instructs the OS to make its best effort to prioritize delivery of values over less important tasks. This is something you can use when you want to update the user interface as fast as possible. To the contrary, if there is less pressure for speedy delivery, you could use the `.background` quality of service. In the context of this example you won't see a real difference since it's the only task running.

Using these options in real applications helps the OS deciding which task to schedule first in situations where you have many queues busy at the same time. It really is fine tuning your application performance!

You're nearly done with schedulers! Hang on a little bit more. You have one last scheduler to learn about.

OperationQueue

The last scheduler you will learn about in this chapter is `OperationQueue`. The documentation describes it as *a queue that regulates the execution of operations*. It is a rich regulation mechanism that lets you create advanced operations with dependencies. But in the context of Combine, you will use none of these mechanisms.

Since `OperationQueue` uses `Dispatch` under the hood, there is little difference on the surface in using one of the other. Or is there?

Give it a go in a simple example. Open the **OperationQueue** playground page and start coding:

```
let queue = OperationQueue()

let subscription = (1...10).publisher
  .receive(on: queue)
  .sink { value in
    print("Received \(value)")
  }
```

You're creating a simple publisher emitting numbers between 1 and 10, making sure values arrive on the `OperationQueue` you created. You then print the value in the `sink`.

Can you guess what happens? Expand the Debug area and execute the playground:

```
Received 4
Received 3
Received 2
Received 7
Received 5
Received 10
Received 6
Received 9
Received 1
Received 8
```

This is puzzling! Items are emitted in order but arrive out of order! How can this be? To find out, you can change the `print` line to display the current thread number:

```
print("Received \(value) on thread \(Thread.current.number)")
```

Execute the playground again:

```
Received 1 on thread 5
Received 2 on thread 4
Received 4 on thread 7
Received 7 on thread 8
Received 6 on thread 9
Received 10 on thread 10
Received 5 on thread 11
Received 9 on thread 12
Received 3 on thread 13
Received 8 on thread 14
```

Ah-ha! As you can see see, each value is *received* on a different thread! If you look up the documentation about `OperationQueue`, there is a note about threading which says that `OperationQueue` uses the `Dispatch` framework (hence `DispatchQueue`) to execute operations. It means it doesn't guarantee it'll use the same underlying thread for each delivered value.

Moreover, there is one parameter in each `OperationQueue` that explains everything: It's `maxConcurrentOperationCount`. It defaults to a system-defined number that allows an operation queue to execute a large number of operations concurrently. Since your publisher emits all its items at roughly the same time, they get dispatched to multiple threads by `Dispatch`'s concurrent queues!

Make a little modification to your code. After defining queue, add this line:

```
queue.maxConcurrentOperationCount = 1
```

Then run the page and look at the debug area:

```
Received 1 on thread 3
Received 2 on thread 3
Received 3 on thread 3
Received 4 on thread 3
Received 5 on thread 4
Received 6 on thread 3
Received 7 on thread 3
Received 8 on thread 3
Received 9 on thread 3
Received 10 on thread 3
```

This time, you get true sequential execution — setting `maxConcurrentOperationCount` to 1 is equivalent to using a serial queue — and your values arrive in order.

OperationQueue options

There is no usable `SchedulerOptions` for `OperationQueue`. It's actually type aliased to `RunLoop.SchedulerOptions`, which itself provides no option.

OperationQueue pitfalls

You just saw that `OperationQueue` executes operations concurrently by default. You need to be very aware of this as it can cause you trouble: By default, an `OperationQueue` behaves like a *concurrent* `DispatchQueue`.

It can be a good tool, though, when you have significant work to perform every time a publisher emits a value. You can control the load by tuning the `maxConcurrentOperationCount` parameter.

Challenges

Phew, this was a long and complex chapter! Congratulations on making it so far! Have some brainpower left for a couple of challenges? Let's do it!

Challenge 1: Stop the timer

This is an easy one. In this chapter's section about `DispatchQueue` you created a cancellable timer to feed your source publisher with values.

Devise two different ways of stopping the timer after 4 seconds. Hint: You'll need to use `DispatchQueue.SchedulerTimeType.advanced(by:)`.

Found the solutions? Compare them to the ones in the **projects/challenge/challenge1/** final playground:

1. Use the serial queue's scheduler protocol `schedule(after:_:)` method to schedule the execution of a closure which cancels the `subscription`.

2. Use serialQueue's normal `asyncAfter(_:_:)` method (pre-Combine) to do the same thing.

Challenge 2: Discover optimization

Earlier in this chapter, you read about an intriguing question: Is Combine optimizing when you're using the same scheduler in successive `receive(on:)` calls, or is it a Dispatch framework optimization?

To find out, you'll want to turn over to challenge 2. Your challenge is to devise a method that will bring an answer to this question. It's not very complicated, but it's not trivial either.

Could you find a solution? Read on to compare yours!

In the Dispatch framework, the initializer for `DispatchQueue` takes an optional `target` parameter. It lets you specify a queue on which to execute your code. In other words, the queue you create is just a shadow while the real queue on which your code executes is the target queue.

So the idea to try and guess whether Combine or Dispatch is performing the optimization is to use two different queues having one targeting the other. So at the Dispatch framework level, code all executes on the same queue, but (hopefully) Combine doesn't notice.

Therefore, if you do this and see all values being received on the same thread, it is most likely that Dispatch is performing the optimizations for you. The steps you take to code the solution are:

1. Create the second serial queue, targeting the first one.
2. Add a `.receive(on:)` for the second serial queue, as well as a `.recordThread` step.

The full solution is available in the **projects/challenge/challenge2** final playground.

Key points

- A `Scheduler` defines the execution context for a piece of work.

- Apple's operating systems offer a rich variety of tools to help you schedule code execution.

- Combine tops these schedulers with the `Scheduler` protocol to help you pick the best one for the job in any given situation.

- Every time you use `receive(on:)`, further operators in your publisher execute on the specified scheduler. That is, unless they themselves take a `Scheduler` parameter!

Where to go from here?

You've learned a lot, and your brain must be melting with all this information! The next chapter is even more involved as it teaches you about creating your own publishers and dealing with backpressure. Make sure you *schedule* a much-deserved break now, and come back refreshed for the next chapter!

Chapter 18: Custom Publishers & Handling Backpressure
By Florent Pillet

At this point in your journey to learn Combine, you may feel like there are plenty of operators missing from the framework. This may be particularly true if you have experience with other reactive frameworks, which typically provide a rich ecosystem of operators, both built-in and third-party. Combine allows you to create your own publishers. The process can be mind-boggling at first, but rest assured, it's entirely within your reach! This chapter will show you how.

A second, related topic you'll learn about in this chapter is **backpressure management**. This will require some explanation: What is this backpressure thing? Is that some kind of back pain induced by too much leaning over your chair, scrutinizing Combine code? You'll learn what backpressure is and how you can create publishers that handle it.

Creating your own publishers

The complexity of implementing your own publishers varies from "easy" to "pretty involved." For each operator you implement, you'll reach for the simplest form of implementation to fulfill your goal. In this chapter, you'll look at three different ways of crafting your own publishers:

- Using a simple extension method in the `Publisher` namespace.
- Implementing a type in the `Publishers` namespace with a `Subscription` that produces values.
- Same as above, but with a subscription that transforms values from an upstream publisher.

> **Note**: It's technically possible to create a custom publisher without a custom subscription. If you do this, you lose the ability to cope with subscriber demands, which makes your publisher illegal in the Combine ecosystem. Early cancellation can also become an issue. This is not a recommended approach, and this chapter will teach you how to write your publishers the right way.

Publishers as extension methods

Your first task is to implement a simple operator just by reusing existing operators. This is as simple as you can get.

To do it, you'll add a new `unwrap()` operator, which unwraps optional values and ignores their `nil` values. It's going to be a very simple exercise, as you can reuse the existing `compactMap(_:)` operator, which does just that, although it requires you to provide a closure.

Using your new `unwrap()` operator will make your code easier to read, and it will make what you're doing very clear. The reader won't even have to look at the contents of a closure.

You'll add your operator in the `Publisher` namespace, as you do with all other operators.

Open the starter playground for this chapter, which can be found in **projects/ Starter.playground** and open its **Unwrap operator** page from the **Project Navigator**.

Then, add the following code:

```
extension Publisher {
  // 1
  func unwrap<T>() -> Publishers.CompactMap<Self, T> where
Output == Optional<T> {
    // 2
    compactMap { $0 }
  }
}
```

1. The most complicated part of writing a custom operator as a method is the signature. Read on for a detailed description.

2. Implementation is trivial: Simply use `compactMap(_:)` on `self`!

The method signature can be mind-boggling to craft. Break it down to see how it works:

```
func unwrap<T>()
```

Your first step is to make the operator generic, as its `Output` is the type the upstream publisher's optional type wraps.

```
-> Publishers.CompactMap<Self, T>
```

The implementation uses a single `compactMap(_:)`, so the return type derives from this. If you look at `Publishers.CompactMap`, you see it's a generic type: `public struct CompactMap<Upstream, Output>`. When implementing your custom operator, `Upstream` is `Self` (the publisher you're extending) and `Output` is the wrapped type.

```
where Output == Optional<T> {
```

Finally, you constrain your operator to `Optional` types. You conveniently write it to match the wrapped type `T` with your method's generic type... *et voilà*!

> **Note**: When developing more complex operators as methods, such as when using a chain of operators, the signature can quickly become very complicated. A good technique is to make your operators return an `AnyPublisher<OutputType, FailureType>`. In the method, you'll return a publisher that ends with `eraseToAnyPublisher()` to type-erase the signature.

Testing your custom operator

Now you can test your new operator. Add this code below the extension:

```
let values: [Int?] = [1, 2, nil, 3, nil, 4]

values.publisher
  .unwrap()
  .sink {
    print("Received value: \($0)")
  }
```

Run the playground and, as expected, only the non-nil values are printed out to the debug console:

```
Received value: 1
Received value: 2
Received value: 3
Received value: 4
```

Now that you've learned about making simple operator methods, it's time to dive into richer, more complicated publishers. You can group publishers like so:

- Publishers that act as "producers" and directly produce values themselves.

- Publishers that act as "transformers," transforming values produced by upstream publishers.

In this chapter, you'll learn how to use both, but you first need to understand the details of what happens when you subscribe to a publisher.

The subscription mechanism

Subscriptions are the unsung heroes of Combine: While you see publishers everywhere, they are mostly inanimate entities. When you subscribe to a publisher, it instantiates a subscription which is responsible for receiving demands from the subscribers and producing the events (for example, values and completion).

Here are the details of the lifecycle of a subscription:

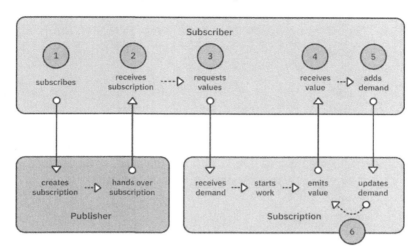

1. A subscriber **subscribes** to the publisher.

2. The publisher **creates a Subscription** then hands it over to the subscriber (calling receive(subscription:)).

3. The subscriber **requests** values from the subscription by sending it the number of values it wants (calling the subscription's request(_:) method).

4. The subscription begins the work and starts emitting values. It sends them one by one to the subscriber (calling the subscriber's receive(_:) method).

5. Upon receiving a value, the subscriber returns a new Subscribers.Demand, which adds to the previous total demand.

6. The subscription keeps sending values until the number of values sent reaches the total requested number.

If the subscription has sent as many values as the subscriber has requested, it should wait for a new demand request before sending more. You can bypass this mechanism and keep sending values, but that breaks the contract between the subscriber and the subscription and can cause undefined behavior in your publisher tree based on Apple's definition.

Finally, if there is an error or the subscription's values source completes, the subscription calls the subscriber's receive(completion:) method.

Publishers emitting values

In Chapter 11, "Timers," you learned about `Timer.publish()` but found that using Dispatch Queues for timers was somewhat uneasy. Why not develop your own timer based on Dispatch's `DispatchSourceTimer`?

You're going to do just that, checking out the details of the `Subscription` mechanism while you do.

To get started, open the **DispatchTimer publisher** page of the playground.

You'll start by defining a configuration structure, which will make it easy to share the timer configuration between the subscriber and its subscription. Add this code to the playground:

```
struct DispatchTimerConfiguration {
  // 1
  let queue: DispatchQueue?
  // 2
  let interval: DispatchTimeInterval
  // 3
  let leeway: DispatchTimeInterval
  // 4
  let times: Subscribers.Demand
}
```

If you've ever used `DispatchSourceTimer`, some of these properties should look familiar to you:

1. You want your timer to be able to fire on a certain queue, but you also want to make the queue optional if you don't care. In this case, the timer will fire on a queue of its choice.

2. The interval at which the timer fires, starting from the subscription time.

3. The leeway, which is the maximum amount of time after the deadline that the system may delay the delivery of the timer event.

4. The number of timer events you want to receive. Since you're making your own timer, make it flexible and able to deliver a limited number of events before completing!

Adding the DispatchTimer publisher

You can now start creating your `DispatchTimer` publisher. It's going to be straightforward because all the work occurs inside the subscription!

Add this code below your configuration:

```
extension Publishers {
  struct DispatchTimer: Publisher {
    // 5
    typealias Output = DispatchTime
    typealias Failure = Never
    // 6
    let configuration: DispatchTimerConfiguration

    init(configuration: DispatchTimerConfiguration) {
      self.configuration = configuration
    }
  }
}
```

5. Your timer emits the current time as a `DispatchTime` value. Of course, it never fails, so the publisher's `Failure` type is `Never`.

6. Keeps a copy of the given configuration. You don't use it right now, but you'll need it when you receive a subscriber.

> **Note**: You'll start seeing compiler errors as you write your code. Rest assured that you'll remedy these by the time you're done implementing the requirements.

Now, implement the `Publisher` protocol's required `receive(subscriber:)` method by adding this code to the `DispatchTimer` definition, below your initializer:

```
// 7
func receive<S: Subscriber>(subscriber: S)
  where Failure == S.Failure,
        Output == S.Input {
  // 8
  let subscription = DispatchTimerSubscription(
    subscriber: subscriber,
    configuration: configuration
  )
  // 9
  subscriber.receive(subscription: subscription)
}
```

7. The function is a generic one; it needs a compile-time specialization to match the subscriber type.

8. The bulk of the action will happen inside the `DispatchTimerSubscription` that you're going to define in a short while.

9. As you learned in Chapter 2, "Publishers & Subscribers," a subscriber receives a `Subscription`, which it can then send requests for values to.

That's really all there is to the publisher! The real work will happen inside the subscription itself.

Building your subscription

The subscription's role is to:

- Accept the initial demand from the subscriber.
- Generate timer events on demand.
- Add to the demand count every time the subscriber receives a value and returns a demand.
- Make sure it doesn't deliver more values than requested in the configuration.

This may sound like a lot of code, but it's not that complicated!

Start defining the subscription below the extension on `Publishers`:

```
private final class DispatchTimerSubscription
  <S: Subscriber>: Subscription where S.Input == DispatchTime {
}
```

The signature itself gives a lot of information:

- This subscription is not visible externally, only through the `Subscription` protocol, so you make it `private`.
- It's a class because you want to pass it by reference. The subscriber may then add it to a `Cancellable` collection, but also keep it around and call `cancel()` independently.
- It caters to subscribers whose `Input` value type is `DispatchTime`, which is what this subscription emits.

Adding required properties to your subscription

Now add these properties to the subscription class' definition:

```
// 10
let configuration: DispatchTimerConfiguration
// 11
var times: Subscribers.Demand
// 12
var requested: Subscribers.Demand = .none
// 13
var source: DispatchSourceTimer? = nil
// 14
var subscriber: S?
```

This code contains:

10. The configuration that the subscriber passed.

11. The maximum number of times the timer will fire, which you copied from the configuration. You'll use it as a counter that you decrement every time you send a value.

12. The current demand; e.g., the number of values the subscriber requested — you decrement it every time you send a value.

13. The internal `DispatchSourceTimer` that will generate the timer events.

14. The subscriber. This makes it clear that **the subscription is responsible for retaining the subscriber for as long as it doesn't complete, fail or cancel**.

> **Note**: This last point is crucial to understand the ownership mechanism in Combine. A subscription is **the link between a subscriber and a publisher**. It keeps the subscriber — for example, an object holding closures, like `AnySubscriber` or `sink` — around for as long as necessary. This explains why, if you don't hold on to a subscription, your subscriber never seems to receive values: Everything stops as soon as the subscription is deallocated. Internal implementation may of course vary according to the specifics of the publisher you are coding.

Initializing and canceling your subscription

Now, add an initializer to your `DispatchTimerSubscription` definition:

```
init(subscriber: S,
     configuration: DispatchTimerConfiguration) {
  self.configuration = configuration
  self.subscriber = subscriber
  self.times = configuration.times
}
```

This is pretty straightforward. The initializer sets `times` to the maximum number of times the publisher should receive timer events, as the configuration specifies. Every time the publisher emits an event, this counter decrements. When it reaches zero, the timer completes with a `finished` event.

Now, implement `cancel()`, a required method that a `Subscription` must provide:

```
func cancel() {
  source = nil
  subscriber = nil
}
```

Setting `DispatchSourceTimer` to `nil` is enough to stop it from running. Setting the `subscriber` property to `nil` releases it from the subscription's reach. Don't forget to do this in your own subscriptions to make sure you don't retain objects in memory that are no longer needed.

You can now start coding the core of the subscription: `request(_:)`.

Letting your subscription request values

Do you remember what you learned in Chapter 2, "Publishers & Subscribers?" Once a subscriber obtains a subscription by subscribing to a publisher, it must **request** values from the subscription.

This is where all the magic happens. To implement it, add this method to the class, above the `cancel` method:

```
// 15
func request(_ demand: Subscribers.Demand) {
  // 16
  guard times > .none else {
    // 17
    subscriber?.receive(completion: .finished)
    return
  }
}
```

15. This required method receives demands from the subscriber. **Demands are cumulative: They add up** to form a total number of values that the subscriber requested.

16. Your first test is to verify whether you've already sent enough values to the subscriber, as specified in the configuration. That is, if you've sent the maximum number of expected values, independent of the demands your publisher received.

17. If this is the case, you can notify the subscriber that the publisher has finished sending values.

Continue the implementation of this method by adding this code after the `guard` statement:

```
// 18
requested += demand

// 19
if source == nil, requested > .none {

}
```

18. Increment the total number of values requested by adding the new demand.

19. Check whether the timer already exists. If not, and if requested values exist, then it's time to start it.

Configuring your timer

Add this code to the body of this last `if` conditional:

```
// 20
let source = DispatchSource.makeTimerSource(queue:
configuration.queue)
// 21
source.schedule(deadline: .now() + configuration.interval,
                repeating: configuration.interval,
                leeway: configuration.leeway)
```

20. Create the `DispatchSourceTimer` from the queue you configured.

21. Schedule the timer to fire after every `configuration.interval` seconds.

Once the timer has started, you'll never stop it, even if you don't use it to emit events to the subscriber. It will keep running until the subscriber cancels the subscription — or you deallocate the subscription.

You're now ready to code the core of your timer, which emits events to the subscriber. Still inside the `if` body, add this code:

```
// 22
source.setEventHandler { [weak self] in
  // 23
  guard let self = self,
        self.requested > .none else { return }

  // 24
  self.requested -= .max(1)
  self.times -= .max(1)
  // 25
  _ = self.subscriber?.receive(.now())
  // 26
  if self.times == .none {
    self.subscriber?.receive(completion: .finished)
  }
}
```

22. Set the **event handler** for your timer. This is a simple closure the timer calls every time it fires. Make sure to keep a weak reference to `self` or the subscription will never deallocate.

23. Verify that there are currently requested values — the publisher could be paused with no current demand, as you'll see later in this chapter when you learn about backpressure.

24. Decrement both counters now that you're going to emit a value.

25. Send a value to the subscriber.

26. If the total number of values to send meets the maximum that the configuration specifies, you can deem the publisher **finished** and emit a completion event!

Activating your timer

Now that you've configured your source timer, store a reference to it and activate it by adding this code *after* `setEventHandler`:

```
self.source = source
source.activate()
```

That was a lot of steps, and it would be easy to inadvertently misplace some code along the way. This code should have cleared all the errors in the playground. If it hasn't, you can double-check your work by reviewing the above steps or by comparing your code with the finished version of the playground in **projects/ Final.playground**.

Last step: Add this extension after the entire definition of `DispatchTimerSubscription`, to define an operator that makes it easy to chain this publisher:

```
extension Publishers {
  static func timer(queue: DispatchQueue? = nil,
                    interval: DispatchTimeInterval,
                    leeway: DispatchTimeInterval
= .nanoseconds(0),
                    times: Subscribers.Demand = .unlimited)
    -> Publishers.DispatchTimer {
    return Publishers.DispatchTimer(
      configuration: .init(queue: queue,
                           interval: interval,
                           leeway: leeway,
                           times: times)
    )
  }
}
```

Testing your timer

You're now ready to test your new timer!

Most parameters of your new `timer` operator, except the `interval`, have a default value to make it easier to use in common use cases. These defaults create a timer that never stops, has minimal leeway and don't specify which queue it wants to emit values on.

Add this code after the extension to test your timer:

```
// 27
var logger = TimeLogger(sinceOrigin: true)
// 28
let publisher = Publishers.timer(interval: .seconds(1),
                                 times: .max(6))
// 29
let subscription = publisher.sink { time in
  print("Timer emits: \(time)", to: &logger)
}
```

27. This playground defines a class, `TimeLogger`, that's very similar to the one you learned to create in Chapter 10, "Debugging." The only difference is this one can display either the time difference between two consecutive values, or the elapsed time since the timer was created. Here, you want to display the time since you started logging.

28. Your timer publisher will fire exactly six times, once every second.

29. Log each value you receive through your `TimeLogger`.

Run the playground and you'll see this nice output — or something similar, since the timing will vary slightly:

```
+1.02668s: Timer emits: DispatchTime(rawValue: 183177446790083)
+2.02508s: Timer emits: DispatchTime(rawValue: 183178445856469)
+3.02603s: Timer emits: DispatchTime(rawValue: 183179446800230)
+4.02509s: Timer emits: DispatchTime(rawValue: 183180445857620)
+5.02613s: Timer emits: DispatchTime(rawValue: 183181446885030)
+6.02617s: Timer emits: DispatchTime(rawValue: 183182446908654)
```

There's a slight offset at setup — and there can also be some added delay coming from Playgrounds — and then the timer fires every second, six times.

You can also test canceling your timer, for example, after a few seconds. Add this code to do so:

```
DispatchQueue.main.asyncAfter(deadline: .now() + 3.5) {
  subscription.cancel()
}
```

Run the playground again. This time, you only see three values. It looks like your timer works just fine!

Although it's barely visible in the Combine API, `Subscription` does the bulk of the work, as you just discovered.

Enjoy your success. You've got another deep dive coming up next!

Publishers transforming values

You've made serious progress in building your Combine skills! You can now develop your own operators, even fairly complex ones. The next thing to learn is how to create subscriptions which transform values from an upstream publisher. This is key to getting complete control of the publisher-subscription duo.

In Chapter 9, "Networking," you learned about how useful sharing a subscription is. When the underlying publisher is performing significant work, like requesting data from the network, you want to **share** the results with multiple subscribers. However, you want to avoid issuing the same request multiple times to retrieve the same data.

It can also be beneficial to **replay** the results to future subscribers if you don't need to perform the work again.

Why not try and implement `shareReplay()`, which can do exactly what you need? This will be an interesting task! To write this operator, you'll create a publisher that does the following:

- Subscribes to the upstream publisher upon the first subscriber.
- Replays the last `N` values to each new subscriber.
- Relays the completion event, if one emitted beforehand.

Beware that this will be far from trivial to implement, but you've definitely got this! You'll take it step by step and, by the end, you'll have a shareReplay() that you can use in your future Combine-driven projects.

Open the **ShareReplay operator** page in the playground to get started.

Implementing a ShareReplay operator

To implement shareReplay() you'll need:

- A type conforming to the Subscription protocol. This is the subscription each subscriber will receive. To make sure you can cope with each subscriber's demands and cancellations, each one will receive a separate subscription.

- A type conforming to the Publisher protocol. You'll implement it as a class because all subscribers want to share the same instance.

Start by adding this code to create your subscription class:

```
// 1
fileprivate final class ShareReplaySubscription<Output, Failure: Error>: Subscription {
  // 2
  let capacity: Int
  // 3
  var subscriber: AnySubscriber<Output,Failure>? = nil
  // 4
  var demand: Subscribers.Demand = .none
  // 5
  var buffer: [Output]
  // 6
  var completion: Subscribers.Completion<Failure>? = nil
}
```

From the top:

1. You use a generic `class`, not a `struct`, to implement the subscription: Both the `Publisher` and the `Subscriber` need to access and mutate the subscription.

2. The replay buffer's maximum capacity will be a constant that you set during initialization.

3. Keeps a reference to the subscriber for the duration of the subscription. Using the type-erased `AnySubscriber` saves you from fighting the type system. :]

4. Tracks the accumulated demands the publisher receives from the subscriber so that you can deliver exactly the requested number of values.

5. Stores pending values in a buffer until they are either delivered to the subscriber or thrown away.

6. This keeps the potential completion event around, so that it's ready to deliver to new subscribers as soon as they begin requesting values.

> **Note**: If you feel that it's unnecessary to keep the completion event around when you'll just deliver it immediately, rest assured that's not the case. The subscriber should receive its subscription *first*, then receive a completion event — if one was previously emitted — as soon as it is ready to accept values. The first `request(_:)` it makes signals this. The publisher doesn't know when this request will happen, so it just hands the completion over to the subscription to deliver it at the right time.

Initializing your subscription

Next, add the initializer to the subscription definition:

```
init<S>(subscriber: S,
        replay: [Output],
        capacity: Int,
        completion: Subscribers.Completion<Failure>?)
    where S: Subscriber,
          Failure == S.Failure,
          Output == S.Input {
  // 7
  self.subscriber = AnySubscriber(subscriber)
  // 8
  self.buffer = replay
  self.capacity = capacity
  self.completion = completion
}
```

This initializer receives several values from the upstream publisher and sets them on this subscription instance. Specifically, it:

7. Stores a type-erased version of the subscriber.

8. Stores the upstream publisher's current buffer, maximum capacity and completion event, if emitted.

Sending completion events and outstanding values to the subscriber

You'll need a method which relays completion events to the subscriber. Add the following to the subscription class to satisfy that need:

```
private func complete(with completion:
Subscribers.Completion<Failure>) {
  // 9
  guard let subscriber = subscriber else { return }
  self.subscriber = nil
  // 10
  self.completion = nil
  self.buffer.removeAll()
  // 11
  subscriber.receive(completion: completion)
}
```

This private method does the following:

9. Keeps the subscriber around for the duration of the method, but sets it to `nil` in the class. This defensive action ensures any call the subscriber may *wrongly* issue upon completion will be ignored.

10. Makes sure that completion is sent only once by *also* setting it to `nil`, then empties the buffer.

11. Relays the completion event to the subscriber.

You'll also need a method that can emit outstanding values to the subscriber. Add this method to emit values as needed:

```
private func emitAsNeeded() {
  guard let subscriber = subscriber else { return }
  // 12
  while self.demand > .none && !buffer.isEmpty {
    // 13
    self.demand -= .max(1)
    // 14
    let nextDemand = subscriber.receive(buffer.removeFirst())
    // 15
    if nextDemand != .none {
      self.demand += nextDemand
    }
  }
  // 16
  if let completion = completion {
    complete(with: completion)
  }
}
```

First, this method ensures there is a subscriber. If there is, the method will:

12. Emit values only if it has some in the buffer and there's an outstanding demand.

13. Decrement the outstanding demand by one.

14. Send the first outstanding value to the subscriber and receive a new demand in return.

15. Add that new demand to the outstanding total demand, but only if it's not `.none`. Otherwise, you'll get a crash, because Combine doesn't treat `Subscribers.Demand.none` as zero and adding or subtracting `.none` will trigger an exception.

16. If a completion event is pending, send it now.

Things are shaping up! Now, implement `Subscription`'s all-important requirement:

```
func request(_ demand: Subscribers.Demand) {
  if demand != .none {
    self.demand += demand
  }
  emitAsNeeded()
}
```

That was an easy one. Remember to check for `.none` to avoid crashes — and to keep an eye out to see future versions of Combine fix this issue — and then proceed emitting.

> **Note**: calling `emitAsNeeded()` even if the demand is `.none` guarantees that you properly relay a completion event that has already occurred.

Canceling your subscription

Canceling the subscription is even easier. Add this code:

```
func cancel() {
  complete(with: .finished)
}
```

As with a subscriber, you'll need to implement both methods that accept values and a completion event. Start by adding this method to accept values:

```
func receive(_ input: Output) {
  guard subscriber != nil else { return }
  // 17
  buffer.append(input)
  if buffer.count > capacity {
    // 18
    buffer.removeFirst()
  }
  // 19
  emitAsNeeded()
}
```

After ensuring there is a subscriber, this method will:

17. Add the value to the outstanding buffer. You could optimize this for most common cases, such as unlimited demands, but this will do the job perfectly for now.

18. Make sure not to buffer more values than the requested capacity. You handle this on a rolling, first-in-first-out basis – as an already-full buffer receives each new value, the current first value is removed.

19. Deliver the results to the subscriber.

Wrapping up your subscription

Now, add the following method to accept completion events and your subscription class will be complete:

```
func receive(completion: Subscribers.Completion<Failure>) {
    guard let subscriber = subscriber else { return }
    self.subscriber = nil
    self.buffer.removeAll()
    subscriber.receive(completion: completion)
}
```

This method removes the subscriber, empties the buffer – because that's just good memory management – and sends the completion downstream.

You're done with the subscription! Isn't this fun? Now, it's time to code the publisher.

Coding your publisher

Publishers are usually value types (struct) in the Publishers namespace. Sometimes it makes sense to implement a publisher as a class like Publishers.Multicast, which multicast() returns, or Publishers.Share which share() returns. For this publisher, you'll need a class, similarly to share(). This is the exception to the rule, though, as most often you'll use a struct.

Start by adding this code to define your publisher class *after* your subscription:

```
extension Publishers {
  // 20
  final class ShareReplay<Upstream: Publisher>: Publisher {
    // 21
    typealias Output = Upstream.Output
    typealias Failure = Upstream.Failure
  }
}
```

20. You want multiple subscribers to be able to share a single instance of this operator, so you use a `class` instead of a `struct`. It's also generic, with the final type of the upstream publisher as a parameter.

21. This new publisher doesn't change the output or failure types of the upstream publisher – it simply uses the upstream's types.

Adding the publisher's required properties

Now, add the properties your publisher will need to the definition of `ShareReplay`:

```
// 22
private let lock = NSRecursiveLock()
// 23
private let upstream: Upstream
// 24
private let capacity: Int
// 25
private var replay = [Output]()
// 26
private var subscriptions = [ShareReplaySubscription<Output, Failure>]()
// 27
private var completion: Subscribers.Completion<Failure>? = nil
```

What this code does:

22. Because you're going to be feeding multiple subscribers at the same time, you'll need a lock to guarantee exclusive access to your mutable variables.

23. Keeps a reference to the upstream publisher. You'll need it at various points in the subscription lifecycle.

24. You specify the maximum recording capacity of your replay buffer during initialization.

25. Naturally, you'll also need storage for the values you record.

26. You feed multiple subscribers, so you'll need to keep them around to notify them of events. Each subscriber gets its values from a dedicated `ShareReplaySubscription` — you're going to code this in a short while.

27. The operator can **replay** values even after completion, so you need to remember whether the upstream publisher completed.

Phew! By the look of it, there's some more code to write! In the end, you'll see it's not that much, but there is housekeeping to do, like using proper locking, so that your operator will run smoothly under all conditions.

Initializing and relaying values to your publisher

Firstly, add the necessary initializer to your `ShareReplay` publisher:

```
init(upstream: Upstream, capacity: Int) {
  self.upstream = upstream
  self.capacity = capacity
}
```

Nothing fancy here, just storing the upstream publisher and the capacity. Next, you'll add a couple of methods to help split the code into smaller chunks.

Add the method that relays incoming values from upstream to subscribers:

```
private func relay(_ value: Output) {
  // 28
  lock.lock()
  defer { lock.unlock() }

  // 29
  guard completion == nil else { return }

  // 30
  replay.append(value)
  if replay.count > capacity {
    replay.removeFirst()
  }
  // 31
  subscriptions.forEach {
    $0.receive(value)
  }
}
```

This code does the following:

28. Since multiple subscribers share this publisher, you must protect access to mutable variables with locks. Using `defer` here is not strictly needed, but it's good practice just in case you later modify the method, add an early `return` statement and forget to unlock your lock.

29. Only relays values if the upstream hasn't completed yet.

30. Adds the value to the rolling buffer and only keeps the latest values of `capacity`. These are the ones to replay to new subscribers.

31. Relays the buffered values to each connected subscriber.

Letting your publisher know when it's done

Secondly, add this method to handle completion events:

```
private func complete(_ completion:
Subscribers.Completion<Failure>) {
  lock.lock()
  defer { lock.unlock() }
  // 32
  self.completion = completion
  // 33
  subscriptions.forEach {
    $0.receive(completion: completion)
  }
}
```

With this code, you're:

32. Saving the completion event for future subscribers.

33. Relaying it to each connected subscriber.

You are now ready to start coding the **receive** method that every publisher must implement. This method will receive a subscriber. Its duty is to create a new subscription and then hand it over to the subscriber.

Add this code to begin defining this method:

```
func receive<S: Subscriber>(subscriber: S)
  where Failure == S.Failure,
        Output == S.Input {
  lock.lock()
  defer { lock.unlock() }
}
```

This standard prototype for `receive(subscriber:)` specifies that the subscriber, whatever it is, must have `Input` and `Failure` types that match the publisher's `Output` and `Failure` types. Remember this from Chapter 2, "Publishers & Subscribers?"

Creating your subscription

Next, add this code to the method to create the subscription and hand it over to the subscriber:

```
// 34
let subscription = ShareReplaySubscription(
  subscriber: subscriber,
  replay: replay,
  capacity: capacity,
  completion: completion)

// 35
subscriptions.append(subscription)
// 36
subscriber.receive(subscription: subscription)
```

34. The new subscription references the subscriber and receives the current replay buffer, the capacity, and any outstanding completion event.

35. You keep the subscription around to pass future events to it.

36. You send the subscription to the subscriber, which may — either now or later — start requesting values.

Subscribing to the upstream publisher and handling its inputs

You are now ready to subscribe to the upstream publisher. You only need to do it once: When you receive your first subscriber.

Add this code to `receive(subscriber:)` – note that you are intentionally not including the closing } because there's more code to add:

```
// 37
guard subscriptions.count == 1 else { return }

let sink = AnySubscriber(
  // 38
  receiveSubscription: { subscription in
    subscription.request(.unlimited)
  },
  // 39
  receiveValue: { [weak self] (value: Output) ->
Subscribers.Demand in
    self?.relay(value)
    return .none
  },
  // 40
  receiveCompletion: { [weak self] in
    self?.complete($0)
  }
)
```

With this code you:

37. Subscribe only once to the upstream publisher.

38. Use the handy `AnySubscriber` class which takes closures, and immediately request `.unlimited` values upon subscription to let the publisher run to completion.

39. Relay values you receive to downstream subscribers.

40. Complete your publisher with the completion event you get from upstream.

> **Note**: You could initially request `.max(self.capacity)` and receive just that, but remember that Combine is demand-driven! If you don't request as many values as the publisher is capable of producing, you may never get a completion event!

To avoid retain cycles, you only keep a weak reference to `self`.

You're nearly done! Now, all you need to do is subscribe `AnySubscriber` to the upstream publisher.

Finish off the definition of this method by adding this code:

```
upstream.subscribe(sink)
```

Once again, all errors in the playground should be clear now. Remember that you can double-check your work by comparing it with the finished version of the playground in **projects/final**.

Adding a convenience operator

Your publisher is complete! Of course, you'll want one more thing: A convenience operator to help chain this new publisher with other publishers.

Add it as an extension to the `Publishers` namespace at the end of your playground:

```
extension Publisher {
  func shareReplay(capacity: Int = .max)
    -> Publishers.ShareReplay<Self> {
    return Publishers.ShareReplay(upstream: self,
                                  capacity: capacity)
  }
}
```

You now have a fully functional `shareReplay(capacity:)` operator. This was a lot of code, and now it's time to try it out!

Testing your subscription

Add this code to the end of your playground to test your new operator:

```
// 41
var logger = TimeLogger(sinceOrigin: true)
// 42
let subject = PassthroughSubject<Int,Never>()
// 43
let publisher = subject.shareReplay(capacity: 2)
// 44
subject.send(0)
```

Here's what this code does:

41. Use the handy `TimeLogger` object defined in this playground.

42. To simulate sending values at different times, you use a subject.

43. Share the subject and replay the last two values only.

44. Send an initial value through the subject. No subscriber has connected to the shared publisher, so you shouldn't see any output.

Now, create your first subscription and send some more values:

```
let subscription1 = publisher.sink(
  receiveCompletion: {
    print("subscription1 completed: \($0)", to: &logger)
  },
  receiveValue: {
    print("subscription1 received \($0)", to: &logger)
  }
)

subject.send(1)
subject.send(2)
subject.send(3)
```

Next, create a second subscription and send a couple more values and then a completion event:

```
let subscription2 = publisher.sink(
  receiveCompletion: {
    print("subscription2 completed: \($0)", to: &logger)
  },
  receiveValue: {
    print("subscription2 received \($0)", to: &logger)
  }
)

subject.send(4)
subject.send(5)
subject.send(completion: .finished)
```

These two subscriptions display every event they receive, along with the time that's elapsed since start.

Add one more subscription with a small delay to make sure it occurs after the publisher has completed:

```
var subscription3: Cancellable? = nil

DispatchQueue.main.asyncAfter(deadline: .now() + 1) {
  print("Subscribing to shareReplay after upstream completed")
  subscription3 = publisher.sink(
    receiveCompletion: {
      print("subscription3 completed: \($0)", to: &logger)
    },
    receiveValue: {
      print("subscription3 received \($0)", to: &logger)
    }
  )
}
```

Remember that a subscription terminates when it's deallocated, so you'll want to use a variable to keep the deferred one around. The one-second delay demonstrates how the publisher replays data in the future. You're ready to test! Run the playground to see the following results in the debug console:

```
+0.02967s: subscription1 received 1
+0.03092s: subscription1 received 2
+0.03189s: subscription1 received 3
+0.03309s: subscription2 received 2
+0.03317s: subscription2 received 3
+0.03371s: subscription1 received 4
+0.03401s: subscription2 received 4
+0.03515s: subscription1 received 5
+0.03548s: subscription2 received 5
+0.03716s: subscription1 completed: finished
+0.03746s: subscription2 completed: finished
Subscribing to shareReplay after upstream completed
+1.12007s: subscription3 received 4
+1.12015s: subscription3 received 5
+1.12057s: subscription3 completed: finished
```

Your new operator is working beautifully:

- The 0 value never appears in the logs, because it was emitted **before** the first subscriber subscribed to the shared publisher.

- Every value propagates to current and future subscribers.

- You created `subscription2` after three values have passed through the subject, so it only sees the last two (values 2 and 3)

- You created `subscription3` after the subject has completed, but the subscription still received the last two values that the subject emitted.

- The completion event propagates correctly, even if the subscriber comes after the shared publisher has completed.

Verifying your subscription

Fantastic! This works exactly as you wanted. Or does it? How can you verify that the publisher is being subscribed to only once? By using the `print(_:)` operator, of course! You can try it by inserting it before `shareReplay`.

Find this code:

```
let publisher = subject.shareReplay(capacity: 2)
```

And change it to:

```
let publisher = subject
  .print("shareReplay")
  .shareReplay(capacity: 2)
```

Run the playground again and it will yield this output:

```
shareReplay: receive subscription: (PassthroughSubject)
shareReplay: request unlimited
shareReplay: receive value: (1)
+0.03004s: subscription1 received 1
shareReplay: receive value: (2)
+0.03146s: subscription1 received 2
shareReplay: receive value: (3)
+0.03239s: subscription1 received 3
+0.03364s: subscription2 received 2
+0.03374s: subscription2 received 3
shareReplay: receive value: (4)
+0.03439s: subscription1 received 4
+0.03471s: subscription2 received 4
```

```
shareReplay: receive value: (5)
+0.03577s: subscription1 received 5
+0.03609s: subscription2 received 5
shareReplay: receive finished
+0.03759s: subscription1 received completion: finished
+0.03788s: subscription2 received completion: finished
Subscribing to shareReplay after upstream completed
+1.11936s: subscription3 received 4
+1.11945s: subscription3 received 5
+1.11985s: subscription3 received completion: finished
```

All the lines beginning with **shareReplay** are logs showing what happens with the original subject. Now you are sure that it's performing the work only once and sharing the results with all current and future subscribers. Job very well done!

This chapter taught you several techniques to create your own publishers. It's been long and complex, as there was quite some code to write. You're nearly done now, but there's one last topic you'll want to learn about before moving on.

Handling backpressure

In fluid dynamics, backpressure is *a resistance or force opposing the desired flow of fluid through pipes*. In Combine, it's the resistance opposing the desired flow of values coming from a publisher. But what is this resistance? Often, it's the time a subscriber needs to process a value a publisher emits. Some examples are:

- Processing high-frequency data, like input from sensors.
- Performing large file transfers.
- Rendering complex UI upon data update.
- Waiting for user input.
- More generally, processing incoming data that the subscriber can't keep up with at the rate it's coming in.

The publisher-subscriber mechanism offered by Combine is flexible. It is a **pull** design, as opposed to a **push** one. It means that subscribers ask publishers to emit values and specify how many they want to receive. This request mechanism is adaptive: The demand updates every time the subscriber receives a new value. This allows subscribers to deal with backpressure by "closing the tap" when they don't want to receive more data, and "opening it" later when they are ready for more.

> **Note**: Remember, you can only adjust demand in an additive way. You can *increase* demand each time the subscriber receives a new value, by returning a new `.max(N)` or `.unlimited`. Or you can return `.none`, which indicates that the demand should not increase. However, the subscriber is then "on the hook" to receive values at least up to the new max demand. For example, if the previous max demand was to receive three values and the subscriber has only received one, returning `.none` in the subscriber's `receive(_:)` will not "close the tap." The subscriber will still receive at most two values when the publisher is ready to emit them.

What happens when more values are available is totally up to your design. You can:

- **Control** the flow by managing demand to prevent the publisher from sending more values than you can handle.
- **Buffer** values until you can handle them — with the risk of exhausting available memory.
- **Drop** values you can't handle right away.
- Some combination of the above, according to your requirements.

Going through all possible combinations and implementations could take several chapters. In addition to the above, dealing with backpressure can take the form of:

- A publisher with a custom `Subscription` dealing with congestion.
- A subscriber delivering values at the end of a chain of publishers.

In this introduction to backpressure management, you'll focus on implementing the latter. You're going to create a pausable variant of the `sink` function, which you already know well.

Using a pausable sink to handle backpressure

To get started, switch to the **PausableSink** page of the playground.

As a first step, create a protocol that lets you resume from a pause:

```
protocol Pausable {
  var paused: Bool { get }
  func resume()
}
```

You don't need a `pause()` method here, since you'll determine whether or not to pause when you receive each value. Of course, a more elaborate pausable subscriber could have a `pause()` method you can call at any time! For now, you'll keep the code as simple and straightforward as possible.

Next, add this code to start defining the pausable `Subscriber`:

```
// 1
final class PausableSubscriber<Input, Failure: Error>:
  Subscriber, Pausable, Cancellable {
  // 2
  let combineIdentifier = CombineIdentifier()
}
```

1. Your pausable subscriber is both `Pausable` and `Cancellable`. This is the object your `pausableSink` function will return. This is also why you implement it as a class and not as a struct: You don't want an object to be copied, and you need mutability at certain points in its lifetime.

2. A subscriber must provide a unique identifier for Combine to manage and optimize its publisher streams.

Now add these additional properties:

```
// 3
let receiveValue: (Input) -> Bool
// 4
let receiveCompletion: (Subscribers.Completion<Failure>) -> Void
// 5
private var subscription: Subscription? = nil
// 6
var paused = false
```

3. The `receiveValue` closure returns a `Bool`: `true` indicates that it may receive more values and `false` indicates the subscription should pause.

4. The completion closure will be called upon receiving a completion event from the publisher.

5. Keep the subscription around so that it can request more values after a pause. You need to set this property to `nil` when you don't need it anymore to avoid a retain cycle.

6. You expose the `paused` property as per the `Pausable` protocol.

Next, add the following code to `PausableSubscriber` to implement the initializer and to conform to the `Cancellable` protocol:

```
// 7
init(receiveValue: @escaping (Input) -> Bool,
     receiveCompletion: @escaping
    (Subscribers.Completion<Failure>) -> Void) {
  self.receiveValue = receiveValue
  self.receiveCompletion = receiveCompletion
}

// 8
func cancel() {
  subscription?.cancel()
  subscription = nil
}
```

7. The initializer accepts two closures, which the subscriber will call upon receiving a new value from the publisher and upon completion. The closures are like the ones you use with the `sink` function, with one exception: The `receiveValue` closure returns a Boolean to indicate whether the receiver is ready to take more values or whether you need to put the subscriptions on hold.

8. When canceling the subscription, don't forget to set it to `nil` afterwards to avoid retain cycles.

Now add this code to satisfy `Subscriber`'s requirements:

```
func receive(subscription: Subscription) {
  // 9
  self.subscription = subscription
  // 10
  subscription.request(.max(1))
}

func receive(_ input: Input) -> Subscribers.Demand {
  // 11
  paused = receiveValue(input) == false
  // 12
  return paused ? .none : .max(1)
```

```
}
func receive(completion: Subscribers.Completion<Failure>) {
  // 13
  receiveCompletion(completion)
  subscription = nil
}
```

9. Upon receiving the subscription created by the publisher, store it for later so that you'll be able to resume from a pause.

10. Immediately request one value. Your subscriber is pausable and you can't predict when a pause will be needed. The strategy here is to request values one by one.

11. When receiving a new value, call `receiveValue` and update the `paused` status accordingly.

12. If the subscriber is paused, returning `.none` indicates that you don't want more values right now — remember, you initially requested only one. Otherwise, request one more value to keep the cycle going.

13. Upon receiving a completion event, forward it to `receiveCompletion` then set the subscription to `nil` since you don't need it anymore.

Finally, implement the rest of `Pausable`:

```
func resume() {
  guard paused else { return }

  paused = false
  // 14
  subscription?.request(.max(1))
}
```

14. If the publisher is "paused", request one value to start the cycle again.

Just as you did with previous publishers, you can now expose your new pausable sink in the `Publishers` namespace.

Add this code at the end of your playground:

```
extension Publisher {
  // 15
  func pausableSink(
    receiveCompletion: @escaping
((Subscribers.Completion<Failure>) -> Void),
    receiveValue: @escaping ((Output) -> Bool))
    -> Pausable & Cancellable {
```

```
    // 16
    let pausable = PausableSubscriber(
      receiveValue: receiveValue,
      receiveCompletion: receiveCompletion)
    self.subscribe(pausable)
    // 17
    return pausable
  }
}
```

15. Your `pausableSink` operator is very close to the `sink` operator. The only difference is the return type for the `receiveValue` closure: `Bool`.

16. Instantiate a new `PausableSubscriber` and subscribe it to `self`, the publisher.

17. The subscriber is the object you'll use to resume and cancel the subscription.

Testing your new sink

You can now try your new sink! To make things simple, simulate cases where the publisher should stop sending values. Add this code:

```
let subscription = [1, 2, 3, 4, 5, 6]
  .publisher
  .pausableSink(receiveCompletion: { completion in
    print("Pausable subscription completed: \(completion)")
  }) { value -> Bool in
    print("Receive value: \(value)")
    if value % 2 == 1 {
      print("Pausing")
      return false
    }
    return true
  }
```

An array's publisher usually emits all its values sequentially, one right after the other. Using your pausable sink, this publisher will pause when values 1, 3 and 5 are received.

Run the playground and you'll see:

```
Receive value: 1
Pausing
```

To resume the publisher, you need to call `resume()` asynchronously. This is easy to do with a timer. Add this code to set up a timer:

```
let timer = Timer.publish(every: 1, on: .main, in: .common)
  .autoconnect()
  .sink { _ in
    guard subscription.paused else { return }
    print("Subscription is paused, resuming")
    subscription.resume()
  }
```

Run the playground again and you'll see the pause/resume mechanism in action:

```
Receive value: 1
Pausing
Subscription is paused, resuming
Receive value: 2
Receive value: 3
Pausing
Subscription is paused, resuming
Receive value: 4
Receive value: 5
Pausing
Subscription is paused, resuming
Receive value: 6
Pausable subscription completed: finished
```

Congratulations! You now have a functional pausable sink and you've gotten a glimpse into handling backpressure in your code!

> **Note**: What if your publisher can't hold values and wait for the subscriber to request them? In this situation, you'd want to buffer values using the `buffer(size:prefetch:whenFull:)` operator. This operator can buffer values up to the capacity you indicate in the `size` parameter and deliver them when the subscriber is ready to receive them. The other parameters determine how the buffer fills up – either at once when subscribing, keeping the buffer full, or upon request from its subscriber – and what happens when the buffer is full – i.e., drop the last value(s) it received, drop the oldest one(s) or terminate with an error.

Key points

Wow, this was a long and complex chapter! You learned a lot about publishers:

- A publisher can be a simple method that leverages other publishers for convenience.
- Writing a custom publisher usually involves creating an accompanying `Subscription`.
- The `Subscription` is the real link between a `Subscriber` and a `Publisher`.
- In most cases, the `Subscription` is the one that does all the work.
- A `Subscriber` can control the delivery of values by adjusting its `Demand`.
- The `Subscription` is responsible for respecting the subscriber's `Demand`. Combine does not enforce it, but you definitely *should* respect it as a good citizen of the Combine ecosystem.

Where to go from here?

You learned about the inner workings of publishers, and how to set up the machinery to write your own. Of course, any code you write — and publishers in particular! — should be thoroughly tested. Move on to the next chapter to learn all about testing Combine code!

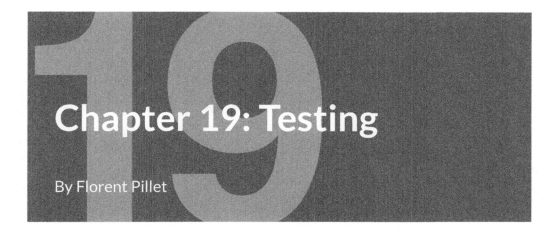

Chapter 19: Testing

By Florent Pillet

Studies show that there are two reasons why developers skip writing tests:

1. They write bug-free code.

2. Are you still reading this?

If you *cannot* say with a straight face that you always write bug-free code — and presuming you answered *yes* to number two — this chapter is for you. Thanks for sticking around!

Writing tests is a great way to ensure intended functionality in your app as you are developing new features and *especially* after the fact, to ensure your latest work did not introduce a regression in some previous code that worked fine.

This chapter will introduce you to writing unit tests against your Combine code, and you'll have some fun along the way. You'll write tests against this handy app:

ColorCalc was developed using Combine and SwiftUI. It's got some issues though. If it only had some decent unit tests to help find and fix those issues. Good thing you're here!

Getting started

Open the starter project for this chapter in the **projects/starter** folder. This is designed to give you the red, green, blue, and opacity — aka *alpha* — values for the hex color code you enter in. It will also adjust the background color to match the current hex if possible and give the color's name if available. If a color cannot be derived from the currently entered hex value, the background will be set to white instead. This is what it's designed to do. But something is rotten in the state of Denmark — or more like some *things*.

Fortunately, you've got a thorough QA team that takes their time to find and document issues. It's your job to streamline the development-QA process by not only fixing these issues but also writing some tests to verify correct functionality after the fix. Run the app and confirm the following issues reported by your QA team:

Issue 1

- Action: Launch the app.
- Expected: The name label should display **aqua**.
- Actual: The name label displays **Optional(ColorCalc.ColorNam…**.

Issue 2

- Action: Tap the ← button.
- Expected: The last character is removed in the hex display.
- Actual: The last *two* characters are removed.

Issue 3

- Action: Tap the ← button.
- Expected: The background turns white.
- Actual: The background turns red.

Issue 4

- Action: Tap the ⊗ button.
- Expected: The hex value display clears to #.
- Actual: The hex value display does not change.

Issue 5

- Action: Enter hex value **006636**.
- Expected: The red-green-blue-opacity display shows 0, 102, 54, 255.
- Actual: The red-green-blue-opacity display shows 0, 62, 32, 155.

You'll get to the work on writing tests and fixing these issues shortly, but first, you'll learn about testing Combine code by — wait for it — testing Combine's *actual* code! Specifically, you'll test a few operators.

> **Note**: The chapter presumes you have some familiarity with unit testing in iOS. If not, you can still follow along, and everything will work fine. However, this chapter will not delve into the details of test-driven development — aka TDD. If you are seeking to gain a more in-depth understanding of this topic, check out iOS Test-Driven Development by Tutorials (https://bit.ly/3m88EwF) from the raywenderlich.com library.

Testing Combine operators

Throughout this chapter, you'll employ the **Given-When-Then** pattern to organize your test logic:

- **Given** a condition.
- **When** an action is performed.
- **Then** an expected result occurs.

Still in the **ColorCalc** project, open **ColorCalcTests/CombineOperatorsTests.swift**.

To start things off, add a `subscriptions` property to store subscriptions in, and set it to an empty array in `tearDown()`. Your code should look like this:

```
var subscriptions = Set<AnyCancellable>()

override func tearDown() {
  subscriptions = []
}
```

Testing collect()

Your first test will be for the `collect` operator. Recall that this operator will buffer the values an upstream publisher emits, wait for it to complete, and then emit an array containing those values downstream.

Employing the **Given — When — Then** pattern, begin a new test method by adding this code below `tearDown()`:

```
func test_collect() {
  // Given
  let values = [0, 1, 2]
  let publisher = values.publisher
}
```

With this code, you create an array of integers, and then a publisher from that array.

Now, add this code to the test:

```
// When
publisher
  .collect()
  .sink(receiveValue: {
    // Then
    XCTAssert(
      $0 == values,
      "Result was expected to be \(values) but was \($0)"
    )
  })
  .store(in: &subscriptions)
```

Here, you use the `collect` operator and then subscribe to its output, asserting that the output equals the values — and store the subscription.

You can run unit tests in Xcode in several ways:

1. To run a single test, click the diamond next to the method definition.

2. To run all the tests in a single test class, click the diamond next to the class definition.

3. To run all the tests in all test targets in a project, press **Command-U**. Keep in mind that each test target may contain multiple test classes, each potentially containing multiple tests.

4. You can also use the **Product ▸ Perform Action ▸ Run "*TestClassName*"** menu — which also has its own keyboard shortcut: **Command-Control-Option-U**.

Run this test by clicking the diamond next to test_collect(). The project will build and run in the simulator briefly while it executes the test, and then report if it succeeded or failed.

As expected, the test will pass and you'll see the following:

The diamond next to the test definition will also turn green and contain a checkmark.

You can also show the Console via the **View ▸ Debug Area ▸ Activate Console** menu item or by pressing **Command-Shift-Y** to see details about the test results (results truncated here):

```
Test Suite 'Selected tests' passed at 2021-08-25 00:44:59.629.
     Executed 1 test, with 0 failures (0 unexpected) in 0.003
(0.007) seconds
```

To verify that this test is working correctly, change the assertion code to:

```
XCTAssert(
  $0 == values + [1],
  "Result was expected to be \(values + [1]) but was \($0)"
)
```

You added a 1 to the values array being compared to the array emitted by collect(), and to the interpolated value in the message.

Rerun the test, and you'll see it fails, along with the message Result was expected to be [0, 1, 2, 1] but was [0, 1, 2]. You may need to click on the error to expand and see the full message or show the Console, and the full message will also print there.

Undo that last set of changes before moving on, and re-run the test to ensure it passes.

> **Note**: In the interest of time *and* space, this chapter will focus on writing tests that test for positive conditions. However, you are encouraged to experiment by testing for negative results along the way if you're interested. Just remember to return the test to the original passing state before continuing.

This was a fairly simple test. The next example will test a more intricate operator.

Testing flatMap(maxPublishers:)

As you learned in Chapter 3, "Transforming Operators," the `flatMap` operator can be used to flatten multiple upstream publishers into a single publisher, and you can optionally specify the maximum number of publishers it will receive and flatten.

Add a new test method for `flatMap` by adding this code:

```
func test_flatMapWithMax2Publishers() {
  // Given
  // 1
  let intSubject1 = PassthroughSubject<Int, Never>()
  let intSubject2 = PassthroughSubject<Int, Never>()
  let intSubject3 = PassthroughSubject<Int, Never>()

  // 2
  let publisher = CurrentValueSubject<PassthroughSubject<Int, Never>, Never>(intSubject1)

  // 3
  let expected = [1, 2, 4]
  var results = [Int]()

  // 4
  publisher
    .flatMap(maxPublishers: .max(2)) { $0 }
    .sink(receiveValue: {
      results.append($0)
    })
    .store(in: &subscriptions)
}
```

You start this test by creating:

1. Three instances of a passthrough subject expecting integer values.

2. A current value subject that *itself* accepts and publishes integer passthrough subjects, initialized with the first integer subject.

3. Expected results and an array to hold actual results received.

4. A subscription to the publisher, using `flatMap` with a max of two publishers. In the handler, you append each value received to the results array.

That takes care of **Given**. Now add this code to your test to create the action:

```
// When
// 5
intSubject1.send(1)

// 6
publisher.send(intSubject2)
intSubject2.send(2)

// 7
publisher.send(intSubject3)
intSubject3.send(3)
intSubject2.send(4)

// 8
publisher.send(completion: .finished)
```

Because the publisher is a current value subject, it will replay the current value to new subscribers. So with the above code, you continue that publisher's work and:

5. Send a new value to the first integer publisher.

6. Send the second integer subject through the current value subject and then send that subject a new value.

7. Repeat the previous step for the third integer subject, except passing it two values this time.

8. Send a completion event through the current value subject.

All that's left to complete this test is to assert these actions will produce the expected results. Add this code to create this assertion:

```
// Then
XCTAssert(
  results == expected,
  "Results expected to be \(expected) but were \(results)"
)
```

Run the test by clicking the diamond next to its definition and you will see it passes with flying colors!

If you have previous experience with reactive programming, you may be familiar with using a test scheduler, which is a virtual time scheduler that gives you granular control over testing time-based operations.

At the time of this writing, Combine does not include a formal test scheduler. An open-source test scheduler called Entwine (https://github.com/tcldr/Entwine) is already available though, and it's worth a look if a formal test scheduler is what you seek.

However, *given* that this book is focused on using Apple's native Combine framework, *when* you want to test Combine code, *then* you can definitely use the built-in capabilities of XCTest. This will be demonstrated in your next test.

Testing publish(every:on:in:)

In this next example, the system under test will be a `Timer` publisher.

As you might remember from Chapter 11, "Timers," this publisher can be used to create a repeating timer without a lot of boilerplate setup code. To test this, you will use XCTest's expectation APIs to wait for asynchronous operations to complete.

Start a new test by adding this code:

```
func test_timerPublish() {
  // Given
  // 1
  func normalized(_ ti: TimeInterval) -> TimeInterval {
    return Double(round(ti * 10) / 10)
  }

  // 2
  let now = Date().timeIntervalSinceReferenceDate
  // 3
  let expectation = self.expectation(description: #function)
  // 4
```

```
    let expected = [0.5, 1, 1.5]
    var results = [TimeInterval]()
    
    // 5
    let publisher = Timer
      .publish(every: 0.5, on: .main, in: .common)
      .autoconnect()
      .prefix(3)
}
```

In this setup code, you:

1. Define a helper function to normalize time intervals by rounding to one decimal place.
2. Store the current time interval.
3. Create an expectation that you will use to wait for an asynchronous operation to complete.
4. Define the expected results and an array to store actual results.
5. Create a timer publisher that auto-connects, and only take the first three values it emits. Refer back to Chapter 11, "Timers" for a refresher on the details of this operator.

Next, add this code to test this publisher:

```
// When
publisher
  .sink(
    receiveCompletion: { _ in expectation.fulfill() },
    receiveValue: {
      results.append(
        normalized($0.timeIntervalSinceReferenceDate - now)
      )
    }
  )
  .store(in: &subscriptions)
```

In the subscription handler above, you use the helper function to get a normalized version of each of the emitted dates' time intervals and append then to the results array.

With that done, it's time to wait for the publisher to do its work and complete and then do your verification.

Add this code to do so:

```
// Then
// 6
waitForExpectations(timeout: 2, handler: nil)

// 7
XCTAssert(
  results == expected,
  "Results expected to be \(expected) but were \(results)"
)
```

Here you:

6. Wait for a maximum of 2 seconds.

7. Assert that the actual results are equal to the expected results.

Run the test, and you'll get another pass — +1 for the Combine team at Apple, everything here is working as advertised!

Speaking of which, so far you've tested operators built-in to Combine. Why not test a custom operator, such as the one you created in Chapter 18, "Custom Publishers & Handling Backpressure?"

Testing shareReplay(capacity:)

This operator provides a commonly-needed capability: To share a publisher's output with multiple subscribers while also replaying a buffer of the last N values to new subscribers. This operator takes a `capacity` parameter that specifies the size of the rolling buffer. Once again, refer back to Chapter 18, "Custom Publishers & Handling Backpressure" for additional details about this operator.

You'll test both the *share* and *replay* components of this operator in the next test. Add this code to get started:

```
func test_shareReplay() {
  // Given
  // 1
  let subject = PassthroughSubject<Int, Never>()
  // 2
  let publisher = subject.shareReplay(capacity: 2)
  // 3
  let expected = [0, 1, 2, 1, 2, 3, 3]
  var results = [Int]()
}
```

Similar to previous tests, you:

1. Create a subject to send new integer values to.
2. Create a publisher from that subject, using `shareReplay` with a capacity of two.
3. Define the expected results and, create an array to store the actual output.

Next, add this code to trigger the actions that should produce the expected output:

```
// When
// 4
publisher
    .sink(receiveValue: { results.append($0) })
    .store(in: &subscriptions)

// 5
subject.send(0)
subject.send(1)
subject.send(2)

// 6
publisher
    .sink(receiveValue: { results.append($0) })
    .store(in: &subscriptions)

// 7
subject.send(3)
```

From the top, you:

4. Create a subscription to the publisher and store any emitted values.
5. Send some values through the subject that the publisher is share-replaying.
6. Create another subscription and also store any emitted values.
7. Send one more value through the subject.

With that done, all that's left is to make sure this operator is up-to-snuff is create an assertion. Add this code to wrap up this test:

```
XCTAssert(
    results == expected,
    "Results expected to be \(expected) but were \(results)"
)
```

This is the same assertion code as the previous two tests.

Run this test and *voilà*, you have a bonafide member worthy of use in your Combine-driven projects!

By learning how to test this small variety of Combine operators, you've picked up the skills necessary to test almost anything Combine can throw at you. In the next section, you'll put these skills to practice by testing the ColorCalc app you saw earlier.

Testing production code

At the beginning of the chapter, you observed several issues with the ColorCalc app. It's now time to do something about it.

The project is organized using the MVVM pattern, and all the logic you'll need to test and fix is contained in the app's only view model: `CalculatorViewModel`.

> **Note**: Apps can have issues in other areas such as SwiftUI `View` files, however, UI testing is not the focus of this chapter. If you find yourself needing to write *unit* tests against your UI code, it could be a sign that your code should be reorganized to separate responsibilities. MVVM is a useful architectural design pattern for this purpose. If you'd like to learn more about MVVM with Combine, check out the tutorial MVVM with Combine Tutorial for iOS (https://bit.ly/2kgGVxF).

Open **ColorCalcTests/ColorCalcTests.swift**, and add the following two properties at the top of the `ColorCalcTests` class definition:

```
var viewModel: CalculatorViewModel!
var subscriptions = Set<AnyCancellable>()
```

You'll reset both properties' values for every test, `viewModel` right before and `subscriptions` right after each test. Change the `setUp()` and `tearDown()` methods to look like this:

```
override func setUp() {
  viewModel = CalculatorViewModel()
}

override func tearDown() {
  subscriptions = []
}
```

Issue 1: Incorrect name displayed

With that setup code in place, you can now write your first test against the view model. Add this code:

```
func test_correctNameReceived() {
  // Given
  // 1
  let expected = "rwGreen 66%"
  var result = ""

  // 2
  viewModel.$name
    .sink(receiveValue: { result = $0 })
    .store(in: &subscriptions)

  // When
  // 3
  viewModel.hexText = "006636AA"

  // Then
  // 4
  XCTAssert(
    result == expected,
    "Name expected to be \(expected) but was \(result)"
  )
}
```

Here's what you did:

1. Store the expected name label text for this test.

2. Subscribe to the view model's $name publisher and save the received value.

3. Perform the action that should trigger the expected result.

4. Assert that the actual result equals the expected one.

Run this test, and it will fail with this message: `Name expected to be rwGreen 66% but was Optional(ColorCalc.ColorName.rwGreen)66%`. Ah, the `Optional` bug bites once again!

Open **View Models/CalculatorViewModel.swift**. At the bottom of the class definition is a method called `configure()`. This method is called in the initializer, and it's where all the view model's subscriptions are set up. First, a `hexTextShared` publisher is created to, well, share the `hexText` publisher.

How's that for self-documenting code? Right after that is the subscription that sets name:

```
hexTextShared
  .map {
    let name = ColorName(hex: $0)

    if name != nil {
      return String(describing: name) +
        String(describing: Color.opacityString(forHex: $0))
    } else {
      return "-----------"
    }
  }
  .assign(to: &$name)
```

Review that code. Do you see what's wrong? Instead of just *checking* that the local name instance of `ColorName` is not `nil`, it should use optional binding to unwrap non-`nil` values.

Change the entire map block of code to the following:

```
.map {
  if let name = ColorName(hex: $0) {
    return "\(name) \(Color.opacityString(forHex: $0))"
  } else {
    return "-----------"
  }
}
```

Now return to **ColorCalcTests/ColorCalcTests.swift** and rerun `test_correctNameReceived()`. It passes!

Instead of fixing and rerunning the project *once* to verify the fix, you now have a test that will verify the code works as expected *every* time you run tests. You've helped to prevent a future regression that could be easy to overlook and make it into production. Have you ever seen an app in the App Store displaying `Optional(something...)`?

Nice job!

Issue 2: Tapping backspace deletes two characters

Still in **ColorCalcTests.swift**, add this new test:

```swift
func test_processBackspaceDeletesLastCharacter() {
  // Given
  // 1
  let expected = "#0080F"
  var result = ""

  // 2
  viewModel.$hexText
    .dropFirst()
    .sink(receiveValue: { result = $0 })
    .store(in: &subscriptions)

  // When
  // 3
  viewModel.process(CalculatorViewModel.Constant.backspace)

  // Then
  // 4
  XCTAssert(
    result == expected,
    "Hex was expected to be \(expected) but was \(result)"
  )
}
```

Similarly to the previous test, you:

1. Set the result you expect and create a variable to store the actual result.

2. Subscribe to `viewModel.$hexText` and save the value you get after dropping the first replayed value.

3. Call `viewModel.process(_:)` passing a constant string that represents the ← character.

4. Assert the actual and expected results are equal.

Run the test and, as you might expect, it fails. The message this time is `Hex was expected to be #0080F but was #0080`.

Head back to `CalculatorViewModel` and find the `process(_:)` method. Check out the switch case in that method that deals with the backspace:

```
case Constant.backspace:
  if hexText.count > 1 {
    hexText.removeLast(2)
  }
```

This must've been left behind by some manual testing during development. The fix couldn't be more straightforward: Delete the 2 so that `removeLast()` is only removing the last character.

Return to **ColorCalcTests**, rerun `test_processBackspaceDeletesLastCharacter()`, and it passes!

Issue 3: Incorrect background color

Writing unit tests can very much be a rinse-and-repeat activity. This next test follows the same approach as the previous two. Add this new test to `ColorCalcTests`:

```
func test_correctColorReceived() {
  // Given
  let expected = Color(hex: ColorName.rwGreen.rawValue)!
  var result: Color = .clear

  viewModel.$color
    .sink(receiveValue: { result = $0 })
    .store(in: &subscriptions)

  // When
  viewModel.hexText = ColorName.rwGreen.rawValue

  // Then
  XCTAssert(
    result == expected,
    "Color expected to be \(expected) but was \(result)"
  )
}
```

You're testing the view model's `$color` publisher this time, expecting the color's hex value to be `rwGreen` when `viewModel.hexText` is set to `rwGreen`. This may seem to be doing nothing at first, but remember that this is testing that the `$color` publisher outputs the correct value for the entered `hex` value.

Run the test, and it passes! Did you do something wrong? Absolutely not! Writing tests is meant to be proactive as much if not more reactive. You now have a test that verifies the correct color is received for the entered hex. So definitely keep that test to be alerted for possible future regressions.

Back to the drawing board on this issue though. Think about it. What's causing the issue? Is it the hex value you *entered*, or is it... wait a minute, it's that ← button again!

Add this test that verifies the correct color is received when the ← button is tapped:

```
func test_processBackspaceReceivesCorrectColor() {
  // Given
  // 1
  let expected = Color.white
  var result = Color.clear

  viewModel.$color
    .sink(receiveValue: { result = $0 })
    .store(in: &subscriptions)

  // When
  // 2
  viewModel.process(CalculatorViewModel.Constant.backspace)

  // Then
  // 3
  XCTAssert(
    result == expected,
    "Hex was expected to be \(expected) but was \(result)"
  )
}
```

From the top, you:

1. Create local values for the expected and actual results, and subscribe to viewModel.$color, the same as in the previous test.

2. Process a backspace input this time — instead of explicitly setting the hex text as in the previous test.

3. Verify the results are as expected.

Run *this* test and it fails with the message: `Hex was expected to be white but was  red`. The last word here is the most important one: red. You may need to open the Console to see the entire message.

Now you're cooking with gas! Jump back to **CalculatorViewModel** and check out the subscription that sets the color in `configure()`:

```
colorValuesShared
  .map { $0 != nil ? Color(values: $0!) : .red }
  .assign(to: &$color)
```

Maybe setting the background to red was another quick development-time test that was never replaced with the intended value? The design calls for the background to be white when a color cannot be derived from the current hex value. Make it so by changing the `map` implementation to:

```
.map { $0 != nil ? Color(values: $0!) : .white }
```

Return to **ColorCalcTests**, run `test_processBackspaceReceivesCorrectColor()`, and it passes.

So far your tests have focused on testing positive conditions. Next you'll implement a test for a negative condition.

Testing for bad input

The UI for this app will prevent the user from being able to enter bad data for the hex value.

However, things can change. For example, maybe you change the hex `Text` to a `TextField` someday, to allow for pasting in values. So it would be a good idea to add a test now to verify the expected results for when bad data is input for the hex value.

Add this test to `ColorCalcTests`:

```
func test_whiteColorReceivedForBadData() {
  // Given
  let expected = Color.white
  var result = Color.clear

  viewModel.$color
    .sink(receiveValue: { result = $0 })
    .store(in: &subscriptions)

  // When
  viewModel.hexText = "abc"
```

```
    // Then
    XCTAssert(
      result == expected,
      "Color expected to be \(expected) but was \(result)"
    )
}
```

This test is almost identical to the previous one. The only difference is, this time, you pass bad data to `hexText`.

Run this test, and it will pass. However, if logic is ever added or changed such that bad data could be input for the hex value, your test will catch this issue before it makes it into the hands of your users.

There are still two more issues to test and fix. However, you've already acquired the skills to pay the bills here. So you'll tackle the remaining issues in the challenges section below.

Before that, go ahead and run *all* your *existing* tests by using the **Product ▸ Test** menu or press **Command-U** and bask in the glory: They all pass!

Challenges

Completing these challenges will help ensure you've achieved the learning goals for this chapter.

Challenge 1: Resolve Issue 4: Tapping clear does not clear hex display

Currently, tapping ⊗ has no effect. It's supposed to clear the hex display to #. Write a test that fails because the hex display is not correctly updated, identify and fix the offending code, and then rerun your test and ensure it passes.

Tip: The constant `CalculatorViewModel.Constant.clear` can be used for the ⊗ character.

Solution

This challenge's solution will look almost identical to the `test_processBackspaceDeletesLastCharacter()` test you wrote earlier. The only difference is that the expected result is just #, and the action is to pass ⊗ instead of ←.

Here's what this test should look like:

```swift
func test_processClearSetsHexToHashtag() {
  // Given
  let expected = "#"
  var result = ""

  viewModel.$hexText
    .dropFirst()
    .sink(receiveValue: { result = $0 })
    .store(in: &subscriptions)

  // When
  viewModel.process(CalculatorViewModel.Constant.clear)

  // Then
  XCTAssert(
    result == expected,
    "Hex was expected to be \(expected) but was \"\(result)\""
  )
}
```

Following the same step-by-step process you've done numerous times already in this chapter, you would:

- Create local values to store the expected and actual results.
- Subscribe to the `$hexText` publisher.
- Perform the action that should produce the expected result.
- Assert that expected equals actual.

Running this test on the project as it stands will fail with the message `Hex was expected to be # but was ""`.

Investigating the related code in the view model, you would've found the case that handles the `Constant.clear` input in `process(_:)` only had a `break` in it. Maybe the developer who wrote this code was itching to take a break?

The fix is to change `break` to `hexText = "#"`. Then, the test will pass, and you'll be guarded against future regressions in this area.

Challenge 2: Resolve Issue 5: Incorrect red-green-blue-opacity display for entered hex

Currently, the red-green-blue-opacity (RGBO) display is incorrect after you change the initial hex displayed on app launch to something else. This can be the sort of issue that gets a "could not reproduce" response from development because it "works fine on my device." Luckily, your QA team provided the explicit instructions that the display is incorrect after entering in a value such as **006636**, which should result in the RGBO display being set to 0, 102, 54, 170.

So the test you would create that will fail at first would look like this:

```
func test_correctRGBOTextReceived() {
  // Given
  let expected = "0, 102, 54, 170"
  var result = ""

  viewModel.$rgboText
    .sink(receiveValue: { result = $0 })
    .store(in: &subscriptions)

  // When
  viewModel.hexText = "#006636AA"

  // Then
  XCTAssert(
    result == expected,
    "RGBO text expected to be \(expected) but was \(result)"
  )
}
```

Narrowing down to the cause of this issue, you would find in CalculatorViewModel.configure() the subscription code that sets the RGBO display:

```
colorValuesShared
  .map { values -> String in
    if let values = values {
      return [values.0, values.1, values.2, values.3]
        .map { String(describing: Int($0 * 155)) }
        .joined(separator: ", ")
    } else {
      return "---, ---, ---, ---"
    }
  }
  .assign(to: &$rgboText)
```

This code currently uses the incorrect value to multiply each of the values returned in the emitted tuple. It should be 255, not 155, because each red, green, blue and opacity string should represent the underlying value from 0 to 255.

Changing 155 to 255 resolves the issue, and the test will subsequently pass.

Key points

- Unit tests help ensure your code works as expected during initial development and that regressions are not introduced down the road.

- You should organize your code to separate the business logic you will unit test from the presentation logic you will UI test. MVVM is a very suitable pattern for this purpose.

- It helps to organize your test code using a pattern such as **Given-When-Then**.

- You can use expectations to test time-based asynchronous Combine code.

- It's important to test both for positive as well as negative conditions.

Where to go from here?

Excellent job! You've tackled testing several different Combine operators and brought law and order to a previously untested and unruly codebase.

One more chapter to go before you cross the finish line. You'll finish developing a complete iOS app that draws on what you've learned throughout the book, including this chapter. Go for it!

Section V: Building a Complete App

Mastery takes practice, and practice you shall!

You've made it through this entire book, an amazing feat by all means. It's time to truly solidify the knowledge you've acquired throughout this chapter and build an entire app using Combine and SwiftUI.

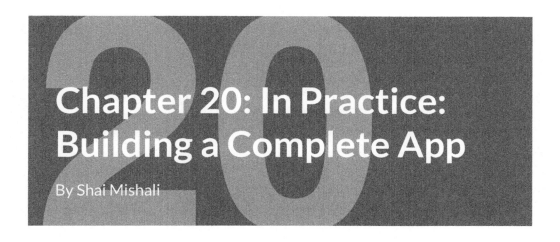

Chapter 20: In Practice: Building a Complete App
By Shai Mishali

By introducing Combine and integrating it throughout their frameworks, Apple has made it clear: Declarative and reactive programming in Swift is a fantastic way to develop tomorrow's greatest apps for their platforms.

In the last three sections, you acquired some awesome Combine skills. In this final chapter, you'll use everything that you've learned to finish developing an app that lets you fetch Chuck Norris jokes. But wait, there's more! You'll also see how to use Core Data with Combine to persist and retrieve your favorite jokes.

Getting started

Open the starter project for this chapter. Before you start adding code to the project, take a moment to review what is already implemented in the starter project.

> **Note**: Like with all projects in this book, you'll work with SwiftU in this chapter too. If you'd like to learn more about it, check out SwiftUI by Tutorials (http://bit.ly/2OMLYmp) from the raywenderlich.com library.

Select the **ChuckNorrisJokes** project at the top of the Project navigator:

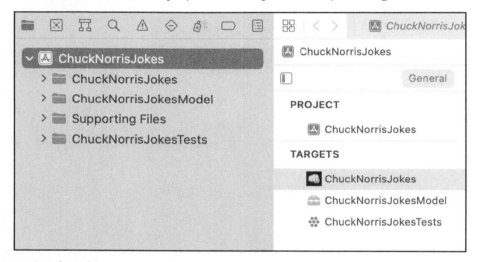

The project has three targets:

1. **ChuckNorrisJokes**: The main target, which contains all your UI code.
2. **ChuckNorrisJokesModel**: You'll define your models and services here. Separating the model into its own target is a great way to manage access for the main target while also allowing test targets to access methods with a relatively strict `internal` access level.
3. **ChuckNorrisJokesTests**: You'll write some unit tests in this target.

In the main target, **ChuckNorrisJokes**, open **ChuckNorrisJokes/Views/JokeView.swift**. This is the main view of the app. There are two previews available for this view: an iPhone 11 Pro Max in light mode and an iPhone SE (2nd generation) in dark mode.

You can see previews by clicking the **Adjust Editor Options** button in the top-right corner of Xcode and checking **Canvas**.

If Xcode fails to render some of your in-progress code, it will stop updating the Canvas. You may have to periodically click the **Resume** button in the jump bar at the top to re-start the previews.

Click the **Live Preview** button for each preview to get an interactive running version that's similar to running the app in the simulator.

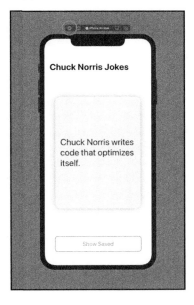

Currently, you can swipe on the joke card view, and not much else. Not for long, though!

> **Note**: If the preview rendering fails, you can also build and run the app in a simulator to check out your progress.

Before getting to work on putting the finishing touches on this app's development, you should set some goals.

Setting goals

You've received several user stories that go like this: As a user, I want to:

1. See indicators when I swipe a joke card all the way to the left or right, to show that I have disliked or liked a joke.

2. Save liked jokes to peruse later.

3. See the background color of a joke card change to red or green as I swipe toward the left or right.

4. Fetch a new joke after I dislike or like the current joke.

5. See an indicator when fetching a new joke.

6. Display an indication if something goes wrong when fetching a joke.

7. Pull up a list of saved jokes.

8. Delete saved jokes.

These goals are your mission, should you choose to accept it. Can someone say Mission *Possible*?! It's time to get started!

Every one of the above user stories relies on logic, so you'll need to implement that logic before you can wire it up to the UI and start checking off that list.

Implementing JokesViewModel

This app will use a single view model to manage the state that drives several UI components, and triggers fetching and saving a joke.

In the **ChuckNorrisJokesModel** target, open **View Models/JokesViewModel.swift**. You'll see a bare-bones implementation that includes:

- Imports of Combine and SwiftUI.
- A `DecisionState` enum.
- A `JSONDecoder` instance.
- Two `AnyCancellable` collections.
- An empty initializer and several empty methods.

Time to fill in all those blanks!

Implementing state

SwiftUI uses several pieces of state to determine how to render your views. Add this code below the line that creates the `decoder`:

```
@Published public var fetching = false
@Published public var joke = Joke.starter
@Published public var backgroundColor = Color("Gray")
@Published public var decisionState = DecisionState.undecided
```

Here, you create several `@Published` properties, synthesizing a publisher for each of them. You can access the publishers for these properties with the $ prefix — e.g., `$fetching`. Their names and types give you a good indication of their purpose, but you'll put them all to use soon enough and see exactly how to utilize them.

Before you can flesh out the rest of this view model, you'll need to implement a few more things.

Implementing services

Open **Services/JokesService.swift**. You'll use `JokesService` to fetch a random joke from the `chucknorris.io` database. It will also provide a publisher of the data returned from a fetch.

To be able to mock this service in unit tests later, you'll need to finish defining a protocol outlining the publisher's requirement. Open **Protocols/JokeServiceDataPublisher.swift**. Combine is already imported for you here, as it is in most of the files that need it throughout this chapter.

Change the `protocol` definition to the following:

```
public protocol JokeServiceDataPublisher {
  func publisher() -> AnyPublisher<Data, URLError>
}
```

Now, open **Services/JokesService.swift** and, similarly, implement its conformance to `JokeServiceDataPublisher`:

```
extension JokesService: JokeServiceDataPublisher {
  public func publisher() -> AnyPublisher<Data, URLError> {
    URLSession.shared
      .dataTaskPublisher(for: url)
      .map(\.data)
      .eraseToAnyPublisher()
  }
}
```

If you build your project's test target at this point, you'll get a compiler error. This error points to the stubbed implementation of a mock service in the test target. To silence this error, open **ChuckNorrisJokesTests/Services/MockJokesService.swift** and add this method to `MockJokesService`:

```
func publisher() -> AnyPublisher<Data, URLError> {
  // 1
  let publisher = CurrentValueSubject<Data, URLError>(data)

  // 2
  DispatchQueue.global().asyncAfter(deadline: .now() + 0.1) {
    if let error = error {
      publisher.send(completion: .failure(error))
    } else {
      publisher.send(data)
    }
  }
}
```

```
    // 3
    return publisher.eraseToAnyPublisher()
}
```

With this code, you:

1. Create a mock publisher that emits `Data` values and may fail with a `URLError`, initialized with the `data` property of the mocked service.

2. Send either the `error` if provided or the `data` value through the subject.

3. Return the type-erased publisher.

You use `DispatchQueue.asyncAfter(deadline:)` to simulate a slight delay in fetching the data, which you'll need for a unit test later in this chapter.

Finish implementing JokesViewModel

With that boilerplate done, return to **View Models/JokesViewModel.swift** and add the following property after the `@Published` ones:

```
private let jokesService: JokeServiceDataPublisher
```

The view model uses the default implementation, while unit tests can use a mock version of this service.

Update the initializer to use the default implementation and set the service to its respective property:

```
public init(jokesService: JokeServiceDataPublisher =
JokesService()) {
  self.jokesService = jokesService
}
```

Still in the initializer, add a subscription to the `$joke` publisher:

```
$joke
  .map { _ in false }
  .assign(to: &$fetching)
```

You'll use the `fetching` published property to indicate when the app is fetching a joke.

Fetching jokes

Speaking of fetching, change the implementation of `fetchJoke()` to match this code:

```
public func fetchJoke() {
  // 1
  fetching = true

  // 2
  jokesService.publisher()
    // 3
    .retry(1)
    // 4
    .decode(type: Joke.self, decoder: Self.decoder)
    // 5
    .replaceError(with: Joke.error)
    // 6
    .receive(on: DispatchQueue.main)
    // 7
    .assign(to: &$joke)
}
```

From the top, you:

1. Set `fetching` to `true`.

2. Start a subscription to the joke service publisher.

3. Retry fetching one time if an error occurs.

4. Pass the data received from the publisher to the decode operator.

5. Replace an error with a `Joke` instance that displays an error message.

6. Receive the result on the main queue.

7. Assign the joke received to the `joke` `@Published` property.

Changing the background color

The `updateBackgroundColorForTranslation(_:)` method should update `backgroundColor` based on the position of the joke card view — aka, its translation. Change its implementation to the following to make that work:

```
public func updateBackgroundColorForTranslation(_ translation: Double) {
  switch translation {
  case ...(-0.5):
```

```
        backgroundColor = Color("Red")
    case 0.5...:
        backgroundColor = Color("Green")
    default:
        backgroundColor = Color("Gray")
    }
}
```

Here, you simply switch over the passed in `translation` and return a red color if it's up to `-0.5` (-50%), green if it's `0.5+` (50%+), and gray if it's in the middle. These colors are defined in the main target's asset catalog in **Supporting Files**, in case you want to check them out.

You'll also use the position of the joke card to determine whether or not the user liked the joke, so change the implementation of `updateDecisionStateForTranslation(_:andPredictedEndLocationX:inBounds:)` to:

```
public func updateDecisionStateForTranslation(
    _ translation: Double,
    andPredictedEndLocationX x: CGFloat,
    inBounds bounds: CGRect) {
    switch (translation, x) {
    case (...(-0.6), ..<0):
        decisionState = .disliked
    case (0.6..., bounds.width...):
        decisionState = .liked
    default:
        decisionState = .undecided
    }
}
```

This method's signature seems more daunting than it actually is. Here, you switch over the `translation` and x values. If the percent is -/+ 60%, you consider that a definitive decision by the user. Otherwise, they're still undecided.

You use the x and `bounds.width` values to prevent a decision state change if the user is hovering inside a decision state area. In other words, if there's not enough velocity to predict an end location beyond these values, they haven't made a decision yet — however, if there is enough velocity, it's a good sign that they intend to complete that decision.

Preparing for the next joke

You have one more method to go. Change `reset()` to:

```
public func reset() {
  backgroundColor = Color("Gray")
}
```

When the user likes or dislikes a joke, the joke card will be reset so that it is ready for the next joke. The only part you need to manually handle is to reset its background color to gray.

Making the view model observable

There's one more thing you'll do in this view model before moving on: Make it conform to `ObservableObject` so that it can be observed throughout the app. Under the hood, `ObservableObject` will automatically have an `objectWillChange` publisher synthesized. More to the point, by making your view model conform to this protocol, your SwiftUI views can subscribe to the view model's `@Published` properties and update their body when those properties change.

That took a lot more time to explain than it will to implement. Change the class definition to the following:

```
public final class JokesViewModel: ObservableObject {
```

You've finished implementing the view model — the brains of this whole operation!

> **Note**: At this point in a real setting, you'd probably write all your tests against this view model, ensure everything passes, check in your work, and go to lunch or home for the day. Instead, you'll proceed with using the view model you just implemented to drive the app's UI. You'll circle back to writing the unit tests in the challenges section.

Wiring JokesViewModel up to the UI

There are two View components on the main screen of the app: a JokeView that's essentially the background and a floating JokeCardView. Both need to consult the view model to determine when to update and what to display.

Open **Views/JokeCardView.swift**. The **ChuckNorrisJokesModel** module is already imported. To get a handle to the view model, add this property to the top of the JokeCardView definition:

```
@ObservedObject var viewModel: JokesViewModel
```

You annotated this property with the @ObservedObject property wrapper. Used in conjunction with the view model's adoption of ObservableObject, you now get the objectWillChange publisher. You get a compiler error in this file now, because the preview provider at the bottom is expecting the view model parameter from JokeCardView's initializer.

The error should point you right to it, but if not, locate the JokeCardView() initializer at the bottom — inside JokeCardView_Previews — and add a default initialization of the view model. The resulting struct implementation should look like this:

```
struct JokeCardView_Previews: PreviewProvider {
  static var previews: some View {
    JokeCardView(viewModel: JokesViewModel())
      .previewLayout(.sizeThatFits)
  }
}
```

You have a compiler error in JokeView to deal with now, but that's also an easy fix.

Open **Views/JokeView.swift** and add the following at the top of the private properties, above showJokeView:

```
@ObservedObject private var viewModel = JokesViewModel()
```

Next, locate the jokeCardView computed property and change the JokeCardView() initialization to:

```
JokeCardView(viewModel: viewModel)
```

The error disappears. Now, switch back to **Views/JokeCardView.swift**. At the top of the body implementation, locate the line `Text(ChuckNorrisJokesModel.Joke.starter.value)` and change it to:

```
Text(viewModel.joke.value)
```

With this code, you switch from using the starter joke to the current value of the view model's joke publisher.

Setting the joke card's background color

Now, head back to **JokeView.swift**. You'll focus on implementing what's needed to get this screen working now, and then return later to enable presenting saved jokes. Locate the `private var jokeCardView` property and change its `.background(Color.white)` modifier to:

```
.background(viewModel.backgroundColor)
```

The view model now determines the joke card view's background color. As you may recall, the view model sets the color based on the card's translation.

Indicating if a joke was liked or disliked

Next, you'll want to set a visual indication of whether the user liked or disliked a joke. Find the two uses of `HUDView`: One displays the `.thumbDown` image and the other displays the `.rofl` image. These image types are defined in **HUDView.swift** and correspond to images drawn using Core Graphics.

Change the two usages of the `.opacity(0)` modifier as follows:

- For `HUDView(imageType: .thumbDown)`:

```
.opacity(viewModel.decisionState == .disliked ? hudOpacity : 0)
```

- For `HUDView(imageType: .rofl)`:

```
.opacity(viewModel.decisionState == .liked ? hudOpacity : 0)
```

This code lets you display the correct image for the `.liked` and `.disliked` states, and no image when the state is `.undecided`.

Handling decision state changes

Now, find `updateDecisionStateForChange(_:)` and change it to:

```
private func updateDecisionStateForChange(_ change:
DragGesture.Value) {
  viewModel.updateDecisionStateForTranslation(
    translation,
    andPredictedEndLocationX: change.predictedEndLocation.x,
    inBounds: bounds
  )
}
```

This method calls through to the view model's `updateDecisionStateForTranslation(_:andPredictedEndLocationX:inBounds:)` method, which you implemented earlier. It passes through the values obtained by the view based on user interaction with the joke card view.

Right below this method, change `updateBackgroundColor()` to:

```
private func updateBackgroundColor() {
  viewModel.updateBackgroundColorForTranslation(translation)
}
```

This method also calls through to a method on the view model, passing in the translation obtained by the view based on user interaction with the joke card view.

Handling when the user lifts their finger

One more method to implement, then you can take the app for a spin.

The `handle(_:)` method is responsible for handling when the user lifts their finger — i.e., touches up. If the user touches up while in an `.undecided` state, it resets the position of the joke view card. Otherwise, if the user touches up while in a *decided* state — `.liked` or `.disliked` — it directs the view model to reset and fetch a new joke.

Change the implementation of `handle(_:)` to the following:

```
private func handle(_ change: DragGesture.Value) {
  // 1
  let decisionState = viewModel.decisionState

  switch decisionState {
  // 2
  case .undecided:
```

```
      cardTranslation = .zero
      self.viewModel.reset()
  default:
    // 3
    let translation = change.translation
    let offset = (decisionState == .liked ? 2 : -2) *
bounds.width
    cardTranslation = CGSize(
      width: translation.width + offset,
      height: translation.height
    )
    showJokeView = false

    // 4
    reset()
  }
}
```

Breaking down what you did with this code:

1. Create a local copy of the view model's current `decisionState` and then switch over it.

2. If the decision state is `.undecided`, set the `cardTranslation` back to zero and tell the view model to reset — which will cause the background color to be reset to gray.

3. Otherwise, for `.liked` or `.disliked` states, determine the new offset and translation for the joke card view based on the state, and temporarily hide the joke card view.

4. Call `reset()`, which hides and then moves the joke card view back to its original position, tells the view model to fetch a new joke, and then shows the joke card view.

There are two things related to this code you haven't touched yet:

- The `cardTranslation` property tracks the joke card's current translation. Don't confuse this with the `translation` property, which uses this value to calculate a translation based the screen's current width, then passes the result to the view model in several areas.

- The joke card view's initial y offset is `-bounds.height`. That is, it sits immediately above the visible view, ready to animate in from the top when `showJokeView` changes to `true`.

Finally, in the `reset()` method immediately below `handle(_:)`, add the following two lines after setting `cardTranslation` to `.zero`:

```
self.viewModel.reset()
self.viewModel.fetchJoke()
```

Here, you ask the view model to fetch a new joke whenever `reset()` is called — i.e., when a joke is liked or disliked, or when the view appears.

That is all you need to do with `JokeView` for now.

Trying out your app

To check out your progress thus far, show the preview, click **Resume** if necessary, and click the **Live Preview** play button.

> **Note**: You can also build run the app in a simulator or on a device to check your progress.

You can swipe all the way left or right to dislike or like a joke, respectively. Doing so will also display the thumb down or ROFL image and the "fetching" animation. If you release the card while in an undecided state, the joke card will snap back to its original position.

If your app encounters an error, it will display the error joke. You'll write a unit test to verify this later, but if you'd like to see the error joke now, temporarily shut off your Mac's Wi-Fi, run the app and swipe left to fetch a new joke. You'll see the error joke: "Houston we have a problem — no joke. Check your Internet connection and try again."

This is, no doubt, a minimal implementation. If you're feeling ambitious, you can implement a more robust error-handling mechanism, applying what you learned in Chapter 16, "Error Handling."

Your progress so far

That takes care of the implementation side of these features:

- ☑ 1. See indicators when I swipe a joke card all the way to the left or right, to show that I have disliked or liked a joke.
- ☑ 3. See the background color of a joke card change to red or green as I swipe toward the left or right.
- ☑ 4. Fetch a new joke after I dislike or like the current joke.
- ☑ 5. See an indicator when a new joke is being fetched.
- ☑ 6. Display an indication if something goes wrong when fetching a joke.

Nice job! All that's left is to:

- 2. Save liked jokes to peruse later.
- 8. Pull up a list of saved jokes.
- 9. Delete saved jokes.

Time to save some jokes!

Implementing Core Data with Combine

The Core Data team has been hard at work these past few years. The process of setting up a Core Data stack couldn't get much easier, and the newly-introduced integrations with Combine make it even more appealing as *the* first choice for persisting data in Combine and SwiftUI apps.

> **Note**: This chapter doesn't delve into the details of using Core Data. It only walks you through the necessary steps to use it with Combine. If you'd like to learn more about Core Data, check out Core Data by Tutorials (http://bit.ly/2BqtbVX) from the raywenderlich.com library.

Review the data model

The data model has already been created for you. To review it, open **Models/ChuckNorrisJokes.xcdatamodeld** and select **JokeManagedObject** in the **ENTITIES** section. You'll see the following attributes have been defined, along with a unique constraint on the `id` attribute:

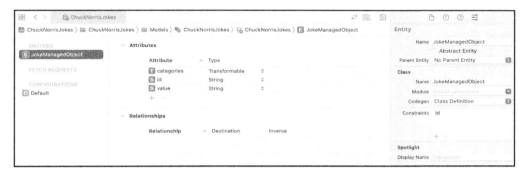

Core Data will auto-generate a class definition for `JokeManagedObject`. Next, you'll create a couple of helper methods in extensions on `JokeManagedObject` and collections of `JokeManagedObject` to save and delete jokes.

Extending JokeManagedObject to save jokes

Right-click on the **Models** folder in the Project navigator for the main target and select **New File…**. Select **Swift File**, click **Next**, and save the file with name **JokeManagedObject+.swift**.

Replace the entire body of this file with the following piece of code:

```
// 1
import Foundation
import SwiftUI
import CoreData
import ChuckNorrisJokesModel

// 2
extension JokeManagedObject {
  // 3
  static func save(joke: Joke, inViewContext viewContext: NSManagedObjectContext) {
    // 4
    guard joke.id != "error" else { return }
    // 5
    let fetchRequest = NSFetchRequest<NSFetchRequestResult>(
      entityName: String(describing: JokeManagedObject.self))
```

```swift
    // 6
    fetchRequest.predicate = NSPredicate(format: "id = %@",
joke.id)

    // 7
    if let results = try? viewContext.fetch(fetchRequest),
      let existing = results.first as? JokeManagedObject {
      existing.value = joke.value
      existing.categories = joke.categories as NSArray
    } else {
      // 8
      let newJoke = self.init(context: viewContext)
      newJoke.id = joke.id
      newJoke.value = joke.value
      newJoke.categories = joke.categories as NSArray
    }

    // 9
    do {
      try viewContext.save()
    } catch {
      fatalError("\(#file), \(#function), \
(error.localizedDescription)")
    }
  }
}
```

Walking through the comments, here's you do with this code:

1. Import Core Data, SwiftUI and your model module.

2. Extend your auto-generated `JokeManagedObject` class.

3. Add a static method to save the passed-in joke using the passed-in view context. If you're unfamiliar with Core Data, you can think of the view context as Core Data's scratchpad. It's associated with the main queue.

4. The error joke used to indicate when a problem occurs has the ID error. There's no reason to save that joke, so you guard against it being the error joke before proceeding.

5. Create a fetch request for the `JokeManagedObject` entity name.

6. Set the fetch request's predicate to filter the fetch to jokes with the same ID as the passed-in joke.

7. Use `viewContext` to try to execute the fetch request. If it succeeds, that means the joke already exists, so update it with the values from the passed-in joke.

8. Otherwise, if the joke doesn't exist yet, create a new one with the values from the passed-in joke.

9. Attempt to save `viewContext`.

That takes care of saving.

Extending collections of JokeManagedObject to delete jokes

To also make deleting easier, add this extension on `Collections` of `JokeManagedObject`:

```
extension Collection where Element == JokeManagedObject, Index == Int {
  // 1
  func delete(at indices: IndexSet, inViewContext viewContext: NSManagedObjectContext) {
    // 2
    indices.forEach { index in
      viewContext.delete(self[index])
    }

    // 3
    do {
      try viewContext.save()
    } catch {
      fatalError("\(#file), \(#function), \(error.localizedDescription)")
    }
  }
}
```

In this extension, you:

1. Implement a method to delete objects at the passed-in indices using the passed-in view context.

2. Iterate over the indices and call `delete(_:)` on `viewContext`, passing each element of `self` — i.e., the collection of `JokeManagedObjects`.

3. Attempt to save the context.

Create the Core Data stack

There are several ways to set up a Core Data stack. In this chapter, you'll take advantage of access control to create a stack that only the SceneDelegate can access.

Open **App/SceneDelegate.swift** and start by adding these imports at the top:

```
import Combine
import CoreData
```

Next, add the CoreDataStack definition at the bottom of the file:

```
// 1
private enum CoreDataStack {
  // 2
  static var viewContext: NSManagedObjectContext = {
    let container = NSPersistentContainer(name: "ChuckNorrisJokes")

    container.loadPersistentStores { _, error in
      guard error == nil else {
        fatalError("\(#file), \(#function), \(error!.localizedDescription)")
      }
    }

    return container.viewContext
  }()

  // 3
  static func save() {
    guard viewContext.hasChanges else { return }

    do {
      try viewContext.save()
    } catch {
      fatalError("\(#file), \(#function), \(error.localizedDescription)")
    }
  }
}
```

With this code, you:

1. Define a `private` enum called `CoreDataStack`. Using an case-less enum is useful here, since it can't be initialized. `CoreDataStack` only serves as a namespace — you don't actually want to be able to create an instance of it.

2. Create a persistent container. This is the *actual* Core Data stack, encapsulating the managed object model, persistent store coordinator, and managed object context. Once you have a container, you return its view context. You'll use SwiftUI's `Environment` API in a moment to share this context across the app.

3. Create a static `save` method that only the scene delegate can use to save the context. It's always a good idea to verify that the context has changed before you initiate a save operation.

Now that you have defined the Core Data stack, move up to the `scene(_:willConnectTo:options:)` method at the top and change `let contentView = JokeView()` to:

```
let contentView = JokeView()
  .environment(\.managedObjectContext,
CoreDataStack.viewContext)
```

Here, you add the Core Data stack's view context to the environment, making it globally available.

When the app is about to move to the background, you want to save the `viewContext` — otherwise, any work done in it will be lost. Locate the `sceneDidEnterBackground(_:)` method and add this code to the bottom of it:

```
CoreDataStack.save()
```

You now have a bona fide Core Data stack and can go about the business of putting it to good use.

Fetching jokes

Open **Views/JokeView.swift** and add this code right before the `@ObservedObject private var viewModel` property definition to get a handle to the `viewContext` from the environment:

```
@Environment(\.managedObjectContext) private var viewContext
```

Now, move to `handle(_:)` and, at the top of the `default` case, before `let translation = change.translation`, add this code:

```
if decisionState == .liked {
  JokeManagedObject.save(
    joke: viewModel.joke,
    inViewContext: viewContext
  )
}
```

With this code, you check if the user liked the joke. If so, you use the helper method you implemented a little while ago to save it, using the view context you retrieved from the environment.

Showing saved jokes

Next, find the `LargeInlineButton` block of code in `JokeView`'s body and change it to:

```
LargeInlineButton(title: "Show Saved") {
  self.presentSavedJokes = true
}
.padding(20)
```

Here, you change the state of `presentSavedJokes` to `true`. Next, you'll use this to present saved jokes — imagine that!

Apply the `sheet` modifier to the *end* of the `NavigationView` block of code:

```
.sheet(isPresented: $presentSavedJokes) {
  SavedJokesView()
    .environment(\.managedObjectContext, self.viewContext)
}
```

This code is triggered whenever `$presentSavedJokes` emits a new value. When it's `true`, the view will instantiate and present the saved jokes view, passing along the `viewContext` to it.

For your reference, the entire `NavigationView` should now look like this:

```
NavigationView {
  VStack {
    Spacer()

    LargeInlineButton(title: "Show Saved") {
      self.presentSavedJokes = true
    }
    .padding(20)
  }
  .navigationBarTitle("Chuck Norris Jokes")
}
.sheet(isPresented: $presentSavedJokes) {
  SavedJokesView()
    .environment(\.managedObjectContext, self.viewContext)
}
```

That's it for `JokeView`.

Finishing the saved jokes view

Now, you need to finish implementing the saved jokes view, so open **Views/SavedJokesView.swift**. The model has already been imported for you.

First, add this property below the body property:

```
@Environment(\.managedObjectContext) private var viewContext
```

You've already set the `viewContext` a couple times — nothing new here.

Next, replace `private var jokes = [String]()` with the following:

```
@FetchRequest(
  sortDescriptors: [NSSortDescriptor(
                      keyPath: \JokeManagedObject.value,
                      ascending: true
                    )],
  animation: .default
) private var jokes: FetchedResults<JokeManagedObject>
```

You'll immediately see a compiler error. You'll fix it next while enabling the ability to delete jokes.

This gem of a property wrapper from SwiftUI does a lot for you. It:

- Takes an array of sort descriptors to sort fetched objects and updates the `List` that will display them with the given animation type.

- Automatically performs fetches for you whenever the persistent store changes, which you can then use to trigger the view to re-render itself with the updated data.

Variations of the underlying `FetchRequest`'s initializers allow you to pass a `fetchRequest` like the one you created earlier. However, in this case, you want *all* jokes, so the only thing you need to pass are instructions on how to sort the results.

Deleting jokes

Locate the `ForEach(jokes, id: \.self)` block of code, including the `.onDelete` block of code, and changing it to the following:

```
ForEach(jokes, id: \.self) { joke in
  // 1
  Text(joke.value ?? "N/A")
}
.onDelete { indices in
  // 2
  self.jokes.delete(
    at: indices,
    inViewContext: self.viewContext
  )
}
```

Here, you:

1. Show the joke text or "N/A" if there isn't a joke.

2. Enable swiping to delete a joke and call the `delete(at:inViewContext:)` method you defined earlier.

With that, `SavedJokesView` is now done!

Resume the app preview or build and run the app. Save a few jokes, then tap **Show Saved** to display your saved jokes. Try swiping left on a few jokes to delete them. Re-run the app and confirm that your saved jokes are, indeed, still there — and the ones you deleted are not!

Challenge

You now have a great app, but your exceptional work ethic — and your manager — won't allow you to check in your work without accompanying unit tests. So this chapter's challenge section asks you to write unit tests to ensure your logic is sound, and to help prevent regressions down the road.

This is the final challenge of the book. Take it on and finish strong!

Challenge: Write unit tests against JokesViewModel

In the **ChuckNorrisJokesTests** target, open **Tests/JokesViewModelTests.swift**. You'll see the following:

- Some preliminary setup code.
- A test that verifies the sample joke can be successfully created, called `test_createJokesWithSampleJokeData`.
- Five test stubs, which you'll complete to exercise each of the responsibilities of the view model.

The `ChuckNorrisJokesModel` module has already been imported for you, giving you access to the view model — aka the system under test.

First, you'll need to implement a factory method to vend new view models. It should take parameters to indicate if it should emit an error for "fetching" a joke. It should then return a new view model that uses the mock service you implemented earlier.

For an extra challenge, see if you can implement this yourself first, then check your work against this implementation:

```
private func viewModel(withJokeError jokeError: Bool = false) -> JokesViewModel {
  JokesViewModel(jokesService: mockJokesService(withError: jokeError))
}
```

With that method in place, you're ready to go about filling in each test stub. You don't need any new knowledge to write these tests — you learned everything you need to know in the last chapter.

Some tests are fairly straightforward. Others require a slightly more advanced implementation, such as using an expectation to wait for asynchronous operations to complete.

Take your time, and good luck — you've got this!

When you're done — or if you get stuck on anything along the way — you can check your work against the solution in **projects/challenge/final**. The tests in this solution demonstrate one approach — i.e., they're not etched in stone as the *only* way. The most important thing is that your tests pass when the system works as it's supposed to, and fail when it does not.

Key points

Here are some of the main things you learned in this chapter:

- Combine works hand-in-hand with SwiftUI, Core Data and other frameworks to provide a streamlined and unified approach to managing asynchronous operations.
- Use `@ObservedObject` in conjunction with `@Published` to drive SwiftUI views with Combine publishers.
- Use `@FetchRequest` to automatically execute a Core Data fetch when the persistent store has changed, and to drive UI based on the updated data.

Where to go from here?

Bravo! Finishing a book of this magnitude is no small accomplishment. We hope you feel extremely proud of yourself and are excited to put your newly-acquired skills into action!

In software development, the possibilities are endless. Developers who keep their skills sharp and up-to-date will create tomorrow's apps that are truly adored by their users. You are one such developer.

You may already have an app or an idea that you want to use Combine to develop. If so, there's no better experience than *real-world* experience — and no one ever learned to swim from a book alone. So dive in!

Not ready to jump into your own project with Combine yet? No worries, there are several ways you can improve the app you developed in this chapter and further hone your Combine chops — including, but not limited to, these enhancements:

- Add the ability to sort saved jokes.

- Add the ability to search saved jokes.

- Add the ability to share a joke via social media, or even with other users.

- Implement a more robust error-management system that provides different messages based on the various errors a user might receive.

- Implement displaying saved jokes in a different way, such as in a `LazyVGrid`.

Additionally, you can visit the forum for this book at bit.ly/combineBookForum if you have any questions, discover errata, or just want to see if you can help fellow Combiners.

Whatever you decide to do with your Combine skills, we wish you good luck — and don't hesitate to reach out to us to say hello or to share your accomplishments.

Conclusion

You're finally here! Congratulations on completing this book, and we hope you enjoyed learning about Combine from the book as much as we've enjoyed making it.

In this book, you've learned about how Combine enables you to write apps in a declarative and expressive way while also making your app reactive to changes as they occur. This makes your app code much more versatile and easier to reason about, along with powerful compositional abilities between different pieces of logic and data.

You started off as a complete Combine beginner, and look at you now; oh, the things you've been through—operators, networking, debugging, error handling, schedulers, custom publishers, testing, and you've even worked with SwiftUI.

This is where we part ways, but we have full confidence in you! We hope you'll continue experimenting with Combine and constantly enhancing your "Combine muscles." As the saying goes—"practice makes perfect."

And like anything new you learn—don't forget to enjoy the ride.

If you have any questions or comments about the projects in this book, please stop by our forums at http://forums.raywenderlich.com.

Thank you again for purchasing this book. Your continued support is what makes the books, tutorials, videos and other things we do at raywenderlich.com possible. We truly appreciate it!

— Florent, Marin and Shai

The *Combine: Asynchronous Programming with Swift* team

Printed in Great Britain
by Amazon